AMERICAN VOICES

Prize-winning Essays on Freedom of Speech,
Censorship and Advertising Bans

PHILIP MORRIS USA
New York
1987

DISCLAIMER
The essays in this book were submitted by members of
the public in response to a nationwide essay competition
sponsored by *Philip Morris Magazine* and were selected as
prize-winning essays by an independent panel of judges.
The ideas, views and content of the essays in this book are
solely those of the authors. Philip Morris Companies Inc.,
Philip Morris USA and *Philip Morris Magazine* do not
necessarily endorse the ideas, views or content of these
essays, and do not assume liability for the essays' contents.

Designed by Allan Mogel
Manufactured in the United States of America

10 9 8 7 6 5 4 3 2 1

Library of Congress Catalog-in-Publication Data
American voices.
    1. Censorship—United States.   2. Freedom of speech—
United States.   3. Advertising—Censorship—United
States.
Z658.U5A45   1987   323.44'5   87-20340
ISBN 0-934037-01-9

Grateful acknowledgment is made for permission to reprint
portions of E. E. Cummings' "as freedom is a breakfastfood" (reprinted on page 424 of this volume). Copyright
1940 by E. E. Cummings, renewed 1968 by Marion
Morehouse Cummings. Reprinted from *Complete Poems
1913–1962* by E. E. Cummings by permission of Harcourt
Brace Jovanovich, Inc.

CONTENTS

CONTENTS

FOREWORD

Americans are often described as self-reliant, resourceful, creative, energetic and outspoken. Judging from the prize-winning essays in this volume, the essayists whose work is presented here personify these qualities.

Each writer entering the *Philip Morris Magazine* Essay Competition was charged with addressing the same issues—censorship, the First Amendment's application to American business and the ramifications of proposed tobacco advertising bans on free expression in a free market economy.

Considered as a whole, this book of winning essays presents a compelling case against censorship in general and advertising bans in particular. Each essay shares the strong central theme of freedom of expression as the cornerstone of American government, culture and life.

Taken individually, the essays consist of styles and content that are as remarkably diverse as the authors themselves. The reader is provided with legal arguments, historical analyses, personal reflections, political science and science fiction. The authors come from every state in the Union. The occupations represented by the essayists range from attorney to antique dealer, law professor to librarian, reporter to retiree, dentist to design consultant, editor to locomotive engineer, minister to tariff analyst. The essays exemplify the American people at their best— their strength, diversity and their unbending commitment to the protection of individual freedom.

In the last analysis, the medium through which the theme of freedom of speech is presented here—the essay—is the message. The fact that these prize-winning essays were written, along with thousands of others submitted in the course of the competition, is itself a refutation of censorship. The success of the *Philip Morris Magazine* Essay Competition, reflected in the pages that follow, should be encouraging to every American who believes in the central freedoms upon which this nation is founded.

Frank E. Resnik
President and CEO, Philip Morris USA
New York City, June, 1987

INTRODUCTION

In September 1986, an advertisement with a reproduction of the First Amendment appeared in major magazines and newspapers throughout the country. The headline for the ad was "Is Liberty Worth Writing For? Our Founders Thought So. And We Think So Too." With that premise, we launched the *Philip Morris Magazine* Essay Competition.

The ad set forth the rules of the Competition, requirements for submissions and the prize structure. Significant prizes were offered for winning essays: $15,000 for the first place national winner; national runner-up prizes of $7,500, $5,000 and $2,500; and prizes of $1,000 for state winners from each of the 50 states and the District of Columbia.

A panel of seven distinguished judges selected the winning essays. The panel consisted of:

- Bonnie Angelo, Eastern Regional Bureau Chief, *Time* magazine
- Thomas J. Broome, Esq., President, National Bar Association
- Elizabeth Carpenter, journalist, author and former Press Secretary for Lady Bird Johnson
- Robert Cornet, Vice President, Corporate Affairs, NBC
- Richard Locke, journalist, literary critic and Lecturer, Department of English, Columbia University
- Hugh Sidey, Washington Contributing Editor, *Time* magazine
- James Thomson, Jr., Professor of International Relations, Journalism and History, Boston University.

The winning essays selected by the panel and published in the present volume are remarkable. Each essay is concise, thoughtful and provocative; each makes a powerful case for free commercial speech.

The publishers, editors and staff of *Philip Morris Magazine* are deeply gratified with the results of the magazine's Essay Competition. We congratulate the winning essayists. And we thank those who entered the Competition and did not win. In the last analysis, all those who entered are "winners" for having expressed themselves on so vital an issue.

Our purpose in conducting the Competition was to raise public awareness of the threat to free speech posed by proposed advertising bans. The essays presented in the present volume, and the thousands of essays written by Americans throughout the country and submitted to the Competition, testify to the successful achievement of our goal.

Guy L. Smith, Publisher
Philip Morris Magazine

Mary A. Taylor, Associate Publisher
Philip Morris Magazine

AMERICAN VOICES

Barbara Rubenstein
New York, New York

Occupation: Actress/Writer
Interests: Reading, cheering the Mets in person,
classes in screenwriting and other aspects of the
acting profession, some tennis and horseback riding
Entered the Competition because of: "Concern and
fear over various attempts to ride roughshod over the
First Amendment in this—of all years—the Year of
the Constitution. As someone whose job is to bring
other people's words to life, I thought it finally time
to find my own words."

The First Amendment holds . . . because we cannot suspend it and remain all we think we are.

America is a nation that invented itself. There was no other way. All known formulas, all history, led to the tidy equation of power plus prejudice.

But how not to repeat history? How to form duties and powers, principles and obligations and still have an entity both responsive and free?

We live the answer—the First Amendment to the Constitution of these United States. It is this amendment which has upheld the vision that designed this country. A vision of words and of personal choice.

We were born out of wrenching debate. Our principal legacy is the guarantee of continued debate. We are a people who persuade and counterpersuade; who insist the truth be spoken aloud and printed for all to see. As a nation we continue to invent ourselves still, through open discovery of what we believe.

We have been denigrated as noisy children for this by elder, "sophisticated" nations. Give us time, they say, and we will change. We shall weary of information; we shall become paralyzed by consensus. We will finally desire one thing: that adults simply lay down the law.

But the law Americans have before all others grants us the prerogative of childhood, to speak what we think and feel without censorship. In the scared, silent hiding places of this world, we are the collective hero of an important story—that little boy who insists the Emperor isn't wearing any clothes.

We are as elastic as the old joke: a nation of two people with three opinions. Yet we are fragile, and any time we become a nation of 240 million with no choice but *one* choice, then we have destroyed ourselves without help from any outside enemy. No part of our lives, personal or public, can escape from the consequences.

Do we really save our children—and from what—if a religious world view, waving the banner of the Ten Commandments, censures student reading about supposed disobedience to authority? We were granted the very right to practice religion by men who took arms against a king.

Do we really protect our egos—and from what—if we smother a creative work that shows us in a light we may not recognize? The artist is part of the checks and balances of our society as surely as any tangible procedure.

Do we protect our modesty—at the expense of our lives—when information about disease is silenced because it might involve open discussion about sex?

America is a melting pot but not because our individual beliefs and backgrounds have vanished. They have willingly linked instead, and any shift by one piece can cause dislocation to another.

The result is friction, sparks. Our forefathers chose to give them all the room they need through the avenue of the First Amendment. They knew that to suppress debate, to smother opinion, was even more dangerous. Whoever might claim sway as the final authority could never put all the fires out.

Is there ever a time when it is justified to suspend the First Amendment, when circumstances and moral repugnance shout that someone is crying an alarm in a crowded theater? The question is as durable as our freedom.

We now have spiritual leaders praying publicly for the death of certain judges. Is this prayer a tacit invitation to pick up a gun and become the hand of God?

We have had a neo-Nazi group insist on the right to march through a Chicago suburb, chosen precisely because it contained some who had survived the genocide of Hitler's Europe.

The First Amendment holds, even in these most extreme and painful cases, because we cannot suspend it and remain all that we think we are.

We cannot be a nation of self-government whose people cannot know or express any certain opinion by which to govern.

We cannot congratulate ourselves on individual pursuit of happiness when the expressions of what might please us have been cut to a predefined shape.

The First Amendment demands from us as much as it offers. It demands we not fear someone else's thoughts, only a forced imposition of those thoughts upon our own.

It demands we accuse no viewpoint as illegal, only actions taken upon that viewpoint which step outside the law.

We do not advocate the violent overthrow of our own government. We may advocate nearly everything else. A few things we hear infuriate us. Some things make us smile. Many things can change our lives. Each of these categories is fluid to each one of us and they cannot be mandated. A prior mandate exists—that of individual choice.

It's ironic to consider business as a special case for this freedom. Its voice—its advertising—becomes our right to choose heard aloud. It becomes our need for speech used creatively. It is, finally, America's words played back.

Advertising stems from within each of us or its message couldn't find a listener. If our own voice finds shelter under the First Amendment, then so must the voice of business.

If we speak up to announce our feelings, so does advertising. If we speak out for something in particular and to urge that option over another, so does advertising.

We must voice our needs to survive. The goods and services offered by American business are tangible evidence of those words. These products become free expressions within themselves.

Yet what of the differences that seem to move us apart? We speak for individual reasons in our lives while advertising uses a common motive. We communicate on a one-to-one basis but advertising speaks to us at large. We may simply choose not to speak. Industry can never have that option.

These are only special distinctions of business speech. They equal its range and inflection and emphasis. They form a particular sound and not particular reasons for thereby claiming business exempt from a law that embraces language whatever its form.

What of the reasons we hold business responsible for whatever its open speech creates? The advertising voice is singular. It touches us en masse.

We cannot assume more responsibility takes up all the space needed for freedom. What do we do then with those who run for office, who are charged with holding the public trust?

We vote to put them out of a job when we hear a promise that cannot be delivered. When advertising speaks to the same effect, we vote dollars for an equal result.

In our other endeavors we are expected to speak the truth. In business, advertising is required to do so.

This is a recognition that our needs must not be turned back on us via shoddy or misleading results. It is not an accusation that business has forfeited its right to stand with the rest of us under the First Amendment.

Advertising, overall, is a menu of choices—what we may pick at any one moment to create results in our daily lives.

Yet U.S. industry has learned the hard way that consumers can divorce it. When a relationship is vital, both sides listen closely. Business must use our free speech as the actual gateway between need and product. Business must find that gate open when it makes the return trip back.

7

This country has prospered through salesmanship even as we shy away from that image. Yet a talent which makes us ambivalent has grown from a First Amendment right. We were born of speechmakers and persuaders. We produce those who talk as directly and colorfully as their own natures will allow.

Advertising takes this inherent salesmanship to move our country further. We cannot boast of our accomplishments, of the strength and scope of American business, while fighting the opportunity to advance ourselves all at the very same time.

We cannot fear business speech because of its focus, because of its motive. Advertising has power but only to the degree anyone *listens*.

We cannot assume that persuasion will harden into coercion. We cannot confuse motive with force, shaping a legal prejudice as a result. We must remember that our freedom to say no is in place under the First Amendment. The result is we have room for speech that specifically asks us to say yes.

We do not speak at all unless we know someone is there to hear us. American business cannot know who's listening unless first, it may speak.

An even deeper irony exists, for the Constitutional Convention was originally proposed due to commerce. The vehement trade quarrels among the colonies were tearing our independence apart.

Business was both a tool in our survival and a catalyst for fitting this nation together. We cannot call business a stepchild when it comes to our freedoms. It has a living claim to being a founding father of those rights.

The gift of human speech is also a tool in our survival. Business' right to the First Amendment is nothing more than that.

Today one business voice—one particular group—faces silence.

Today one business voice—one particular group—faces silence. A proposed bill by the House Subcommittee on Health and Environment may erase all speech by the tobacco industry.

Will this ban on advertising and promotion do more that that? Will it, in effect, edit the First Amendment, pasting the word "but . . ." at the end of a law we know as absolute?

The underlying issues of the ban, public health, legislative responsibility, can only circle home to the First Amendment since tobacco products will still be legal to sell. Does this ban create a third irony in regard to free expression in a free market? Yet one that is the most serious? Can we now produce a product but go to jail for producing information?

If a product is such that it causes concern, we cannot find ourselves like Alice in Wonderland, lost, searching for rules that might make some sense.

A tobacco advertising ban is more than simply one wedge in one application of the First Amendment because any wedge is a tool that is used for force. It deliberately admits space for a wider tool to enter until the object in question may be cracked apart.

How does a free market conduct itself, then, among these pieces? When the avenue to reach the buyer is closed or narrowed beyond the call of the product itself, what impetus is there to make the product? If goods and services are a response to our own words, yet the market can no longer announce that it has heard us, will the market give up certain attempts to even answer us at all?

A ban on tobacco advertising seeks just that. It uses advertising as a weapon against the beginning and end of the free market chain. Unless Congress is willing to confront directly freedom of choice by the producer, promotion to the public may mean a considered defense instead.

We do not all drive cars but we are all potential victims of the speed of a car. Will the auto industry find it cannot show its product traveling over thirty-five miles an hour? The possibility is not out of line with a tobacco advertising ban.

Americans across the board face serious health dangers from overweight. Will certain bakery goods now have to protect themselves? Announce they should only be eaten if one meets the limits of a life insurance chart? It is not a far-fetched question when related to a tobacco advertising ban.

Should this law be passed, free expression in a free economy will have to cut and weigh its own motives. It will no longer reach out as effectively as possible but as carefully as it knows how. It will not have the choice to look toward us. It will need to look back to see who might be watching.

It will have to know the difference between appearance and reality. Is it free to say anything it likes? Of course. *But...*

We have tried out this word before, and we failed, with Prohibition. At what point will a tobacco advertising ban mean that we try it again? At what point might "a public concern" be stretched by a minority? Be interpreted to mean open lifestyles that some products and advertising promote?

9

Free expression will mislead despite federal regulations against it. It cannot help but do so because it will not address our real selves.

We are a people who dream aloud. We have been promised choice by the First Amendment. Free expression in the future may include words but never our dreams.

We are a people who plan aloud. We try on our possibilities and we are free to take them off again if they do not fit. The voice of business in the future may be to announce that we are out of possibilities.

We are a people who change and grow through open discovery of what we believe. What we may discover in the future are market promptings to stay right where we are.

If free expression becomes both constricted and tentative, it may lose more than just its voice. It will face the prospect of losing what it needs most. An audience.

If free expression becomes both constricted and tentative, it may lose more than just its voice. It will face the prospect of losing what it needs most. An audience.

For every word or image we may turn away from now, there's another that captures our attention. For every point of information we know we've heard before, there's another point that tells us something new. For every product that's already part of our lives, we have an introduction to something we might like to consider.

Advertising must keep us watching and listening. It is the job business has asked it to do. It is able to do so now, precisely because it is free to find new ways to seek our attention. In the future, limited and cautious from the effects of a tobacco advertising ban, it may speak only to find nobody will want to hear.

The question may be not whether a free market will be able to have equally free expression in the future, but whether the freedom that remains to this expression can still accomplish its purpose. If it cannot, if neither Americans nor American business can clearly see their own potential, then the freedom of the market may become valueless as well.

Don G. Campbell
Los Angeles, California

Occupation: Journalist
Interests: Reading, the theater, travel, tennis and swimming
Entered the Competition because: "I have experienced an increasing resentment at the current trend to redefine the Constitution to champion what is 'popular' at any given moment. This document was never intended to be 'trendy.'"

Continually, the Supreme Court has had to shore up the First Amendment as its bulwarks have been battered under the guise of protecting the American people from a never-ending series of "perils."

Then, as now, Little White Lick Creek dawdles its serpentine way along the west edge of Brownsburg, Indiana. But in 1931 it was the western boundary of the town—there wasn't anything past it until you got to Pittsboro, four miles away—and we could skinny-dip with impunity at almost any bend of its muddy banks because the few houses that were in hooting distance lined a tree-shaded bluff one hundred yards away. And when you're nine years old, sprawled on the damp broad-leaf grass with the warm summer sun drying your skin and the aerodynamically incongruous dragonflies skipping gingerly around you, who cares what the old fogies up there might see, anyway?

Today, the Little White Lick simply separates downtown Brownsburg from the suburbs that have grown up to the west along Ind. 136, and the broad field on its banks where the Gypsies used to camp in the summer—next to the squat and gray concrete bridge that the WPA had recently built to replace the old covered wooden bridge—now houses a television satellite station. But it isn't as romantic or as scary a setting as it was in 1931 when, at night, we would spy on the ragtail Gypsies from across the creek, watch their fires and listen to the strange babble of a language so foreign to our Midwestern ears. Scary, because here was proof for sure, that there really *were* Gypsies in the world—the people your mother had threatened to sell you to so often when, even younger than you were then, you'd been bad.

1931, a long-ago but not so simple time, as our little sheltered community finally found itself caught up in the Depression that—I was to find out later—had started two years before with the collapse of the stock market. Something meaningless to a nine-year-old at first but then, as the backwash of it began ebbing and flowing around us and over us, it became an extremely personal thing—an itch that Calamine lotion didn't ease, a hollowness that wouldn't go away.

Outwardly, at least, not much was different. Our family, people said, still "ran the town." Or my dad did, at least. Not because he was all

13

that much richer than anybody else, or snapped orders at people, or anything like that. But because he published *The Brownsburg Record*—circulation 1,200—he, and Old George who cleaned up and, if he were sober enough, ran the big flatbed Miehle printing press, and Brownie, whose strong, tapered fingers could hand-set the type that the old, battered Linotype couldn't, with a speed that was dazzling and could transfix me for hours.

It was funny the way Mr. Hunter, the banker who could buy and sell my dad a hundred times over, never made a business move without coming over and huddling with him. How snooty Mrs. Bailey (that's not her real name, because she's still got kin around Hendricks County) would come in and kind of fawn over Dad when she was plugging the Junior Bazaar. And how all of the members of the town council would cotton up to him.

It was a puzzling thing because—while he was smart, all right—my dad was strictly self-taught. He'd had his first weekly newspaper when he was just fifteen years old in Fort Recovery, Ohio, which hadn't left him much time for any formal kind of upbringing. But our house always had been alive with books and magazines, and the upright Philco radio in our living room wasn't there so much for "Amos 'n' Andy" as it was for the news programs.

But there were others in Brownsburg who were just as well-read as my dad was, so why did everyone treat him so differently? He'd look at me a little blankly when I'd try to bring it up and then he'd grin his lopsided grin and most likely give Brownie a big wink.

" 'Cause if they aren't nice to me we'll gang up on 'em, and make sure that their name *never* gets spelled right in the *Record*. Ain't that right, Brownie?"

And Brownie'd guffaw and go right back to slamming those little tiny s's and t's and e's out of the font and into his metal stick.

But by then, of course, I was reading the *Record* a lot more closely than I had as a little kid and some things were beginning to fall into place. And now it was becoming clear that it wasn't always a coincidence when, on Thursday afternoons—press day—somebody or other would come into the office and huddle with my dad by his desk behind the tall counter where my mom sold ads. And sometimes you could see it wasn't all that friendly a chat, and that my dad wasn't just selling *Records* at a nickel apiece or helping old man Blanck lay out his Chevy ads. He was into something a lot more personal than all that—ideas. Sometimes popular, more often not.

You've got to remember that in 1931, at the height of the Depression that was churning things up so much, a lot of little towns like

Brownsburg weren't all as tranquil and serene as it looked like they were on the surface. Up in the "cut-off," on the north side of town, for instance, some of the people living there—heavily Catholic, heavily Irish ("lace curtain Irish," the other people in town called them)—were beginning to chafe under the hard times. Mostly railroad workers (that's where the "cut-off" came from—because they lived in shanties separated from the rest of the town by railroad tracks) a lot of them had been laid off, and the little bit of pocket change that the wives had always brought in taking in washings from those of us on the south of the tracks was spread pretty thin.

Instead of just taking it quietly, as they'd always handled hard times before, they were starting to pressure the town council for more help and one of them, that bad year, had even taken it into his head to *run* for the council. A leathery old guy who, to my nine-year-old eyes, looked older than the hills—but who was probably my dad's age—would come into the *Record* office early each week with something scratched out on a grocery sack in soft pencil. And he and my dad would huddle over the desk while Dad helped put what he'd written into halfway-understandable English and that's the way the story would come out the following Thursday.

And a lot of people in town were fit to be tied because Dad was giving "that Bolshevik" all that free space. And a lot of them didn't like it, either, when Dad would give the same space to the doings of the tiny Catholic church up in the cut-off as he did to the other churches in town—the Baptists and the Christian Church, mainly—where all of our friends went.

And when I asked him why once, I got one of those rare, earth-burning looks that he normally saved for the Town Marshal every time he caught the Marshal manhandling the hoboes who dropped off in Brownsburg trying to sponge a free meal. Every train coming through town was loaded with them. They weren't real bums, just guys who had lost their jobs and were traveling anywhere there might be work.

"Why?" Dad had snorted. "Why? Are you afraid you're going to wake up some morning a mackerel-snapping Papist just by reading about Father Donovan's fund-raiser? Going to do better in your Bible studies by *not* reading about the Catholics?" Biting my lip, I'd skeedaddled to the back of the *Record* office and to the job I was supposed to be doing—scrubbing down the inky pages, still locked in their forms, with kerosene.

And then there was the time Dad ran the story about the cross-burning out west of town and followed it up with an editorial that would have peeled the hull off a fresh walnut. Today, we forget that the Ku

Klux Klan had come back to life during the Depression that had beaten everybody down so much and that Indianapolis, just fourteen miles away to the east, was the Midwest hub of it.

A lot of folks who'd been embarrassed by the cross-burning thought Dad was wrong to make a big fuss about it and that we'd look bad if the Indianapolis papers picked it up. And there were others in town who didn't like it for entirely different reasons. It was uncomfortable, because I'd taken a lot of heat about it, myself, at school.

"We don't say anything about it, so it didn't happen, right?" he'd snapped at my mother who was afraid of maybe a second cross-burning. "People pay us their good two dollars a year to know what's goin' on. Don't make a tinker's dam whether I like what I see goin' on or not. They gotta right to know. I gotta duty to tell 'em. I let myself get shut up because *they* don't like it, or *I* don't like it, and you and me and George and Brownie—we're just so much dead weight!"

It was as close as I ever heard my dad get to the First Amendment. With all the reading he did he sure had to know about it, but I never heard him mention it, probably because it would have sounded too preachy and too high-falutin' for a weekly editor.

He's been gone a good twenty-five years now, but I'd give a lot to have him back—at least for just an hour or two—so I could watch those heavy white eyebrows furrow and hear that raspy, cigar-brittled voice boom out on the subject of what today's readers are *still* expecting for their nickel. And of all the odd things that are happening to cheapen that nickel's worth: people setting themselves up to decide for today's Mr. Hunter, today's Mrs. Bailey, today's Father Donovan, what's fit and proper for them to know, or not know.

The only thing my dad hated worse than covering a high school basketball game was covering the town council meetings.

"But *somebody's* gotta be there or those fools are gonna start taking themselves seriously. So, half the time, they don't do anything, anyway. Reader's gotta right to know that, in particular."

The nickel reader's got a right to be sheltered from life's unpleasantness, sordidness . . . things he's simply better off not knowing? Today, Dad would frown over that one and finally dismiss it with a weary wave of the once-strong hand that had finally yielded to arthritis. The Depression, the cross-burning, the racial, social and economic prejudices that had lain barely under the surface in 1931 Brownsburg, had been sordid, unpleasant . . . perhaps better off not known. He would find it a silly issue though, that anybody would want, or need, to be "protected" from it.

But "silly" is in the beholder's eye and the First Amendment that my dad so took for granted has an almost unparalleled history of attacks on it—the first, in 1797, just six years after its ratification when an attempt was made to imprison Representative Samuel J. Cabell for "endeavoring at a time of real national danger to disseminate unfounded calumnies against the unhappy government of the United States . . . and to increase or produce a foreign influence, ruinous to the peace, happiness and independence of these United States." All for writing letters to his constituents attacking President Adams' belligerent attitude toward France. And then, just a year later, with the signing of the infamous Sedition Act which was so punitive that a newspaper publisher could be sent to prison for charging the President of the United States with something as frivolous as being cruel to animals.

Restored, reattacked, reaffirmed and continually assaulted, the First Amendment reeled on but was almost completely buried under the anti-German hysteria of World War I and the Espionage Acts of 1917 and 1918. The latter was modeled on the Sedition Act of 1798 and, in the words of historian Irving Brant, "fell just short of making it a penal offense to say *Gesundheit* at a sneeze." A woman, Rose Pastor Stokes, was given a ten-year sentence for writing a letter containing the phrase: "I am for the people and the government is for the profiteers."

Continually, the Supreme Court has had to shore up the First Amendment as its bulwarks have been battered under the guise of protecting the American people from a never-ending series of "perils"— "the disloyal, scurrilous and abusive language" of pro-Socialist, pro-Communist publications. Against scandal sheets and pornographers.

But, in recent years, I think my father would find silliest of all the attempts to pervert the First Amendment by reinterpreting the meaning of "peril" to cover legitimate business practices that are "perilous" only because certain segments of the population find those practices—and rightly so, perhaps—controversial. As if, in denying the protection of the First Amendment to these businesses, the controversial nature of the issue will, itself, die from not being heard—death by muzzlement.

But this flies in the face of philosopher Ralph Barton Parry's observation that: "All important questions are controversial, if by 'controversial' is meant that there are at least two sides that can conceivably be taken. If two sides are not already taken, the attempt to suppress a question on the ground that it is controversial will make it controversial."

I can remember the sly smile that would cross my dad's face in 1931 when I would profoundly solve some of the world's most pressing problems from the height of my nine-year-old wisdom and he would nod, sagely, and say, "Well, now, that's certainly a *thought*, all right." I would see the same look today if I were to tell him that one industry, the tobacco industry, is living under the threat of having its right to tell its side of the controversial smoking issue prohibited by law. A law that would rule out all tobacco advertising despite the guarantees supposedly extended under the badly battered, but still viable, First Amendment.

"I see," he would say with mock profundity. "That way, if they can't advertise their product people won't know it's *there*, and, if they don't know it's there, it'll go away. And there goes your old controversy." Then, drawing his brows together, "Tell you what—I'll give you a silver dollar for every bad habit, every danger, I've managed to steer clear of in my life by *not* readin' about it. Fair enough?" And there'd be that lopsided grin again.

"Tell you what—I'll give you a silver dollar for every bad habit, every danger, I've managed to steer clear of in my life by *not* readin' about it. Fair enough?"

Which, perhaps, is another way of phrasing philosopher George Santayana's thought on the same subject:

A man may not always eat and drink what is good for him; but it is better for him and less ignominious to die of the gout freely than to have a censor officially appointed over his diet, who after all could not render him immortal.

John E. DeWald

Devon, Pennsylvania

Occupation: Attorney
Interests: Jogging, painting in oils and pastels,
photography, languages, travel
Entered the Competition because of: "My belief in
the importance of constitutional issues for all
citizens."

THE FIRST AMENDMENT AND TOBACCO ADVERTISING

Visitors to an ancient Capuchin monastery near Rome report a most peculiar practice. It seems the cemetery vault is too small to hold the bodies of all the monks who pass on to the next life. So the remains of the most recently departed monks are left hanging in an anteroom until their bones are fit for the cramped quarters. And they are left on view for friar and tourist alike. No doubt this strange sight is intended as a silent reminder of the transient aspect of life. But no abstract reflection on death drives home the message as directly as the sign some wit hung across one of the departed friars—"*Me hodie; tu cras*": Me today; you tomorrow.

"Me today; you tomorrow" is an appropriate warning to remember in considering the risks of proposed tobacco ad ban legislation.

We Americans are fortunate to live under a government of laws, not of men. And we all appreciate in the abstract the rockbed of freedom which guarantees our liberties, the Constitution. Yet, somehow, the daily pressures and problems of life make such a persistent claim on our attention, that grand concepts like constitutional freedoms can ebb into the background of our consciousness.

There is a risk in this. We might take our constitutional liberties so much for granted that we are tempted to ignore forces and events which chip away at them.

We can easily be lulled by our own preoccupations into ignoring this cold reality—what happens to someone else's freedom today can diminish our own freedom tomorrow. So concern about cutting corners on constitutional rights is much more than an intellectual exercise, which may be safely left to specialists. It is a matter of vital self-interest to all of us. Eternal vigilance is still the price of liberty.

That is why, as an attorney concerned with preserving the benefits

21

of our basic American freedoms, I am opposed to proposed legislation to ban tobacco advertising, even though I am a nonsmoker myself.

I believe that such proposals are misguided and it is doubtful they will achieve any worthwhile result. More importantly, I worry that any such legislation tampers with the delicate balance between regulation and governmental restraint which is at the heart of democracy. Interference with this balance on a matter of constitutional rights jeopardizes the constitutional freedom of all of us.

Our founding fathers understood that liberty is undermined more often in subtle ways than in dramatic ones. In 1788, Madison told the Virginia Convention:

> I believe there are more instances of the abridgement of the freedom of the people by gradual and silent encroachments of those in power than by sudden and violent usurpations.

Patriots of every generation have understood that the duty to guard against these threats to freedom belongs to all citizens, not just political leaders or special interest groups.

George Washington warned in his first inaugural address that the preservation of the "sacred fire of liberty" is "in the hands of the American people."

In our own time, the late Chief Justice Earl Warren warned that the Bill of Rights is under "subtle and pervasive attack" not only from outside but from "our own indifference and failure of imagination." "The duty to resist these attacks," he said, "rests on the shoulders of every American."

Our founding fathers understood that liberty is undermined more often in subtle ways than in dramatic ones.

This is more than patriotic sloganeering. It is a lesson of history. From the time of the Boston Tea Party until today, the tension between governmental power and individual rights has been tested and redefined in the crucible of public opinion.

Public controversy over the *Dred Scott* decision fanned the debate over slavery, which led eventually to constitutional amendments after the Civil War guaranteeing civil rights to all.

In a different way, the limits on liberty were also tested during

Prohibition. However noble the intent behind the Eighteenth Amendment may have been, most students of history recognize this experiment in social reengineering was a major failure.

Perhaps worse, according to historians such as Samuel Elliot Morrison, Prohibition contributed many unforeseen adverse social effects. These included encouragement of law breaking and the spawning of a criminal class that turned to gambling and drugs when the Eighteenth Amendment was repealed in 1933.

Each generation must face the challenge of protecting America's basic freedoms. In fact, this very process of applying the framers' principles to a new set of circumstances is what keeps the Bill of Rights a vital document instead of a historical relic.

Of all the American freedoms protected by the Bill of Rights, the one most worthy of concern and protection is freedom of speech. In fact, freedom of speech may well be considered the linchpin of all the other freedoms we enjoy.

After all, it is only through freedom of expression that we are able to put into practice freedom of religion, freedom of the press, the flow of information in our free market economy and so on down the line. All other freedoms flow from it; without it, none can survive.

What's more, constitutional experts speak in terms of a "free market of ideas." That is, freedom of speech is *intended* to safeguard our democracy by encouraging a free flow of thought. Ideas expressed in this intellectual "marketplace" are tested in competition with other ideas. Obviously, some ideas will directly contradict others. But ultimately in the continuing ebb and flow of this marketplace, some ideas will fail and some will prevail.

No one guarantees or even imagines that this process is infallible. But in this "free market," each side may offer its best arguments. And, at the very least, no voice may be stifled through prior restraint.

This point is critical. Bear in mind that the Constitution and especially the Bill of Rights is, at root, a protection of individual liberty. It is not, and was never intended to be a rubber stamp endorsement of the prevailing sentiment at any given time.

On the contrary, the glory of the Constitution is that it stands as a bulwark against any such "tyranny of the majority."

This is no accident. The framers of the Constitution, sometimes through heated controversy, deliberately forged a method of government in which power is restrained by checks and balances.

Madison saw that the problem was twofold. In *The Federalist* No. 51 he wrote:

In framing a government which is to be administered by men over men, the great difficulty lies in this: you must first enable the government to control the governed; in the next place, oblige it to control itself.

Government is obliged to control itself not only through the checks and balances in its three branches. It is also controlled by the Bill of Rights' grant of inalienable rights to the governed.

The Constitution draws the "foul lines" for the field of play of American life. The branches of government may not step over each other's boundaries. But even more importantly, none of them may "step over the line" by violating an individual's constitutional rights.

We should proceed then to analyze a legislative ban on tobacco advertising in terms of its potential impact on the constitutional rights to freedom of speech in the prism of Supreme Court opinions on such questions, even though they can seem contradictory.

We may do this without special claim to expertise because, as citizens, we have the duty to do so.

And we do it, despite the hazards of Supreme Court second-guessing, because the Constitution is our common legacy. Theodore Roosevelt wrote in 1901, "I am not a lawyer, but I have never believed that a layman who thought soberly was incompetent to express a judgment upon the Constitution."

Based on these considerations, we can start our analysis with the fundamental observation that a tobacco advertising ban clearly violates the plain meaning of the First Amendment: "Congress shall make no law . . . abridging the Freedom of Speech. . . ."

This is not decisive. But it is not to be taken lightly either. Because by the sheer sweep of their simple, unqualified prohibitions, the framers intended to give these constitutional liberties the broadest scope possible in an orderly society. And, historically, the constitutional guarantee of free speech has been jealously guarded. Its protection has been construed liberally. It has been the American tradition to allow the widest room for discussion and the narrowest for restriction of this freedom.

We know, of course, that no freedom is absolute. In Justice Holmes' famous dictum, there is no freedom to protect a man falsely shouting "Fire" in a theater. This is the Clear and Present Danger Doctrine. But mere tendency or even likelihood of an evil result will not justify the exception, and this test is not generally applied to regulation in interstate commerce.

It was traditionally held that free speech did not restrict the "police power" of the states to promote health, safety and welfare. But this restriction was altered substantially by a line of cases beginning in 1976 which specifically accorded constitutional protection to commercial speech.

Under this rationale the Court has struck down regulations restricting a variety of economic activities including the advertisement of contraceptives, lawyer advertising, prescription price advertising and the like.

In general, these cases confirmed the principle that truthful speech proposing lawful commercial transactions is protected by the First Amendment. Essentially, they reflect the "free market of ideas" approach.

Unfortunately, another string of cases blurs the line. They shift the emphasis to protection of the public from fraud, deception, undue influences and the like. For example, one decision approved a ban on practicing optometry under a trade name; another against in-person attorney solicitation. This approach assumes that consumers may be protected from at least certain categories of commercial speech deemed harmful, despite the First Amendment.

The Court tried to blend these two trends by adopting a four-part test in a 1980 case, *Central Hudson Gas & Electric* v. *Public Service Commission*. The test is composed of a four-part inquiry:

1. Is the expression nonmisleading commercial speech concerning a lawful activity?
2. Is the asserted governmental interest substantial? (That is, significant enough to really matter as opposed to nominal, trivial or illusory.)
3. Does the regulation directly advance the governmental interest asserted?
4. Is it more extensive than necessary to serve that interest?

Unfortunately, that does not end the matter. For in a 1986 case, *Posadas de Puerto Rico Associates* v. *Tourism Co. of Puerto Rico*, a five-to-four majority (led by now-Chief Justice Rehnquist) upheld regulations banning the advertisement of casino gambling to Puerto Rican natives. The holding expressly observed and applied the *Central Hudson* test.

For the tobacco ad ban issue, *Posadas* has become a kind of legal Rorschach test. Opponents of the ban argue persuasively that *Posadas* can only be understood in the light of the Court's conceded deference to Puerto Rican courts' interpretation of its law "given the unique cultural and legal history of Puerto Rico."

This has not prevented ban proponents from gleefully proclaiming that virtually any plausible argument for "consumer protection"–type regulation will be sustained under *Posadas*.

Even though this debate will doubtless go on, we can draw several conclusions from it about a tobacco ad ban.

First, truthful tobacco advertising is commercial speech proposing lawful commercial activity of the type consistently protected by the Court under the First Amendment. (Most pre-*Posadas* cases approving restrictions involved some perceived form of misleading or deception. Tobacco advertisement is *already* subject under existing law to prohibition against false or misleading information.)

Second, truthful advertising serves a beneficial purpose for its audience as well as the advertiser. If information about "tar" and nicotine, filters and the like persuade a smoker who would smoke something anyway to choose even a moderately "safer" brand, the public interest would certainly be served more than not. Furthermore, suppose research produced an indisputably health-risk-free cigarette (or other tobacco product)? Wouldn't advertising such a product substantially *advance* the public interest?

Third, a tobacco ad ban would do little to "directly advance" a governmental purpose of ending or reducing demand. In reality, most evidence confirms that advertising has scant effect on creating additional demand. Its actual purpose and effect is to promote brand loyalty or induce switching among competitive brands.

Finally, a tobacco ad ban would fail the "least restrictive means" test. Numerous alternatives exist. Many are in use now. The traditional approach adopted by the Supreme Court has been to favor remedies which employ more information, not less. The Court clearly *disfavors* suppression:

> It is precisely this kind of choice between the dangers of suppressing information, and the dangers of its misuse if it is freely available, that the First Amendment makes for us.

In fact, by adopting laws which mandate rotating warning messages, ban broadcast ads, and prohibit untruthful content, and by engaging in affirmative "counterspeech" by the Surgeon General, the National Institutes of Health and so on, the government has already gone about as far as a free society ought to go in taking a position on the use of a lawful product by individuals.

To go any further would cross over the line into the manipulation of consumer choice by the restriction of truthful information so rightly disfavored by the Court.

26

For when all is said and done, the acid test of our commitment to free speech is not the acceptance of noncontroversial expressions which enjoy general approval. Just the opposite. It is, in the ringing rhetoric of Justice Holmes, "freedom for the thought we hate."

The government has already gone about as far as a free society ought to go in taking a position on the use of a lawful product by individuals.

The poet John Donne told us that because no man is an island, we need never send to know for whom the bell tolls. In that spirit, those ban proponents who would trade off a little liberty to achieve a goal they believe worthwhile might reflect on the exchange Thomas More has in *A Man For All Seasons* with the impetuous Roper, who says he would cut down every law in England to get after the Devil. More replies:

Oh? And when the last law was down, and the Devil turned round on you—where would you hide, Roper, the laws being flat? This Country's planted thick with laws from coast to coast . . . and if you cut them down—and you're just the man to do it—d'you really think you could stand upright in the winds that would blow then? Yes, I'd give the Devil benefit of law, for my own safety's sake.

Anthony Green
Philadelphia, Pennsylvania

Occupation: Attorney
Interests: Reading, writing, swimming, politics
Entered the Competition because: "As an attorney
and a former journalist, the freedoms provided
by the First Amendment have always been
important to me."

> **Proponents of the bill argue that advertising . . . entices young people to start smoking—despite evidence that advertising does not encourage consumers to start engaging in a new habit.**

They used to have a terrible alcoholism problem in Tlaakii. But not for long.

Tlaakii is a satellite nation of the Soviet Union, nestled in between the Soviet's southern border and Poland's western border. About the size of New York State, it is one of Russia's most obedient protégé nations, adhering to most of the principles of its mentor nation. Tlaakii's government is organized much the same way as the Soviet government and the official language is Tilscha, a mixture of Russian and Polish.

Tlaakii has little in the way of natural resources but for rich forests and some copper. Its major production endeavors include lumber and paper products, strong Stolichnaya-like vodka—Rischa, they call it—ceramic objects and, strangely, metal objects, "chaszkas." Chaszkas are used for hanging things like vacuum cleaner tubes, brooms, mops and the like in closets, which Tlaakii exports to the West and which are very popular with young urban professionals. The people who work in the two chaszka factories in Fikhla and Porisch do not know what the odd objects are used for, and don't particularly care.

The Tlaakiians are a strong, silent people, the men more friendly than Russian men, the women much prettier than Russian women. (The present Soviet premier has a Tlaakiian paramour.) But the Tlaakiians have one weakness: Rischa. Tlaakiians drink Rischa as if it was water; almost as soon as Tlaakiian children are weaned from milk, their parents serve them small glasses of Rischa at bedtime. On special occasions—and Tlaakiians are big on special occasions—they drink Rischa flavored with red hot pepper.

Just as in the Soviet Union, precious commodities like toilet paper, meat, gasoline, and Rischa are rationed out and Tlaakiians must wait in long lines to get their share. Always, the longest lines queue up for Rischa. It is the job of the Ministry of Information to prepare signs advertising when and where the goods will be available. The placards are hung on the kiosks of Tlaakiian cities.

The Ministry of Research and Development performed a study which concluded 1) Tlaakii had a terrible drinking problem and, 2) the problem was having a marked negative effect on production in Tlaakiian factories.

Boris Plitkov, Tlaakii's head of state, woke early one morning, unable to sleep. He poured himself a glass of red-pepper-flavored Rischa and carefully opened the report on alcoholism and production. He was not particularly surprised by the discussion of the extent of the alcoholism problem (a story about Tlaakii's drinking habits appeared in the Tlaakii's censored newspaper, *Pliitkaa*), but was startled by the figures tracking the decline in production. If the rate of decline continued, Tlaakii wouldn't be able to export enough chaszkas to supply the Greenwich Village branch of Conran's. Plitkov set aside his glass of Rischa, only half drunk, and called an emergency meeting of his closest advisers.

Over the next eighteen months, the Tlaakiian government tried various measures to deal with this urgent situation. Billboards suddenly appeared in the cities, hanging between posters of Marx and Juresczku (Tlaakii's founding father), saying MISCKA SULEK P'LNUUTYU. VILEK MISLEK which roughly translated means "Celebrate in moderation. Work hard." Tlaakiian workers coming to the factories drunk were suspended for two weeks. The Ministry of Imports, reversing an earlier decision, allowed the United States to import Coca-Cola and the Tlaakiian government aggressively tried to popularize "Kcuka-Kuzcka"—much to the objection of the Ministry of Dentistry. But it was all to no avail. Long lines still formed at the Rischa ration centers and Tlaakiians still toasted to large glasses of Rischa, "Mityek bleczh," which, roughly translated, means "Down the hatch."

To shut down the Rischa factories would spell economic disaster, putting eighteen percent of the workforce on the streets. The government was dumbfounded, its leading bureaucrats and planners stymied.

Finally, a solution was found. One night, at the Plitkov dinner table, Plitkov's daughter's boyfriend Dmitri Chellov, a young officer in the Ministry of Research and Development, casually offered his idea: "Why not just stop the Ministry of Information from advertising when the Rischa will be available?" Plitkov was stunned for a brief moment but then the premier, who had previously detested young Chellov, put down the glass of Kcuka-Kuzcka he was drinking, rose, strode over to Chellov and kissed both the boy's cheeks.

The next day, the signs advertising the availability of Rischa were torn down from the kiosks.

Rischa was still produced and distributed. But nobody knew when or where to get it.

The drinking problem practically disappeared; production went back to normal. And young Dmitri Chellov was given Plitkov's permission to marry Andri and he was appointed Minister of Information.

* * *

In Tlaakii and the Soviet Union, the government does the "advertising," deciding what the people should know and shouldn't know.

Freedom is ignorance.

Knowledge is slavery.

But we, in the United States, do things differently than in the imaginary nation of Tlaakii and the Soviet Union.

This year, we celebrate the 200th anniversary of the United States Constitution, and one of the most important elements of that precious document is its First Amendment. There the founding fathers held that Congress could make no law abridging the freedom of speech. However brief, those crucial forty-five words are what separate us from a Tlaakii.

Two hundred years ago it was not so clear what the First Amendment specifically protected, but after refinement by the United States Supreme Court, things are more evident. For example, one cannot shout "Fire" in a crowded movie theater, cannot ply pornographic materials without meeting some restraint,* cannot make statements which present a clear and present danger to the security of the United States† and cannot make defamatory statements about another (though the Court has set more liberal rules regarding freedom of speech in public debate).‡

Regarding commercial speech, the Supreme Court has held that the First Amendment guarantees our right to speak as well as to receive information and that the First Amendment protects the right of speech of all persons, including those who happen to be corporations in their effort to advertise their products or services. Under the law, a corporation has the same rights as any "person." The Supreme Court has held, "the free flow of commercial information is indispensible."§

Despite the First Amendment protections and the Court's many decisions interpreting it, the Congress has barred television advertising regarding tobacco sales.‖ Now, some Congressmen seek to expand that prohibition even further. A proposed statute would bar *all* advertising about tobacco.¶ The proponents of the bill argue that such advertising glamorizes the habit and entices young people to start smoking—despite

---

* *E.g. Miller v. California*, 413 U.S. 15 (1973).

† *E.g. Brandenburg v. Ohio*, 395 U.S. 444 (1969).

‡ *New York Times v. Sullivan*, 376 U.S. 254 (1964); *Gertz v. Welch*, 418 U.S. 323 (1974).

§ *Virginia State Board of Pharmacy v. Virginia Citizens Consumer Council, Inc.*, 425 U.S. 748 (1976). In other cases, the Supreme Court consistently invalidated restrictions which would deprive consumers of accurate information about products or services. *E.g. Bates v. State of Arizona*, 433 U.S. 350 (1977) (attorney's advertising); *Carey v. Population Services International*, 431 U.S. 678 (1977) (birth control); *Linmark Associates, Inc. v. Willingboro*, 431 U.S. 85 (1977) (commercial housing).

‖ 15 U.S.C. § 1334; *Capital Broadcasting Co. v. Mitchell*, 333 F.Supp. (D.D.C. 1971), *aff'd mem.* 405 U.S. 1000 (1971)

¶ In the 1985–1986 session, the bill which would bar all tobacco advertising was introduced by Representative Mike Synar (D-Okla.) as H.R. 4972.

evidence that advertising does not encourage consumers to start engaging in a new habit, but that it merely helps the consumers decide which product to choose.

If Congress passes this legislation, what is next? Driving a car after drinking beer causes carnage on our highways. Do we ban Miller Lite and Pontiac commercials? Soft drinks and candy cause the decay of children's teeth. Do we ban ads for Coke and M & M's?

Commerce's ability to advertise is crucial to our economic structure. The implications are great, both to our economic system as well as to our liberty—which is why our Supreme Court has ruled as it has in favor of free commercial speech. The marketplace needs to be able to communicate that it is in business, what is being sold and for how much. Without the power and right to advertise, the American marketplace may as well close down.

In its decisions concerning commercial speech, the Court has consistently applied a four-pronged analysis to determine whether a statute is constitutionally valid: 1) whether the speech is false or misleading; 2) whether the government has a substantial interest; 3) whether the statute advances the governmental interest; and 4) whether the statute is no more restrictive than necessary to advance the governmental interest. *

Our government must try to effect change by allowing the debate in our society to continue.

The analysis concerning the statute under consideration should focus on the fourth element of the test. There can be little question that advertising about cigarettes is *not* misleading—the tobacco industry is bound by the same truth in advertising laws as other corporations. Moreover, there is little doubt that the government *has* an interest in protecting the health of the young. Regarding the third prong of the Court's test, one could argue whether the proposed statute would truly advance the governmental interest considering the marketing evidence suggesting that advertising only leads one to choose a type of product once the consumer is at the store, rather than leading one to pick up an entirely new habit.

The issue is not whether smoking is dangerous. If the government believes that cigarette smoking presents a danger to society and, more

---

* *Central Hudson Gas & Electric Corp.* v. *Public Service Commission*, 447 U.S. 557 (1980). The Supreme Court's most recent decision regarding commercial speech, *Posadas de Puerto Rico Association* v. *Tourism Co. of Puerto Rico*, 106 S.Ct. 2968 (1986), which approved of a statute barring advertising about Puerto Rico's casino industry aimed solely at Puerto Rico citizens did not disturb the *Central Hudson* test.

specifically, to impressionable young people, there are other less intrusive ways to deal with the problem—to use the legal phrase, less restrictive means to advance the governmental interest.

That less restrictive means is education, communications, debate, persuasion, speech. Unlike Tlaakii, the Soviet Union and its minion countries, our government must try to effect change by allowing the debate in our society to continue.

The technology of speech and communications is vast; the tools in the possession of the government almost unlimited. If the Congress is concerned about young people picking up the smoking habit—it should develop curricula for the schools, produce clever public service announcements for television and radio as it has in the war against drug abuse, encourage the heroes of youth (rock stars, television personalities and cartoon characters) to preach the virtues of not smoking . . . The list of the initiatives the government could take to meet its goal is as long as an imaginative, enlightened government can develop.

That list must stop, however, when it interferes with the right to speak and the consumers' right to receive information.

Let the smoking versus nonsmoking debate rage on. But let us not stoop to facile solutions.

Let the smoking versus nonsmoking debate rage on.

But let us not stoop to the facile solutions used by nations like Tlaakii and the Soviet Union.

Predictably, things went awry in Tlaakii.

Minister of Information Chellov started using the censorship device to cope with other problems pinpointed by the Tlaakii government. The Ministry stopped publishing notices about the availability of meat when there was a shortage and, for health reasons, about sweet foods and tobacco, "tobascz." Then, notices about the times for church services were banned. Finally, Chellov had the kiosks removed altogether. There was nothing left for the kiosks to say.

But the quiet people of Tlaakii could remain silent no more. The underground obtained information about when Rischa and tobascz were to be available and published crude leaflets advertising the information. The lines began to form again. After the ban on church service announcements, the underground organized a successful strike of Tlaakiian factories.

Something had to be done. The Kremlin was getting nervous,

fearing another embarrassing situation like Poland.

Plitkov called young Chellov into his chambers. Other means would be used to deal with the nation's problems. Chellov was relieved of his duties as Minister of Information and as Plitkov's son-in-law.

And, again, the kiosks stand in the cities of Tlaakii.

ALABAMA STATE PRIZE WINNER

Brad Rodu, D.D.S.
Birmingham, Alabama

Occupation: Dentist
Interests: Reading history, cycling, beer brewing,
cooking
Entered the Competition because of: "Opportunity
to formally express my hearfelt opinions on this
subject."

> **Of paramount concern is the small but immensely important leverage that will be acquired by those individuals who would utilize this precedent to impose further controls. . . .**

Cancer and its prevention is an emotionally charged issue that has repeatedly stimulated the American public's fascination with the concept of a single sweeping explanation for its cause or cure. In an attempt to appease the accompanying popular demand for action, the American Medical Association has already proposed a ban on advertising of all tobacco products. At first glance this proposal appears especially attractive as an easily implemented legislative remedy which has the support of many conservative health-oriented groups and is opposed only by nonconstituent lobbies such as the "evil, manipulative" (as they are being portrayed) tobacco and advertising empires. But closer examination transforms this from a relatively parochial issue regarding smoking to an immensely important attack on freedom of expression.

In order to propose such a ban the proponents must assume two vital points: first, that tobacco products cause deleterious health effects, and second, that advertising is overwhelmingly successful in selling these products. Each assumption merits more than casual consideration before broaching the principle issue.

There are few health professionals, including myself, who would seriously suggest that consumption of tobacco products as currently practiced does not adversely affect health. But these effects are primarily due to what may be defined as tobacco abuse. Scientists have been eager to characterize, albeit retrospectively, increased health risks following extensive exposure to particular substances, but they remain woefully inadequate when defining a minimum tolerance level, below which exposure carries little or no risk. This inadequacy invokes the controversy concerning the toxicity of products such as saccharin, caffeine and alcohol, the potential health hazards of which, with normal consumption, are extensively debated. For example, if tobacco exposure is reduced to one or two episodes per week (or even per day) rather than the virtually constant exposure now experienced by most users, the associated health risks would likely require a significant downward adjustment. Thus, it can be argued that improper use of a product, rather than the product itself, forms the nucleus of the issue.

This proposed ban also succinctly implies that tobacco advertising is not only effective, but in essence irrevocably so, thereby drastically underestimating the average American's intellectual capacity to process information of an obvious commercial nature. This proposal rather pessimistically suggests that tobacco advertising deviously lures feeble-minded individuals who would otherwise abstain from tobacco consumption into the treacherous clutches of the habit. Although advertising may be directed at generic consumption of a product it is more likely to be specifically aimed at differentiation of competing brand name products. Therefore, a more rational, progressive alternate viewpoint is that these advertisements are only contending for the attention of consumers previously committed to tobacco use.

Thus, careful examination of the foundation for this proposed ban reveals some serious deficiencies. However, the crucial issue is the serious violation of free expression that results from abolishing the advertising of a legal product. While a response to this atrocity can be forged around sophisticated constitutional, philosophical and historical theses, an equally valid and less pretentious approach employs the logical extension of this reasoning to other products of similar potential vulnerability. Of paramount concern is the small but immensely important leverage that will be acquired by those individuals who would utilize this precedent to impose further controls on freedom of expression.

For the moment let me painfully assume the successful implementation of the current plan, which builds tremendous confidence in these advocates of repression and releases new energies for further ventures. Indeed, the attack will shortly be focused on alcoholic beverages. The preliminary groundwork has already begun by the organization of grass roots support by a small but very vocal group of ultraconservatives who quite literally believe that consumption of alcohol in any way, shape or form is a sin. Having dispensed with the formalities of discussions concerning the manipulation of rights of free expression, this debate can be predicted to be short and fall decisively against the alcoholic beverage industry, despite that industry's commendable voluntary adoption of ethical standards of advertising, such as refraining from actually showing imbibition of alcohol on television commercials.

The red meat industry may presently emerge as another vulnerable target in this campaign, and for legitimate reasons. The body of evidence associating diets rich in saturated (i.e. animal) fats with increased risks for colorectal cancer and atherosclerosis (relating to myocardial infarctions) is modest, but expanding at an impressive rate. The American Cancer Society estimates that 140,000 new cases of colorectal cancer have occurred this year (compared to 149,000 cases of lung cancer). In comparison, atherosclerosis-related diseases will kill over 400,000 Americans. A significant dietary reduction in saturated fats, primarily accomplished through decreasing red meat consumption, has been recommended by several prominent nutrition councils to alter mortality from both these diseases. If the strategy developed by the American Medical Association is considered valid and effective, this reduction could be at least partially effected by a prohibition of advertising—both of generic red meat products and by food service companies specializing in their sale to the public (e.g. McDonalds, Burger King, and Bob Evans).

Responsibility requires us to make difficult decisions, but in the proposed ban ... the privilege of the decision-making process is denied.

If the advertising of a product should be prohibited on the basis of its potential detriment to individual or collective public health, no better case could exist than that of the automobile industry. Every year approximately 50,000 Americans die in automobile accidents while hundreds of thousands more are injured and permanently disabled. Following the logic of the prohibitionists, we can expect the withdrawal of automobile advertising to result in a substantial decline in automobile sales and use with a corresponding decrease in automobile-related mortality.

As the debate concerning tobacco advertising turns to its persuasive effects on children, this line of argument may be reoriented to the use of other dangerous products such as motorbikes, which are responsible for 30,000 injuries per year in children from the ages of five to fourteen, despite the fact that six out of every eleven children under the age of thirteen are developmentally incapable of operating these vehicles.

The logic of prohibiting advertising of undesirable products can be extended to absurd lengths by suggesting a ban of advertisements, aimed primarily at children, of heavily sugared food products. In 1977, $10 billion was expended on dental care in this country, most of which was spent on restoration of caries. Foods with a high sugar content are readily available to young children and indiscriminate consumption has definitely been identified as a major contributing factor to this significant health problem. But is the solution a ban on advertising? The Federal Trade Commission, along with the American Dental Association and the American Association of Public Health Dentists, thought so. The FTC proposed such a ban in 1978, in part due to published figures that the average child watches 23.5 hours of television weekly

41

which exposes him/her to 20,000 commercials annually. These are truly incredible statistics, but who is at fault? Is it the government's responsibility to decide what is and is not acceptable for viewing by children?

The current bandwagon, fueled by superficial consideration of emotional issues without regard for significant constitutional concerns, must not be allowed to pass another milestone. . . .

By its very nature, responsibility requires us to make difficult decisions, but in the proposed ban this small fragment of individual and collective responsibility is rejected; the privilege of the decision-making process is therefore denied. When we demand controls of this nature in an emotional attempt to solve complex problems with simple solutions, we invite further repression with open arms. Prohibition never represents a rational (let alone effective) method of confronting society's problems, but rather exemplifies a superficial and palliative attempt to dispose of only the most valuable and accessible expressions of these problems. The reason we are currently at this important juncture is that this dangerous lobby was not satisfied with previous limitations in advertising (which were unfortunately accepted without serious opposition). The current bandwagon, fueled by superficial consideration of emotional issues without regard for significant constitutional concerns, must not be allowed to pass another milestone, to set yet another ominous precedent, from which there may be no return.

Judith M. White
Eagle River, Alaska

Occupation: Utilities Tariff Analyst
Interests: Flower gardening, cooking, canning the
salmon her husband and son catch, reading,
conversation
Entered the Competition because: "It was an
opportunity for me to address a subject about which
I have strong feelings."

It is when we believe that our particular vision of the public interest is so perfect that we indulge in the ultimate self-aggrandizement—the restriction of the rights of those whom we believe to have less perfect vision. . . .

CIGARETTE ADVERTISING AND THE FREE EXPRESSION OF IDEAS

During the last quarter of the eighteenth century, the founding fathers of this country teetered between their desire for an organized and stable society and their commitment to a new society made strong by the recognition of fundamental rights belonging to all men.

In response to a monarchical master accused of "a long train of abuses and usurpations," they penned their signatures to a document of open rebellion whose most fundamental theme was that governments are instituted to secure life, liberty and happiness for those they govern. Following the successful military conclusion of that rebellion, the thirteen states bound together in a loose confederation. The strength of the confederation—the inability of a central government to oppress its members—was also its weakness, for the confederation was so loose that it could not foster an organized and stable society. Faced with overwhelming practical problems and a mandate to "render the constitution of the Federal Government adequate to the exigencies of the Union," an early Congress issued the call for a convention to revise the Articles of Confederation.

Every American child hears the story of that convention. They are told that the delegates ignored their restricted orders and instead compromised on a new document that vastly increased the power of the central government while simultaneously restricting the ability of the government through a complicated series of checks and balances that we know as the separation of powers. For many citizens of the country, this proposed document, which evolved from the desire for an organized and stable society, did not commit the government it created strongly enough to basic human rights. Ratification of the Constitution by the states took place over a three-year period, and some of those states finally ratified only in the strong belief that the document would be immediately amended to protect the "rights of man."

Thus it was that the very first session of the First Congress assembled under the authority of the Constitution submitted to the states ten amendments which were ultimately ratified and are now known as the Bill of Rights. Of those ten amendments, none is more fundamental than the first:

> Congress shall make no law respecting an establishment of religion, or prohibiting the free exercise thereof; or abridging the freedom of speech, or of the press; or the right of the people peaceably to assemble, and to petition the Government for a redress of grievances.

Indeed, ask any American what the Bill of Rights protects, and it will be a rare bird that answers with anything more than the freedom of religion, speech, press and assembly.

The document so laboriously created in Philadelphia during the summer of 1787 was incomplete; the Bill of Rights completed it. There is some argument that all the subsequent revisions to the Constitution simply have been technical window dressings or restatements that have not altered the essential features of the new government: the strength of stability; the nobility of human rights.

The period from 1776 to 1791 in America is truly a marvelous story—comprising actual war, the conflict of ideas and personalities, and best of all, victory not only for generations of Americans but also for millions of other inhabitants of the planet Earth whose leaders were influenced by the powerful ideas and passionate words of Jefferson, Hamilton, Adams and Madison.

In the two hundred intervening years since the Declaration of Independence and the Constitution were the current events of the day, the conflict has continued between the rights of one individual or group to voice their opinions and the desire by others, usually the "majority," to promote their particular visions of the public interest. The most shameful moments of our history have occurred when that "majority" succeeded in oppressing the rights of individuals simply to speak or assemble. Less than ten years after the Bill of Rights had been ratified, Congress passed a Sedition Act making it a crime to publish any statement bringing either the president or Congress into contempt or disrepute. For over sixty years following the ratification of the Bill of Rights, black Americans were systematically denied the right to speak and assemble freely. One hundred and fifty years following the ratification of the Bill of Rights, Americans of Japanese descent were herded into internment camps.

With our hindsight from the end of the twentieth century, the Sedition Act, slavery and Japanese internment seem not simply cruel but irrational and incomprehensible—akin to an earlier insistence that the earth was the center of the universe. How, we wonder, could these things have happened? The First Amendment is so clear—Congress shall make *no* law . . . abridging the freedom of speech, or of the press; or the right of the people peaceably to assemble. . . ." There are no ifs, no conditions, no exceptions: "Congress shall make *no* law. . . ."

The capacity for rational thought and action is the greatest human faculty. The First Amendment does not grant Americans the privilege of free speech; instead it recognizes that we have a fundamental right to exercise this greatest of human faculties.

Almost all our speech is so mundane—so caught up in the daily activities of living and working—that it never occurs to us that someone or some institution would think it worth censoring. Yet events and ideas which to most Americans are mundane today may have been very controversial in the not too distant past: tens of millions of women holding jobs outside their homes; the use of marijuana to benefit glaucoma victims; the "Big Bang" theory in astronomy; nuns in street dress—the list is endless. Can we imagine the nature of our lives had no one been free to voice these ideas?

It is when we believe that our particular vision of the public interest is so perfect that we indulge in the ultimate self-aggrandizement—the restriction of the rights of those whom we believe to have less perfect vision to speak, to worship, to assemble or to publish. It is ironic that these restrictions say more about the restrictor than those restricted. When society or the state has to close a man's mouth, it must either admit that there is no rational answer to what he has to say or assert that those who might hear him have lost their capacity for rational thought and action.

The debate about cigarette advertising is not about cigarettes; it is about speech and the free flow of ideas. And speech, whether radical or conservative, must be met with speech.

The current debate about cigarette advertising illustrates this phenomenon. Those who would censor the advertising of an absolutely legal product are reduced to reliance on a theory of the nature of man that conflicts with the whole fabric of our history, for they argue that men and women are incapable of evaluating information and making rational decisions about their lifestyles, their personal habits, their children. One rarely hears an advocate of cigarette advertising censorship speak on the subject when he does not pronounce that, while he himself is able to discern the true facts about cigarettes, his concern is for the vast majority of the public, which lacks this ability.

The debate about cigarette advertising is not about cigarettes; it is about speech and the free flow of ideas. And speech, whether radical or conservative, must be met with speech.

While I do not smoke cigarettes, I know that I gain from living in a society where manufacturers have the ability to disseminate information about their products; and while I generally ignore cigarette advertising, I may not ignore advertising of some other products which is offensive to other individuals. I have never heard a tobacco company argue that those who oppose cigarettes should be outlawed from voicing their opposition. It seems incongruous that those who argue that they pursue a more perfect future are Machiavellian in their pursuit. I believe that the vast majority of Americans recognize that there is no social goal so noble that it justifies the means of censorship. What idea can be so powerful that it must be protected at the expense of free expression and yet so fragile that it cannot withstand the ordinary advertising applicable to millions of products ranging from asprin to xylophones?

I have never heard a tobacco company argue that those who oppose cigarettes should be outlawed from voicing their opposition.

If tobacco advertising is censored today, what products will be next? Controversial ideas abound today, and individuals hold strong feelings on all sides of these controversial ideas which inevitably have products associated with them. American businesses have traditionally advertised their products and their philosophies. These products and philosophies have conflicted and competed; some succeeded, some failed. But we have all benefitted—not simply from the newspapers and magazines funded from advertising but more importantly from the opportunity to evaluate, to discuss and to accept or discard the advertising information we received.

In 1859, John Stuart Mill articulated the value of free speech in his famous essay, *On Liberty*. It made sense then, and it makes sense today:

> If all mankind minus one were of one opinion, and only one person were of the contrary opinion, mankind would be no more justified in silencing that one person, than he, if he had the power, would be justified in silencing mankind. . . . The peculiar evil of silencing the expression of an opinion is, that it is robbing the human race; posterity as well as the existing generation; those who dissent from the opinion, still more than those who hold it. If the opinion is right, they are deprived of the opportunity of exchanging error for truth; if wrong, they lose, what is almost as great a benefit, the clearer perception and livelier impression of truth produced by its collision with error.

Keith Burgess-Jackson
Tucson, Arizona

Occupation: Graduate Student
Interests: Bicycling, hiking, reading, music
Entered the Competition because: "I'm interested in
the conceptual issues surrounding free speech, as
well as the practical problems."

FREE SPEECH, ADVERTISING AND CENSORSHIP

Americans are and always have been a people of principle. When it
comes to criminal justice, we pride ourselves on the many safeguards
that have been built into our system. Better that ten guilty persons go
free, we say, than that one innocent person be convicted. A similar
commitment appears in connection with speech, assembly and petition.
However easy it may be in the short run to coerce individuals for
pragmatic reasons, for some real or apparent public good, we resist such
coercion in favor of abstract principle. "Congress shall make no law . . .
abridging the freedom of speech. . . ." These ten words summarize our
adherence to a principle of liberty, and in particular the liberty to speak.
In popular terminology, we say that these words confer a *right* to speak
freely.

Nonetheless, there has been considerable debate over the meaning
and effect of the First Amendment, some of it arising from misconcep-
tions about the nature of rights. If a right is anything, it is a bulwark
against the slings and arrows of popular sentiment. In the twenties, it
was sentiment against drinking alcoholic beverages; in the fifties, it was
sentiment against Communists and Communist sympathizers. Today,
among other things, it is sentiment against smoking, smokers and
tobacco. Had we succumbed to the earlier sentiments and thrown
principle to the wind, the world would be a much different—and
undoubtedly worse—place than it is. But fortunately, whenever there
were voices shouting "Censor this! Censor that!" there were others
shouting "Liberty! Liberty!" The forces for liberty ultimately prevailed,
however unpopular they may have been at the time.

The conflict between principle and pragmatism crops up regularly
in our daily lives. We make a promise to a friend. When the time comes
for fulfilling the promise, we notice that it would be convenient—
perhaps even remunerative—to break it. But the principle of promise
keeping leads us to do otherwise, and on reflection we think that this is
for the best. The same process occurs in public life. There is widespread
sentiment for restricting the public access of smokers; there is clamor for

restrictions on tobacco advertising. And yet, we are principled enough in our reflective moments to realize that something important goes by the boards if we submit to these restrictions. However we may feel personally about tobacco and smokers, and whether we are smokers or nonsmokers ourselves, we are sufficiently committed to principles to be willing to sacrifice something for them.

This, in fact, is the essence of a right. A right is a summary of a principle that we hold dear. To say that someone has a right to do X is to admit that, even if X causes harm or offense to others, it has weight on the scale. It may be that the harm or offense is comparatively insignificant, in which case we side with liberty. Or it may be that the harm or offense is comparatively weighty, in which case we restrict liberty for the good of all. The important feature of rights is that they have *extra* weight. They are not just one consideration among many that policymakers put on the scale before making a decision. We think that rights are important enough to confer them on every citizen as protection against an intrusive and coercive government. One of the most important of these rights is the right to free speech.

To override the right to free speech on grounds that the speech in question is likely to harm or offend others is to commit an act of censorship. Not all censorship is unjustified, however, for some speech causes significant and direct harm to others. Examples are maliciously defamatory speech and speech which discloses national secrets to prospective enemies. But there should be a presumption that all speech is protected against censorship. The burden of proof and persuasion should always be on the censor, not the speaker. The would-be censor must show not just that harm or offense to others is likely to result from the speech in question, but that the harm or offense is *significant*. It must also be direct. Given the value of free speech, we should not restrict it on grounds that, in some remote or fanciful way, it will adversely affect others.

Given the value of free speech, we should not restrict it on the grounds that, in some remote or fanciful way, it will adversely affect others.

One implication of a principled approach to free speech is that commercial advertising, like political and scientific speech, should be protected. To conclude otherwise would be to engage in just the sort of pragmatic or ad hoc reasoning that principles are designed to exclude. In other words, since commercial speech is speech, it is protected. The burden of establishing otherwise lies with the would-be censor, not the would-be speaker. This distinction makes sense of most of our intuitions about speech and censorship in everyday life. First of all, most of us agree that the prohibition of commercial fraud is justified. Fraud is an act which harms specific others in significant ways; moreover, it is direct. The same is true of misleading and deceptive advertising. We can admit both that advertising, as speech, is valuable, and that it has its limits. The freedom to speak ends where it causes significant and direct harm to others.

Consider the much-discussed ban on tobacco advertising. Advertising is a form of speech, an attempt to win people over to the virtues of one's product; hence, the burden of demonstrating that it causes harm or offense to others lies with the censor. Given our principle of free speech, we should be willing to sacrifice something—some small bit of harm or offense, perhaps—in order to protect what the right to free speech embodies. What is the harm that tobacco advertising allegedly causes? According to the would-be censors, it is lung cancer and a variety of other physical ailments. The argument goes roughly as follows: Tobacco advertisements cause people to smoke; smoking causes death and disease; and death and disease constitute harms; therefore, we as a society are justified in prohibiting tobacco advertisements.

The problem with this line of reasoning is that it ignores altogether the principle of free speech. It succumbs to the very pragmatism that principles are designed to avoid. It is not enough, as we have seen, to simply point out that such-and-such an act of speech causes or is likely to cause harm to others. As we have conceptualized rights, they are consistent with a certain amount of harm. That is what makes them valuable. So the censor must show more than this: the censor must show not only that tobacco advertisements cause harm, but that the harm prevented through censorship *outweighs* the liberty of tobacco advertisers to speak, and also the liberty of individuals to have information about tobacco products. This alone seems to be an insurmountable task.

But there is more. The censor must show that the harms allegedly caused by tobacco advertising are sufficiently *direct* to justify censorship. We do not restrict liberty simply because, under some conceivable set of circumstances, one's action may cause harm to another. The harm must be direct. It cannot be the joint product of the original action and a self-imposed choice by a willing consumer. In the case of tobacco advertising, if there is any harm at all, it is consented-to harm. The advertisement provides information to prospective consumers, nothing more. It does not coerce them into purchasing tobacco products; nor does it force its way into their homes. If a person desires to avoid tobacco advertisements entirely, he or she can do so by averting the eyes and ears at appropriate times. Any harm or offense that is caused by tobacco advertising is too remote to justify censorship.

Thus, the case for commercial advertising in general, and tobacco advertising in particular, rests solidly on the principle of free speech. The censor's burden is heavy, and probably cannot be carried. What follows are several common objections to the free-speech principle, together with replies and discussion.

First, it might be objected that not all speech is created equal. Political and religious speech, for example, deserve more protection than commercial speech. Whereas it takes significant and direct harm to justify restricting political or religious speech, it takes much less to justify restricting or eliminating commercial speech. But this objection founders for the very reason that principles are important to us. It draws an arbitrary distinction—a distinction based not on the value of speech to the speaker, but on the alleged value of the speech to the prospective listeners. Is there any evidence that American citizens prize political speech more highly than commercial speech? Is it obvious that a rational citizen would trade information on a wide variety of products for a reduction in remote, self-imposed and comparatively insignificant harm to others? Given that we live in and prize a free market economy, any distinction between commercial and other kinds of speech is unsupportable.

A second objection focuses on the alleged *right* to free speech. Rights aren't absolute, one might say, so it is permissible for policy-makers to regulate, restrict and perhaps ban certain forms of advertising. If this is so, then the proposed ban on tobacco advertising is justified. But this objection misses the point. The claim has never been that rights are absolute. Such a view would quickly generate absurdities and moral dilemmas. (For instance, what happens when one of two individuals, each of whom has a right to life, must die?) The claim is rather that rights are *valuable*—so valuable, in fact, that we attach an artificially high weight to them when we formulate public policy and adjudicate between conflicting interests. To have a right to X, as we have seen, means that mere public good is insufficient to deprive one of X. From the fact that rights are not absolute it does not follow that they are worthless.

A third objection pursues a different angle. Surely, one might argue, there is no right to harm or offend others. But this is exactly what tobacco advertisers claim to have. Given the studies which demonstrate a causal link between smoking and lung cancer, and given that individuals are persuaded to smoke by viewing tobacco advertisements, to assert a right to speak freely on this subject is tantamount to asserting a right to harm others. Clearly there can be no such right.

This objection, unlike the previous two, rests upon empirical claims which have not been proven to the satisfaction of many scientists. While a correlation may be *evidence* of a causal connection, it is not, without more, a *demonstration* of a causal connection. But even if the objector is right about these factual claims, even if smoking does cause lung cancer and other ailments, and even if individuals are persuaded to smoke by viewing tobacco advertisements, it does not follow that the right in question is "a right to harm others." As indicated above, rights protect interests which are thought to be important—so important that we are willing to pay a price to protect them. The price that we pay is some small bit of harm or offense to others. This does not mean that any amount of harm is permissible, for we draw the line between significant and insignificant harms. We also require that the harm be direct—that it not be self-imposed. In the case of smoking, the second of these conditions is not satisfied.

The fourth objection centers on the intentions of those who drafted the First Amendment. The framers of our Constitution, it might be argued, did not intend for it to protect tobacco advertisers. The First Amendment was intended to cover political and religious speech, not commercial speech. Since tobacco advertising could not have been before the minds of the framers, it deserves less protection now—if indeed it deserves any protection at all. But this objection again rests on dubious empirical claims. For one thing, the framers were as concerned as any modern American with the viability of an open market, as well as with the viability of commercial advertising. Colonial newspapers were rich sources of information about products and services. Second, tobacco was a mainstay of the colonial economy. To suggest the framers were antagonistic toward smoking, smokers or tobacco is to engage in historical fantasy, not serious history.

But even if these factual claims were true, it would still not follow that the intentions and desires of the framers should govern our current situation. The framers of the Constitution lived in a world that was in many ways much different from our own. They could not have foreseen the geographical growth of the nation, the development of vast commercial networks, and the advent of electronic media. James Madison, prescient as he may have been in other respects, could not have envisioned the modern corporate state or the fragile relationship that has come to exist between production, exchange and marketing. For this reason, it is the merest form of speculation to invoke his intentions. But policy decisions must be made, and we wish them to be rational, so we must invoke some theory or other of the First Amendment. The first part of this essay constitutes a sketch of such a theory. It is a theory based on principles and rights.

But we must make a stand now, for popular sentiment against smoking, smokers and tobacco is at fever pitch. It is ultimately . . . a matter of holding firm to what is valuable.

Finally, it might be objected that we live in a democracy; that if duly elected legislators decide to ban tobacco advertising, the people will have spoken. Anyone who claims otherwise—anyone who claims that the people, through their legislators, are not entitled to do so— must be mistaken at best and antidemocratic or antirepublican at worst. But again, this objection misconceives the nature of rights. Rights are bulwarks against popular sentiment. They protect minorities from the ravages of majorities, however well intentioned those majorities may be. *By definition*, rights protect certain interests even though some harm may befall the public in the process. This conception of rights has served us well throughout our history, and is likely to continue to do so in the future. But we must make a stand now, for popular sentiment against smoking, smokers and tobacco is at fever pitch. It is ultimately a matter of principle, a matter of holding firm to what is valuable.

Edward F. Mazur
Mena, Arkansas

Occupation: Retired Electronics Engineer, now self-employed
Interests: Music, ham radio, crafts, writing, travel
Entered the Competition: "As a challenge; to determine whether my words, opinions and arguments had any power to sway a panel of distinguished experts in the field."

There is a trade-off between risk and benefit which no one but the individual can make.

We are a gregarious, impulsive and energetic people. Ours is a wonderful world, full of vitality, action and competition. We engage in all sorts of activities and pursuits to satisfy and fulfill our individual needs. We jump out of planes with colorful parachutes. We run off cliffs holding on to a kite-like craft made of sticks and fabric. We explore a shipwreck two hundred feet below the ocean. We soar aloft in a hot air balloon traveling at the whim of the wind. We also play the zither and the bagpipes, dance the ballet and the polka, paint a skyline or an abstract vision, partake of French cuisine or Kentucky Fried Chicken. The choice is ours and we are only limited by our abilities, desires and means. If all three of these are present, the way is clear. If not, we are still free to give it a try. There are no restrictions or prohibitions—at least not yet.

And why not? The Declaration of Independence states that among our "unalienable Rights" are those of "Life, Liberty, and the Pursuit of Happiness." The Constitution guarantees it. The American lifestyle encourages it. That's what America is all about. The freedom to challenge the physical world, to defy nature, to confront scientific theory and principle, to stretch human performance to higher and higher limits. The freedom to eat goldfish, grasshoppers or rattlesnake meat—if one has a taste for it—or to drink yak's milk, sarsaparilla or home brew, if that strikes his fancy.

But, while the free exercise of individual will is a precious right that cannot and should not be abridged, it is recognized that such free exercise is not always without cost. For example, sky diving and hang gliding are exhilarating activities but result in some crippling accidents and fatalities. Driving a car, either as a necessity or for pleasure, involves some danger. Each year, nearly 50,000 are killed and many more are maimed in traffic accidents. A game of golf is very enjoyable even though it carries a risk of being hit by a ball or club, struck by lightning, run over by a golf cart or bitten by a snake. Joggers, eager to improve their fitness and well-being, often injure their internal organs, damage their feet and even drop dead of cardiac arrest. Tennis, weight lifting, hunting, fishing, boating, auto racing, motorcycling, swimming, scuba diving and even home gardening are all associated with injuries and fatalities.

And when air and water pollution are considered, along with chemical residues in the food chain, nuclear power radiation, and the danger of high cholesterol foods, one begins to realize that while it is a wonderful, exciting world, it is also a dangerous one. But it always has been dangerous, much more so in the past than now.

Certainly there are far more hazards today than in the Stone Age. But we also have more remedies and countermeasures now than there were then. We know what the weather is going to be and can prepare accordingly. The Stone Age man would drown in a flood or a hurricane and perhaps freeze to death from an unanticipated change in the weather. We have the technology to grow and store vast amounts of food. Stone Age man knew nothing of food cultivation or preservation and very often starved to death. Our medical capabilities and facilities are highly advanced and can be summoned quickly through sophisticated communications systems. But Stone Age man would most likely perish after a minor illness or accident.

It is not surprising that population growth was at such a low rate during that era. It took about 10,000 years for the world population to reach 300 million by the year 1 A.D. It took nearly 1,700 more years for that population to double. But in less than 300 years—from 1700 to 1987—the population increased eight times to nearly 5 billion. The greatest growth occurred in the last 100 years, the same period in which technology and industrialization advanced so rapidly. During that time, the world added 3.5 billion more people to its ranks. It is obvious that if mankind was unable to come to grips with the risks and dangers to life in an advancing society, population growth could not have been possible. So even though the type and number of hazards are increasing, so is our ability to deal with them. The world will continue to be a dangerous place to live. Absolute safety and security will only be found in heaven. Until then, earthlings will have to continue weighing risk against gain in their daily activities.

But guarding against every known danger is not only impossible, it is undesirable as well. Life would become a total bore and the individual would wither away in flesh and in spirit. A zestful life involves a certain amount of excitement and chance. There is a trade-off between risk and benefit which no one but the individual can make. No one can make it for him. No one should make it for him. And yet, there is a growing tendency in our society to do just that.

Control and regulation in many areas of American life are being experienced with increasing frequency. The Bureaucracy appears to be obsessed with the broad aspects of that power. They attempt to control the population of different species of wildlife, the growths of various plants and trees, the breeding of insects, the flow of rivers and even the weather. They issue regulations to control the speeds we drive at, the food we eat, the drugs we take, the beverages we drink and even the way we are born and the way we die. They don't do any of these things very well and in many cases they only aggravate the conditions they set out to improve.

Government officials ought to direct their energies and expertise to the areas they are most knowledgeable in and have the greatest influence on. For example, the reduction of the $2 trillion federal debt; a cut in the runaway federal spending program; elimination of the balance of payments deficit; the rescue of America's industries from foreign encroachment; and restoration of the American standard of living. Governmental control of these crucial problems could yield considerably more in terms of improved national prosperity, personal well-being, and optimistic outlook than the present meddling in the lives of their constituents. But perhaps they are unwilling or unable to grapple with these important issues and are content to exercise their power in more trivial pursuits.

Their attention now appears to be focused on certain products or activities that may be harmful to the public, and it has been suggested that such products be banned from any form of advertising. Many items, it would seem, could be classified as harmful to one degree or another and the list could be quite long. Almost everything we do or everything we consume carries with it some degree of risk. It would also appear that if a product or activity is known to cause ill effects or results in fatalities to the users, its sale and manufacture should be banned, not just its advertising program. This, of course, has been the case with some products which were known to be extremely dangerous, such as DDT, Thalidomide and various other drugs and appliances. Those products quickly disappeared from the marketplace.

The announcement, however, that Congress is now considering a ban on the advertising of tobacco products raises some profound observations. To begin with, the case against tobacco has never been very strong. For example, it has never been explained why many people who have smoked for fifty or more years die of something other than respiratory disease or cancer. Or why others who have never smoked contract lung cancer or emphysema. It has never been determined whether the temperament or personality of the individual that predisposes him to smoke is a factor in the onset of illness. Nor has the alleged offending agent in tobacco ever been isolated and identified.

It is interesting to note that while cigarette smoking has been going on for well over one hundred years, the incidence of lung cancer began to increase only after the end of World War II. The rate of that increase appeared to coincide with the increase in toxic air pollutants rather than in the increase in tobacco consumption. To single out tobacco products as harmful commodities based on dubious and inconclusive evidence is, at best, speculative. Banning the advertising of those products would not only be a disservice to the tobacco industry and the public but would set a dangerous precedent for selective censorship of other firms and products.

Such a ban would also be a violation of traditional American business ethics. It would be contrary to, and in defiance of, the Declaration of Independence and the Preamble to the Constitution. It would constitute an infringement of the First Amendment with regard to free expression of vital information in pursuit of a legitimate and free market enterprise, and would cast a stigma upon the product's merits by suggesting that it was harmful to every user.

In addition, the advertising ban would indirectly violate the product user's rights of free choice by denying him information concerning it and discrediting the product in order to discourage its use—a use which had previously satisfied his needs.

Although the congressional proposition is seriously flawed and there are powerful arguments against it, there is a good possibility that the proposal can pass. Constitutional infringement and censorship are not new in the American experience. Misguided moralists and self-styled benefactors have frequently imposed their dogmas on the nation, but none lasted very long.

The Eighteenth Amendment to the Constitution prohibiting the sale and distribution of intoxicating liquors was passed in 1919. Its real aim was the elimination of alcoholic consumption—without directly saying so—on the grounds that alcohol was harmful to health and to morals. The Prohibition Amendment, however, caused more harm than good. It created more loose morals than it cured, increased the number of criminals and racketeers, and after failing to curb the people's appetite for liquor or their right of free choice, was repealed in 1933 to the cheers of the nation.

A somewhat more successful attempt at control and censorship began in the 1870s and lasted for over forty years. A veteran of the Civil War, Anthony Comstock, devoted his life to a crusade aimed at the removal of objectionable books, paintings and other material. Comstock, who was born in Pennsylvania of Puritan ancestry, established the New York Society for the Suppression of Vice in the year 1873. Later, as an official agent of the U.S. Post Office, he initiated and promoted stronger laws barring obscene materials from the mails. He was instrumental in banning many books and was responsible for the censorship of 500,000 drawings and paintings. Comstock once had

3,000 persons arrested for obscenity and proudly took credit for hounding sixteen persons to their death through mental anguish and suicide. He was successful in banning Margaret Sanger's books on birth control and bragged continually of having destroyed 160 tons of literature and of sending thousands of people to prison.

In 1915, President Woodrow Wilson appointed Anthony Comstock U.S. Delegate to the International Purity Congress meeting in San Francisco. By this time public opposition to Mr. Comstock and his crusade had reached a peak, partly because of a run-in he had with George Bernard Shaw. Mr. Shaw later said, "Comstockery is the world's standing joke at the expense of the U.S. It confirms the deep seated conviction of the Old World that America is a provincial place, a 2nd rate country town." Shortly thereafter Comstock died and so did his crusade, but not without leaving scars.

In some respects this European view of the U.S. is again being revived. The efforts of the crusaders, as in George Bernard Shaw's time, are not going unnoticed. Europeans, including those of the Communist countries, are heavier smokers than their American counterparts. Yet their governments are not imposing restrictions on their decision to do so. For Americans who take immense pride in their birthright of freedom from oppression, liberty and justice for all, this may come as a surprise.

The denial of rights, interference in free trade, and censorship have all been implemented at one time or another by the government and influential groups in the United States. It can be done again, and in the case of the ban on tobacco advertising, the machinery is already in motion. The tobacco industry has been under attack for many years by various groups within the government and in the private sector. The public has become inured to the continuing charges, rebuttals and conflicting statistical data, and at this point might acquiesce to the passage of such an advertising ban. And therein lies the danger. Legislation of this type would be the foot in the door, the nose of the camel poking into the tent, the tip of the iceberg, resulting in still more acts of censorship and paternalistic compulsion.

Legislation of this type would be the foot in the door . . . resulting in still more acts of censorship and paternalistic compulsion.

Americans have come a long way since the first settlers landed on these shores. They carved out a nation second to none as free men, deciding alone what was in their best interest. And when King George and Lord North had other ideas on how they should live, colonists took strong exception to them. That spirit lives on to this day and should be encouraged, not stifled. Let Americans be Americans.

Professor Butler D. Shaffer
Los Angeles, California

Occupation: Law Professor
Interests: Writing and thinking
Entered the Competition: "To express my views re
the importance of totally unfettered freedom of
expression."

There is no shortage of men and women who are so certain of the validity of their own conclusions that they are prepared to restrain others. . . .

DOES THE FIRST AMENDMENT'S PROTECTION OF THE "MARKETPLACE OF IDEAS" ALSO PROTECT THE MARKETPLACE?

There has long been, in both our law and culture, an underlying assumption that First Amendment guarantees of freedom of expression exist primarily—if not exclusively—to protect *political* and *ideological* speech and writing, leaving so-called commercial speech subject to government regulation. While the United States Supreme Court has, in recent years, somewhat extended constitutional protections to commercial advertising, these same decisions have continued to insist upon a demarcation between commercial and noncommercial expression, declaring that "the Constitution . . . accords a lesser protection to commercial speech than to other constitutionally guaranteed expression;"[*] and that "commercial speech" has been afforded "a limited measure of protection, commensurate with its subordinate position in the scale of the First Amendment values. . . ."[†]

This assumption appears to be grounded in the belief that freedoms of speech, press and assembly serve to keep the citizens of a democracy fully informed as to facts, issues and competing policies, so that political decisions can be rendered by a knowledgeable electorate. Without denying that an unrestrained freedom of expression is absolutely essential to even the narrowest definition of a free society, or that restraints on political expression have, throughout human history, posed far more serious threats to our liberty than intrusions on commercial speech, it

[*] *Central Hudson Gas and Electric Corporation v. Public Service Commission*, 447 U.S. 557, at 562–563, 100 S. Ct. 2343, at 2349–2350 (1980).
[†] *Ohralik v. Ohio Bar Association*, 436 U.S. 447, at 456, 98 S. Ct. 1912, at 1918 (1978).

nevertheless totally misconceives of the social value of free expression to maintain this arbitrary distinction between political and commercial expression.

It must be remembered that the "founding fathers" were not only classic political liberals versed in the thoughts of such men as John Locke and Adam Smith. They were also men of reason who, at the dawn of the Industrial Revolution, were able to appreciate the significance of a human understanding, enhanced by discoveries in the physical and biological sciences, to create technologies that would enhance the material well-being of all mankind. In our highly politicized world, we often forget that Benjamin Franklin, for instance, was more than simply a draftsman of the Constitution: he was also an inventor, an important scientist, a publisher and a businessman. We forget that Thomas Jefferson was more than just the architect of the Declaration of Independence: he was also the architect—both figuratively and literally—of the University of Virginia, an institution that reflected the importance Jefferson attached to free thinking and free expression. When Jefferson declared: "I have sworn upon the altar of God, eternal hostility against every form of tyranny over the mind of man,"* he was surely expressing a greater awareness of the importance free thought and free communication had in the lives of men and women than is contained in a doctrine that would limit such liberties only to political matters.

That unrestricted expression has more than simply political or ideological value can be seen from the practice of "brainstorming" used in industrial problem solving. Premised upon the value arising from the cross-fertilization of ideas, brainstorming techniques consist of a group of problem solvers sitting around a table and verbalizing every conceivable solution to the given problem. It is crucial to the success of such a method that no judgments be made of any particular suggestions at the time they are offered. It is understood that 1) all ideas are welcomed, no matter how "far out" or "impractical" they might at first appear, because one "far out" idea might very well trigger a better idea in the mind of another participant, and 2) criticisms made of ideas as they are offered have a chilling effect, and tend to restrict the kind of spontaneous thinking that often produces creative solutions. Once the participants have completed this spontaneous phase of suggestion making, they proceed to evaluate the various offerings. Organizations that use such brainstorming methods will attest to the value that unrestrained free expression has in solving the most practical of problems.

"But how," an advocate of government regulation of commercial

* Thomas Jefferson, *Letter to Benjamin Rush*, September 23, 1800.

70

speech might argue, "does this relate to, let us say, restrictions on tobacco companies advertising their products on television? What possible benefits could be produced by allowing such companies to inform people about their products? After all, everybody knows that cigarette smoking is harmful to one's health."

Such a response is, of course, offered with the same smug self-assurance that led medieval church officials to ban the writings of Copernicus and Galileo, as well as other men of science; that caused many municipalities to pass ordinances in the early 1900s banning the use of automobiles; and that even led one police department, in the nineteenth century, to arrest a man for fraud trying to sell stock in a company that would sell telephones, a device that "everyone knows" could never work! There is no shortage of men and women who are so certain of the validity of their own conclusions that they are prepared to restrain others in the kinds of decisions *they* can make. But the fallacy that always underlies censorship practices is founded on the arrogance of presumed omniscience: he who would censor always believes that he is already possessed of sufficient information and understanding and, by virtue thereof, is able to determine, in advance, what information is and is not valid and relevant for intelligent decision making by others.

Let us take the present television ban on cigarette commercials as an example of the point being made. Let us imagine a woman who is trying to decide whether or not to smoke cigarettes. Let us suppose further that she is not content with simply reacting, in a conditioned way, to all the antismoking arguments that have been presented to her, but is intent on making an intelligent, informed decision. How will she go about doing so? There is an abundance of antismoking "public service" messages on television, but where is there an opportunity for the tobacco companies to present their best case to her?

"But they shouldn't be *allowed* to present their case," our advocate of commercial censorship will counter. "Besides, commercial advertising is never done for the purpose of providing consumers with information. It is *sellers*, not buyers, who benefit from advertising, because sellers are thus able to get people to buy things they really don't want or need."

Again, the arrogance of the censor arises to assert his "right" to "protect" people from experiencing what he does not *want* them to experience: the freedom of self-directed minds exercising independent judgments. The notion that advertising is a form of consumer seduction has been around since long before Vance Packard popularized it in his book *The Hidden Persuaders*. That its basic premise has been refuted both by economic studies and the marketplace reality that buyers will *pay money* to obtain catalogs and other publications containing mostly advertising—not to mention the increasing popularity of televised and computerized "shop at home" services, as well as the importance of a "Yellow Pages" directory in every home—has not diminished the enthusiasm with which it has been advanced by those intent on directing what others may see, read or hear. In assuming that advertisers seek only to overcome the free wills of consumers, the censor may only be projecting his *own* motives.

In assuming that advertisers seek only to overcome the free wills of consumers, the censor may only be projecting his *own* motives.

What those who would ban advertising usually fail to understand is how even their well-intended efforts often produce a far greater harm than what they seek to regulate. A good example can be seen in the media and government's one-sided treatment of the dangers associated with the smoking of marijuana. For decades, young men and women have been subjected to a frenetic *Reefer Madness* scare campaign that told them marijuana use would cause them to lose control over their minds and their behavior and produce irreversible brain damage. Those who tried marijuana soon discovered how overstated these dangers were. Now, when the media and government agencies warn people about the dangers of drugs that may, indeed, have health- and life-threatening consequences, the exaggeration of the antimarijuana campaigns come to mind and lead many to doubt *any* warnings about drugs. A more open discussion on the nature and effects of marijuana, with all interested parties having access to the media, might well have given greater credibility to those who warn against more powerful drugs and, as a consequence, saved many lives in the process.

What the advocates of any form of censorship fail to understand is that a society of free and intelligent human beings must rest upon the premise that minds be free to think about, read about and talk about whatever engages the curiosity or deep conviction of any member of that society. If one looks at the First Amendment more broadly than it has been viewed by the courts, one will discover a purpose of freeing every facet of human consciousness—be it in the form of *speech*, published information and ideas (*press*), *religious* inquiry or meetings to discuss any of the same (*assembly*)—known to men and women of the eighteenth century. Men like Jefferson and Franklin—for whom the practical pursuits of commerce and the philosophical concern for fostering human liberty were but two aspects of living the integrated life—would have understood that liberty cannot be carved up into "protected" and "non-protected" categories without destroying its meaning.

Liberty cannot be carved up into "protected" and "nonprotected" categories without destroying its meaning.

Those who assume that freedom of expression makes for a more informed decision making process in the *political* arena, but are prepared to regulate or censor *commercial* speech, would do well to consider the implications of their position. If, indeed, the political process is enhanced by the unrestrained flow of information and ideas; if there *is* social value having a "marketplace of ideas" in which competing ideologies and policies can freely compete for support from others, how much more so are our personal lives—and, as a consequence, the collective well-being of us all—enhanced by our being free to communicate with one another in matters involving what we will consume, how we shall live and raise our children, and what interests we shall pursue? If freedom of expression improves the quality of our political life, is it not clear that it must have an equally beneficent role to play in enhancing our general quality of life?

If the logic of commercial censorship was applied in the political sphere, we would at once recognize the tyrannical implications of the practice. If, as we have been content to do with the issue of cigarette advertising, we allowed one candidate or one political party or one side of an issue to have access to the media to present their position, all the while denying their opponents access on the grounds of "protecting" the citizenry from "unhealthy" ideas, even the dullest mind would be able to see through the sham.

The issue that underlies every attempt at censorship—whether it be the censorship of political ideas, "pornographic" literature or films, scientific conclusions that conflict with established religious doctrine or commercial advertising—is whether the minds of men and women shall be free of political restraint. "Freedom" is a total proposition. We cannot be "free" to think, write and speak about some matters, while being restrained in our expressions about other matters, particularly when it is government that decides which matters will go into one category or the other. We do not enjoy freedom of thought and expression if we must ask the government to tell us which matters are and which are not "proper" subjects of free speech!

The courts have endeavored to maintain a distinction between political speech, which is protected by the First Amendment, and nonprotected commercial speech. But, when government tries to restrict what our minds may and may not consider; when governments seek to control our minds and regulate what we may see, read or listen to, then, regardless of the subject matter of the regulation, the issue becomes as political as one can make it! The matter becomes political as soon as there is a law prohibiting the conduct and threatening a punishment of violators. This is why the danger to free speech lies not just in the restriction itself, but in the presumed authority of governments to decide what expressions are and are not a subject of First Amendment guarantees.

It has been said that "the price of liberty is eternal vigilance," but we are too often lulled into a state of casualness about our liberties, and soon become content with the assurances of those who would regulate our lives that they seek only to "protect" us. But if we look closely, we will discover that, as often as not, what governments seek to "protect" us from is the pursuit of our own interests. We must relearn, each day of our lives, to be distrusting of political power. We must learn to recognize the inroads on our liberties at the outset. Governments do not suddenly swoop down upon us and strip us of our freedoms—such as by a total censorship—but eat away at our liberties by degrees. Once we learn to accept the "protection" of antipornography laws, laws prohibiting the publication of whatever the government deems in the interest of "national security," and laws banning cigarette commercials on television, it is relatively easy for the same government to persuade us that we need "protection" from wrong opinions, heretical religious viewpoints and divisive ideologies.

Above all else, we need to remember that the First Amendment guarantees of freedom of expression are not so much for the purpose of celebrating the ideas and opinions with which most of us agree— although it *includes* that—but to protect the expression of those views with which most of us disagree. No citizen of Nazi Germany or the Soviet Union ever needed the protection of free speech in order to stand in a public square and praise the regime under which he lived! Free speech is as important or unimportant as we regard our own sense of individuality and value the opportunity to express our sense of self. But we cannot express our sense of being a person if, as every act of censorship necessarily implies, the content of our mind is subject to the supervision of those who, under whatever pretext and for whatever purpose, seek to deny our interests as they enhance their own.

74

Karen A. Olson
Denver, Colorado

Occupation: Secretary/Freelance Writer
Interests: Reading, folk music, theater, film,
bicycling, volleyball, cooking
Entered the Competition because: "I have a long-
standing commitment to civil liberties, including
freedom of expression. The essay competition
provided an opportunity to think, then write,
creatively about censorship issues."

> "I am saddened by my conviction that those people did not know what they were doing. They stumbled down a path they did not want to travel, prodded by vague fears and noble sentiments that they were acting for the common good."

A FUTURE AMERICAN HISTORY REVIEWED

January 12, 2191
Ben Fintz, Editor
American History Revisited
1144886 East Westlake
Boston, Massachusetts 00336-44997-8800 AbD

Dear Ben,

How nice to hear from you again. Yes, I would be interested in writing some new material for AHR. Thanks for thinking of me.

Unfortunately, the assignment you suggested is not one that I feel I can complete successfully. The politilegal history of the late 21st century is not really my field of expertise. I doubt that I could do justice to an article on the merger between the executive and judicial branches of the government.

I'd like to propose an alternative that might be of some interest to your readers. I've recently read some publications from the 1980s and 1990s, and I've run across a few pieces that shed light on the events that preceded the abolition of the First Amendment to the Constitution. Prevailing wisdom maintains that this peculiar little law just withered away of its own irrelevancy. However, I think I could make the case that a series of well-meaning but misdirected efforts was actually responsible for the death of unrestricted freedom of speech and press.

Contrary to popular belief, Americans of the 20th century did appear to place value on the First Amendment. The rhetoric of the period shows that, at least in theory, they held the concept in high esteem. In my article, I would argue that they never intended to abolish any part of the so-called "Bill of Rights"; I will develop the hypothesis that they simply cut away at *certain* applications of the amendment until, ultimately, there was no amendment left.

(You may recall the old-fashioned surgical procedure, well before the widespread use of artificial organs, in which doctors would remove portions of the heart in order to preserve the health of the patient. Their intentions were not to destroy the heart. However, the operation always diminished the patient in some vital way, and the end result of repeated surgery was usually the death of the individual. The deliberate slicing coupled with the benevolent intent resemble the actions I would describe.)

I expect that your initial response to my proposal will be one of bemusement, Ben. But before you dismiss this idea as "cute but unimportant," let me remind you that the original Bill of Rights took effect exactly four hundred years ago this December. Perhaps the nostalgia value of a quatercentennial examination will overcome any objection you might have to an otherwise dead topic.

Please greet Jane and the children for me. I hope to get to Boston soon and would love to sample Jane's exquisite mock clam chowder once again. I'd even spring for the bottled water!

Hoping to hear from you soon—

Karen

February 28, 2191

Dear Karen,

Sorry to take so long to answer your letter. (I had to find someone to write about the executive/judicial merger before I could even begin to consider your proposal. Why do you have to make my life so difficult?)

I confess, though, that the real reason for the delay is that I do not share your enthusiasm for the First Amendment piece. You have already anticipated my objection: Your topic is simply not important enough to warrant an assignment. Everyone agrees that unrestricted freedom of speech is a mad idea. Censorship is the only viable solution to deal with those who would contaminate innocent minds with unwise, false or even dangerous propositions.

Besides the triviality of your topic, I'm afraid that you face another hurdle. You write as though the original intention of the Bill of Rights was to allow anyone to say or write anything he or she pleased. I expect you are mistaken here. Although I have not personally read Thomas Jefferson on the subject, I cannot believe that such a brilliant man would advocate something so reckless.

I am tempted to reject your query outright and save us both some trouble. But in deference to our long friendship and to your distinguished past contributions to AHR, let me only discourage.

I am reluctant to consider your proposed piece at all, but if you insist on writing it, I agree to read it. To assure even the slimmest chance of acceptance, you should take a humorous look at the subject—

a sophisticated view of the superstitions of an unsophisticated people. You might want to broaden the appeal of your article by discussing a whole collection of antiquated blue laws, not just the one. You know what I mean—those laws that ban spitting on Sunday, swearing in public and wearing socks that don't match. Concentrate on the truly funny ones.

I'm sure you can understand why this article must be written on speculation. We simply cannot guarantee payment for something so unlikely to meet our needs.

Finally, as always, our Board of Governors must approve the content. If you decide to go ahead (and I still hope that you decide instead to write something useful), please send periodic summaries of your main points so that we can accept or reject your theses.

On a pleasanter note, Jane and I are looking forward to seeing you whenever you get to Boston. Mock clams are almost impossible to get these days, but if we can find any, you'll have your chowder. Hold off on the bottled water until I can reciprocate with an acceptance check!

Best wishes,
Ben

March 3, 2191

Dear Ben,

I received your letter, and I wanted to send you a quick note telling you that I intend to pursue the First Amendment piece. Rest assured that I will address your objections; I hope you did not confuse my enthusiasm for the topic with any softheaded notion that censorship is wrong.

Nevertheless, I am touched by the naive sincerity of the American public in the last half of the 20th century. The more I read, the more I am convinced that they really supported full freedom of expression. Given their low level of education, simplicity is to be expected. I guess we can only be thankful that some advanced minds were able to see the dangers inherent in a flirtation with anarchy.

(An interesting sidelight to this story is that the masses did not seem to become increasingly convinced, at least from any rational standpoint, of the desirability of censorship. Rather, the advocates had to move slowly, issue by issue. They defined one individual evil and suggested a one-time restriction for the good of all. The masses would adopt that single control, believing it to be essential. The pattern was repeated until restriction was the rule rather than the exception. Had the advocates of censorship been less skilled, the masses might have resisted, and we would all be living in Babel today.)

(One more thought—I seem fated to write in parenthetical statements, but each answer raises a new question. Could it be that this entire issue consists of sidelights and has no real center?

I have just reread the preceding paragraphs and have caught myself in an error. I attribute foresight to those who moved us in the direction of orderly communication, and yet my research shows that they were as unaware as their followers of their destination. They did the right things for the wrong reasons.

The analogy I used in my earlier letter is off base. The surgeons I described meant to do good but did, in fact, do harm. They killed the patient. Here, the surgeons intended to do a small amount of good and did, in fact, do enormous good. So unless I change the object of their scapels from a human heart to a tumor, I will be forced to abandon my comparison.)

I have allowed my thoughts—parenthetical and otherwise—to run away with me. Back to work. . .

Karen

March 23, 2191

Dear Ben,

I will assume that no news is good news. Since I have not heard any recent objections to my article, I am proceeding.

As you know, I had intended to develop the thesis that the authors of the Bill of Rights never intended to permit completely unbridled expression in either speech or printed material. I have hit a snag, however.

I managed to find an old copy of the original Bill of Rights, and I read the amendments themselves. The first one says, "Congress shall make *no* law (emphasis added) . . . abridging the freedom of speech, or of the press. . . ." Now, we were raised to understand that Congress limited any restrictions to those that served the common good. But I can't find language to that effect anywhere in the original document. Can you steer me in the right direction? I have also run across some obscure writings of Thomas Jefferson that disturb me. He may not have been what he seems.

In 1814, he wrote, "Are we to have a censor whose imprimatur shall say what books may be sold, and what we may buy? And who is thus to dogmatize. . . ? Whose foot is to be the measure to which ours are all to be cut or stretched?. . . Shall a layman, simple as ourselves, set up his reason as the rule of what we are to read, and what we must believe?"

80

He continues, "If [a] book be false in its facts, disprove them; if false in its reasoning, refute it. But for God's sake, let us freely hear both sides." Radical, eh?

I need my editor's guidance on this one. Please write quickly.

Karen

April 1, 2191

Dear Karen,

Your editor's guidance is to drop this folly and concentrate on something worthwhile. Let me tempt you with an assignment on the establishment of Ordered Population Zones during the last seventy-five years. Since you delight in exploring chaos, describe the havoc that reigned prior to government direction of population migration. Can you imagine how Arizona and Florida would look today if we had not dispersed the elderly throughout the country? If you really want to get creative, paint a picture of what California would be like if it had survived the earthquake and continued on the path started way back in your beloved 20th century.

This is a serious offer, Karen—one that carries with it the promise of acceptance if written to conform to our standards. Please consider it, and let me know your answer.

As to your quandary, I can only remind you that you proposed to write about an obscure phenomenon that occurred in the late 1900s. Forget about what the founding fathers meant, what Jefferson wrote, what the original Bill of Rights said. None of that is relevant.

I would also remind you that I promised to consider a *humorous* piece on precensorship days. If you must continue with this article, can you liven it up with some of the ridiculous things that were said or written before standards were established?

Let me know about the OPZ's.

Ben

April 16, 2191

Dear Ben,

I am interested in the OPZ article. I'd like to tackle it as soon as I decide what to do about the First Amendment thing.

No, I am not yet ready to abandon my "folly." But I am afraid that you and I will never reach an accord on this topic. Your ideas about infusing the article with humor are good ones and would, in the hands of another writer, be valuable inspiration. Perhaps if we had bantered

81

over a bowl of mock clam chowder (I will dream), I would have developed a different perspective on the issue. Somehow, the satirical vision eludes me.

I have continued to read source documents from the 20th century. And I am saddened by my conviction that those people did not know what they were doing. They stumbled down a path they did not want to travel, prodded by vague fears and noble sentiments that they were acting for the common good. I do not believe that they intended to end up where we are.

You may chuckle (I cannot) to read that restrictions began with someone saying that freedom of speech was never intended to permit someone to yell "Fire" in a crowded theater. How absurd. As though early Americans were overrun with lunatics hollering "Fire" in crowded theaters. As though other, less drastic, safeguards could not have been invoked to deal with those rare circumstances in which one madman did indeed endanger public safety.

We know vaguely of the evil of Naziism. We can understand why people of that age prohibited expressions of sympathy for its evil tenets. Now, the prohibitions seem wise and beneficial. But my reading shows that many of those who supported restrictions did so reluctantly. In their hearts, they supported individual rights and freedom, but they panicked and became practitioners of the very repression they abhorred.

The next steps these primitive people took are laughable in their triviality. They imposed restrictions against the businesses of the day, limiting their rights to promote products. It seems silly to us now: certain goods and services could legally be sold, but they could not legally be discussed.

Their hypocrisy is hardly a matter for debate. Yes, they said one thing and did another. They even said one thing and then said the opposite. But history is replete with examples of addled thinking, it would not be fair to mock this one generation.

"I am convinced that the people of the late 1900s had no desire to abandon the First Amendment. I expect that they felt one little restriction would do no 'harm.' "

The question that intrigues me remains the intention of these people. We are fortunate to live in a society that maintains high standards for what can be publicly said or printed. We are spared the idiot ravings of those who cannot meet our standards. We have mistakenly credited these early Americans with establishing the basis for our standards. We have assumed that they would applaud our success.

We are wrong. I am convinced that the people of the late 1900s had no desire to abandon the First Amendment. I expect that they felt one little restriction would do no "harm." I fear that, given another chance, they would look at our sanitized society and shout "No!"

Surely we are safer than those vulnerable people of the 20th century, protected as we are from the temptations of incorrect thinking. Surely we are happier, free from the anxiety of trying to sort out truths from a tangled mess of competing information. Surely the small price we paid was worth the certainty we gained.

But I cannot help but be haunted by the feeling that those people who gave us the seeds would tremble at the harvest. They would feel betrayed. I keep hearing their voices, raised in a welcome chorus of blessed second chance, shouting, "No!"

Ben, you were right all along. This article should not be written. We are better off without it, and I gratefully accept your offer of a more suitable assignment.

Sincerely,
Karen

William Jay Jacobs
Westport, Connecticut

Occupation: Teacher
Interests: Travel, tennis, chess and much writing
Entered the Competition because: "As a member of
the ACLU I believe passionately that the Bill of
Rights is at the heart of American freedom.
Consequently, I am committed to opposing any
attempts to limit free speech—in this case the right to
advertise a product."

> To Jefferson especially, government was to be neutral—an
> umpire, not a participant in the business of life.

SOCRATES WALKS THE MARKETPLACE

If all mankind minus one, were of one opinion, and only one person were of the contrary opinion, mankind would be no more justified in silencing that one person, than he, if he had the power, would be justified in silencing mankind.
—*John Stuart Mill,* On Liberty

In 399 B.C. an Athenian jury convicted the philosopher Socrates and condemned him to death. His crime: corrupting the minds of the city's youth. His nagging questions, charged the prosecutor, Meletus, had raised doubts among young people about the gods and the laws of Athens. For that, he deserved to die. Spurning the advice of friends that he escape into exile, Socrates drank the poisoned hemlock prescribed in his sentence. Organized society must survive, he reasoned, even if just men sometimes had to become victims of unjust laws.

Now, twenty-four centuries after the death of Socrates, the United States of America still is preoccupied with the issue of whether, or how best, to prevent the minds of free citizens from being "corrupted" into wrongful actions by what they read and hear.

THE FIRST AMENDMENT AND THE MARKETPLACE OF IDEAS

If the struggle for free expression of ideas finds its roots in classical antiquity, the plant perhaps bloomed most fully at the founding of the American republic. Thomas Jefferson proclaimed in the Declaration of Independence that individuals were free to pursue their own values for their own purposes: "We hold these truths to be self-evident, that all men are created equal, that they are endowed by their Creator with certain unalienable Rights; that among those are Life, Liberty, and the pursuit of Happiness."

Or, as stated without qualification in the First Amendment to the Constitution:

> Congress shall make no law respecting an establishment of religion, or
> prohibiting the full exercise thereof; or abridging the freedom of speech,

or of the press; or the right of the people peaceably to assemble, and to petition the government for a redress of grievances.

Today, however, the once "self-evident" freedoms of speech and the press, assumed by the founding fathers, are subjected to relentless, unremitting attack. For example in the field of textbooks for elementary and secondary schools, self-appointed "protectors" of our nation's youth examine books to assure their ideological purity. In response to their concerns hundreds of lines of Shakespeare's *Hamlet* and *Romeo and Juliet* have been deleted in new editions. The phrase "Honest Injun" was removed from Mark Twain's *Tom Sawyer* to avoid offending Native Americans. In one story called "A Perfect Day for Ice Cream" the publisher deleted the story's key scene, a trip by children to an ice cream parlor, in order to avoid being labeled by health critics as an advocate of junk food. One of the major textbook houses removed all references to cowboys from its eighth grade U.S. history text, informing the book's author that the word was "sexist."

How stark is the contrast, then, between such heavy-handed at- tempts at censorship and an incident in Thomas Jefferson's presidency described by historian James A. Eichner. According to Eichner, a German visitor to the White House noticed a newspaper there filled with abuse of the president and asked Jefferson why he did not have the writer hanged. "What? Hang the guardian of public morals?" replied Jefferson. "Put that paper into your pocket, my good friend," he suggested, "and carry it with you to Europe, and when you hear anyone doubt the reality of American freedom, show them that paper, and tell them where you found it."

In our own century President John F. Kennedy restated Jefferson's faith in "the illimitable freedom of the human mind," saying:

> We are not afraid to entrust the American people with unpleasant facts, foreign ideas, alien philosophies, and competitive values. For a nation that is afraid to let its people judge the truth and falsehood in an open market is a nation that is afraid of its people.

Kennedy would scarcely be surprised to know that in Nicaragua, recently, in one of the hundreds of articles cut out of the opposition newspaper *La Prensa* before the Sandinista dictatorship finally shut down the paper completely, the official censor supplied this reason for banning the item: "They accused us of suppressing freedom of expression. That was a lie, and so we clearly could not let them publish it."

A FREE MARKET MAKES A FREE PEOPLE

Along with freedom to think and write and speak comes the practical freedom to act—to make choices in the open market of goods, as well as in the open market of ideas. Such choices must, of necessity, be free choices. For when a robber faces you with "Your money or your life!" that is really no choice at all. Rather, as John Locke put it while preparing the intellectual landscape for Jefferson, governments are created to protect the inherent rights of people to "life, liberty, and property." To Locke, the issue of property remained central. For if a government can presume to take away a person's property, he reasoned, before too long it can presume to take away his liberty and then his life.

As historian Richard Hofstadter has pointed out, the founding fathers represented "a generation of realists." Because of their experience with British colonial rule they distrusted government. In writing the Constitution and, subsequently, the Bill of Rights their principal objective was to shield the individual from excessive intrusion by the state, leaving people free to make their own choices. To Jefferson especially, government was to be neutral—an umpire, not a participant, in the business of life. He hoped for a "wise and frugal government, which should restrain men from injuring one another [and] which shall leave them otherwise free to regulate their own pursuits of industry and improvement."

In the tenscore years since the ratification of our Constitution, government—that intrusive camel—has pushed first its nose and then its whole body into the tent of individual freedom. In most instances the intentions behind such intrusion were (and continue to be) benevolent. Often, however, well-intended legislation has exercised a stultifying, chilling effect on free market enterprise. In New York City, for example, rent controls tend to magnify rather than alleviate the shortage of apartments. Price and wage controls, whether used in the demand economy of the United States or in the command economies of nations like the USSR, seem almost to guarantee the emergence of a thriving black market.

Perhaps the most extreme example in America's history of government intervention to achieve high moral ends was the introduction—by constitutional amendment—of a prohibition on the manufacture, sale and distribution of alcoholic beverages. Never was there a more noble experiment. Clearly, alcohol is a dangerous substance. It takes lives, contributes to the breakup of families and makes ordinarily sensible people behave in an outrageous fashion. As economist Milton Friedman recalls, the onset of Prohibition was marked by a prediction of success by the fiery evangelist Billy Sunday:

> The reign of tears is over. The slums will be only a memory. We will turn our prisons into factories and our jails into corncribs. Men will walk upright now, women will smile, and the children will laugh. Hell will be forever for rent.

Friedman reminds us, too, that "Prohibition was imposed for our own good." It was a morally righteous step "to protect us from ourselves."

We all know what happened. The great gangland empires of Al Capone, Dutch Schultz and Bugs Moran were built on bootleg alcohol. The ventures of those mobsters into prostitution, loan sharking, extortion and drug dealing all came later. Illicit alcohol was the bedrock of their careers. Respectable, law-abiding citizens in search of a drink became lawbreakers. Men and women who never before had considered drinking found it glamorous, exciting, to do what national, state and local governments unanimously—and by force of law—decreed was harmful for them to do.

In the end, the American people did not stop consuming alcohol. Today, in most localities in the United States those who wish to purchase alcoholic beverages may do so legally. Nevertheless, severe legislative restrictions still limit the *advertising* of liquor—even where it is a fully legal commodity—by prohibiting the appearance of ads on radio and television. Such restrictions on advertising, like the Prohibition Amendment itself, necessarily must have as their intent, at least in part, a reduction in the consumption of alcohol. Why, otherwise, would the limitations have been imposed? We next must ask, therefore, whether it is consistent with the First Amendment's guarantee of free speech for society to provide greater freedom to persons trying to *dissuade* citizens from using such products as alcohol and tobacco than to persons trying to persuade them.

CHOOSING ONE'S TOBACCO ON CHANDNI CHOWK

In the crowded bazaar of Chandni Chowk, a narrow street in New Dehli, India, hundreds of sellers display their wares as attractively as possible. There in the marketplace the visitor finds in profusion Oriental spices, jade, cut glass, jewels, vegetables, ivory carvings, rich brocades and, of course, tobacco. Merchants call out to passersby from their booths or from cloths laid by the curbside, imploring potential buyers to come closer. On inspection one quickly learns that, regardless of price, some of the merchandise is extraordinarily good, some of it hopelessly shoddy. Sellers compete with each other to sell goods. Buyers, through free price mechanisms (such as bargaining) try to acquire the best possible merchandise for the lowest possible prices. In that ancient process of free trade many forms of salesmanship are brought into play.

Circumstances on Main Street, U.S.A., are by no means identical to those on exotic, remote Chandni Chowk, India. American consumers expect, and usually receive, important product safeguards when they make their purchases. Yet we have already noted in this essay how, in the context of America's free market system, even such commodities as school textbooks ("packaged ideas," as it were) are subject to the competitive forces of the marketplace. Not every textbook can be adopted. Some will fail and go out of print. The "right to be heard" in the classroom is, therefore, far from absolute. Given the ground rules of democratic capitalism, tests of strength among contending pressure groups—sometimes staged in the political arena—probably are inevitable. It is only when such competition breaks down that we, the public, have something to fear.

When we cater to the special obsessions of what James Madison, "the father of the Constitution," called *factions*, the rights of all of us are abused. And it was precisely that kind of abuse that the founding fathers had in mind when they drafted the First Amendment, protecting free speech and free press for *all* Americans, not just those with righteous causes to purvey.

When we cater to the special obsessions of what James Madison called *factions*, the rights of all of us are abused.

Certainly, the use of such products as alcohol and tobacco is abhorrent to some Americans. Many find the advertising of such items to be obnoxious, erroneous and embarrassing. Yet in every state of the Union today tobacco, for example, is a legal product, openly available to persons above a certain age. People are *permitted* to use it. And as John Stuart Mill, that ardent nineteenth-century champion of British liberty once wrote, "Whatever is *permitted* to do, it must be permitted to *advise* to do."

As in the case of alcohol, there are those who propose to make tobacco excessively expensive and, hence, beyond the economic means of some citizens. Most recently, some groups have argued in favor of a national ban on the advertising of tobacco products, thereby presumably reducing for prospective buyers the frequency of temptation.

Yet it is reasonable to ask whether the men who drafted the First Amendment would have agreed to place a legislative straitjacket on a product any more readily than on the free expression of an idea. Would they have said, "Free speech, yes, but limitations, too, on free speech intended to persuade others to buy a product"? Such restrictions on commercial free speech may be said to limit individual choice just as blatantly as the long chain of historic attempts, extending from the trial of Socrates in 399 B.C., to put a muzzle on intellectual expression. Indeed, is a restriction on the free market mechanism of displaying one's wares—as long as they are legitimate, legal substances—any more tolerable or consistent with the First Amendment than a limitation on the free speech of such "unpopular," "abhorrent," "obnoxious" and "embarrassing" groups as the Nazis, the Communists or the Ku Klux Klan—all of whom are protected by the Constitution?

The real issue, finally, is the maturity of America's citizens. Are we to be treated by those with righteous causes as a nation of preadolescents? Must we, like children, be protected, restrained, by a class of "intellectual nannies" (in the phrase of Yale President Benno C. Schmidt, Jr.) until at some indeterminate time in the future we are at last ready for admission to the full privileges of freedom? Or are we already free men and women—the responsible citizens of a free society, legally able to choose for ourselves precisely which advertised messages we wish to accept and which to reject?

The real issue, finally, is the maturity of America's citizens.

John Stuart Mill, like Jefferson and the authors of the First Amendment before him, thought it unnecessary to qualify his definition of individual freedom: "The only purpose," said Mill, "for which power can be rightfully exercised over any member of a civilized community, against his will, is to prevent harm to others. . . . Over himself, over his body and mind, the individual is sovereign."

And, ultimately, is that not what the First Amendment is all about?

John Micklos, Jr.
Newark, Delaware

Occupation: Editor
Interests: Writing, reading, golf
Entered the Competition because: "I believe strongly
in the importance of First Amendment freedom."

John Micklos, Jr.
Newark, Delaware

Occupation: Editor
Interests: Writing, reading, golf
Entered the Competition because: "I believe strongly
in the importance of First Amendment freedom."

FREEDOM OF SPEECH: IS IT FOR EVERYONE?

The vast majority of Americans do not need or want anyone to decide for them what they should be able to view or read. The proposed ban on cigarette advertising is just one example of a growing trend toward "protecting" all Americans from those things which certain groups deem "bad" for us, even if that protection comes at the expense of our First Amendment rights.

Many of these censorship efforts are spearheaded by small, but vocal, minorities. For example, more than 8,000 convenience stores throughout the United States stopped selling "adult" magazines in 1986 due to pressure and threats of boycott by groups opposing the sale of such magazines. However, a 1986 survey by Americans for Constitutional Freedom found that eighty-four percent of those polled believe that people should have the right to buy all magazines and books that have not been judged illegal. Nearly three out of four respondents who identified themselves as "born again Christians" agreed with this view.

Furthermore, voters in a statewide referendum conducted in Maine in June 1986 voted down by more than a two-to-one margin a proposed law that would have carried fines and possible jail terms for those who sell obscene materials. Still, censorship of adult materials continued to thrive in 1986, spurred by the lengthy report issued in July by the Attorney General's Commission on Pornography. This report concluded that some forms of pornographic materials cause sexual violence.

Adult materials are not the only ones being censored. Some people also feel impelled to protect children from reading textbooks and children's books they consider dangerous. Recently, a federal judge in Tennessee ruled that children of fundamentalist parents did not have to read a reading textbook which included such concepts as working mothers and talking animals, which run contrary to their religious beliefs.

According to People for the American Way, an anticensorship group, the number of reported cases of attempted censorship in American schools has more than doubled in the past four years. Among the works deemed too "dangerous" for students are books by Judy Blume, Kurt Vonnegut and Pulitzer Prize–winner Bernard Malamud. Censors have even targeted seemingly innocuous fairy tales such as "Snow White" for portraying magic and witchcraft.

These actions seem far removed from the intent of those who wrote in the First Amendment to the American Constitution that "Congress shall make no law respecting an establishment of religion, or prohibiting the free exercise thereof; or abridging the freedom of speech, or of the press; or the right of people peaceably to assemble, and to petition the government for a redress of grievances." Most scholars agree that a primary purpose of the Constitution was and is to preserve as many rights as possible for the individual.

Lately, however, America seems to have fallen into a "well, but" complex. Those who would protect us from that which they consider harmful say that of course they agree with the First Amendment in principle. When it comes to specific issues such as "pornographic" magazines, "dangerous" children's literature or cigarette advertising, however, these people say, "Well, but, I think we need to make an exception in this case." While it is possible to understand their concern, it is difficult or impossible to agree with their belief that no one should have access to certain information just because they disagree with it.

Those who support intellectual freedom would probably agree that there is an Orwellian chill in the air. Although we have passed by 1984 without Big Brother telling us what we can read and what we can think, it seems that there is currently a dangerous trend toward allowing censors to tell the American public what it cannot read and what it cannot think, which is a major step in that direction. The most dangerous thing about censorship is that once it starts, there is no telling where it will stop.

The controversy surrounding cigarette advertising goes back well beyond the current censorship controversies, however. Serious concern about the hazards of smoking started with the release of the U.S. Surgeon General's Smoking and Health Hazard Report in early 1964. In 1965, Congress required that warning labels be placed on cigarette packages, and stronger warnings were approved by Congress in 1984. Whether or not these warnings represent a legitimate restriction on First Amendment freedoms is not at issue here. In 1970, the Public Health and Smoking Act banned cigarette advertising on radio and television. Today, there is a proposed ban on *all* tobacco advertising. These bans seem wrong for several reasons. First of all, they run counter to the freedom of speech and freedom of the press clauses in the First Amendment of the Constitution. We can only imagine that the authors specified these freedoms first because they believed these issues to be of paramount importance. Once again, however, those who would protect us from ourselves would say, "Well, but, in this case, the product is clearly dangerous, and we should not allow it to be advertised."

96

However, nowhere in the First Amendment does it state that censorship shall be permitted because a number of people (even a majority) disagree with a given message. As Wendell Willkie, the 1940 Republican candidate for president, believed, "Because we are generous with our freedom, we share our rights with those who disagree with us."

The would-be ban on cigarette advertising is inconsistent. Producers of other arguably dangerous products, such as alcohol, enjoy the freedom to advertise. Most doctors would tell their patients that either heavy drinking or heavy smoking is dangerous to their health. Yet ads for alcohol (beer) appear on nearly all televised sports programs, not to mention on the pages of all popular magazines.

Not only does the proposed ban on cigarette advertising run counter to First Amendment freedoms, but also to the principles of our free market economy. The key to a free market economy is an informed consumer who decides whether or not to buy a product based on the information available about that product. Allowing cigarette manufacturers to advertise and promote their product does not force anyone to smoke. Certainly, there is a wealth of information available to the consumer outlining the possible dangers of smoking. According to our free market system, it should be left up to the consumer to decide whether the benefits of smoking outweigh the possible health hazards.

The only advertising restriction that I would support would be to ensure that cigarette advertising was not directed toward children and teens. Youngsters are not and cannot be expected to be informed consumers. For that reason, they should not be bombarded with messages for cigarettes or alcohol or other substances which might be harmful to them. Of course, the tobacco industry has since 1964 observed a code of self-censorship which prohibits the advertising of cigarettes to people under the age of twenty-one.

On the practical side, there are some serious questions as to whether the 1970 ban on cigarette advertising on television and radio accomplished its purpose. Cigarette ads still appear throughout the various print media, so the consumer still has easy access to information about cigarettes. In fact, I question whether or not even a total ban on cigarette advertising would significantly affect smoking rates. It seems to me that few people base their decision whether or not to smoke on advertising. Rather, I believe that they use ads to help them choose among various brands.

A 1984 report by the World Health Organization showed that tobacco consumption in most industrialized nations is declining at an annual rate of 1.1 percent. This probably can be attributed to the abundance of information available on the dangers of smoking. It is highly questionable whether banning cigarette advertising would augment this trend. But allowing such advertising truly allows the consumer to see all sides of the issue.

The consumer should make the final decision—not the censor.

Just to give some perspective to my opinions in this matter, I am an ex-smoker, and I personally do not think that smoking is a healthy activity. However, I do support the rights of other people to smoke. I also support the rights of tobacco producers to advertise their products through all available media and to let the consumer make the final decision. As the French philosopher Voltaire once said, "I disapprove of what you say, but I will defend to the death your right to say it."

I imagine that Voltaire would make the same statement in regard to cigarette advertising. Whether or not you agree with the wisdom of smoking, the First Amendment would seem to indicate that makers of tobacco products have the fundamental right to advertise these products through the same public outlets that makers of other products use. The consumer should make the final decision—not the censor.

David Bunning
Washington, D.C.

Occupation: Attorney
Interests: Jogging, gardening, beer making
Entered the Competition because: "I wanted to
write in defense of a constitutional right that
addresses an unpopular activity."

> The problem with any restriction on speech, political or commercial, is that it infringes on the public's ability to gather information.

CENSORSHIP AND CIGARETTES: THE RIGHTS OF BUSINESS TO FREEDOM OF SPEECH

Can the government ban the advertising of cigarettes? The Congress is currently considering a law which would do just that, and this has sparked a heated debate on the right of manufacturers and advertisers to First Amendment protection.

The springboard for the proposed law is the recent decision of the Supreme Court in *Posadas de Puerto Rico Associates* v. *Tourism Company of Puerto Rico,* on July 1, 1986. In that decision, Justice Rehnquist wrote the opinion for a Court which was divided five to four. The majority opinion upheld a Puerto Rican law which banned casino advertising in forms calculated to reach residents of Puerto Rico. Casinos are legal in Puerto Rico, and its residents are free to use them. The law did not attempt to ban advertising which would reach tourists or others outside Puerto Rico—only advertising in forms calculated to reach Puerto Ricans. The court, in so doing, acknowledged it was perfectly fine to permit an ad in one newspaper and ban it in another based solely on the perceived circulation of the paper.

The majority opinion based its decision on the freedom of the legislature to regulate certain activities, and noted that it could have banned gambling altogether. From this it reasoned that it was permissible to take the "less intrusive" step of allowing the activity but forbidding any attempt to encourage people to participate. The Court mentioned other products which the state is also free to outlaw, such as cigarettes and liquor.

Four of the nine justices dissented; two, Brennan and Stevens, wrote dissenting opinions. Ironically, it was Justice Brennan, one of the Court's most liberal members, who championed the right of business to

101

freedom of speech. Justice Rehnquist's majority opinion barely questioned the legislature's ability to censor advertising.

Two aspects of this decision led to the current assault on the First Amendment. The Court's ideas that the legislature is free to outlaw cigarettes, and that banning advertising is "less intrusive" and therefore acceptable, gave impetus to the proposal to ban cigarette advertising. That law, however, would be both distasteful and unconstitutional.

To evaluate both the palatability and constitutionality of such a law, we look to the First Amendment to the Constitution. As it relates to freedom of speech, it reads simply, "Congress shall make no law . . . abridging the freedom of speech. . . ." For an understanding of what those words have come to mean, we must look to their interpretation by the Supreme Court.

That body has had many occasions, within the facts of a particular case, to judge whether the government may ban, suppress or censor certain ideas. It has repeatedly held that freedom of speech is not absolute: certain speech, such as libel or obscenity, is entitled to no protection whatsoever. All speech is subject to certain restrictions on its presentation and means of expression, so long as those restrictions do not discriminate on the content of the speech.

The Court has also repeatedly held that "commercial speech," speech about a product or service, can be more easily restricted than can "political speech," expressions about political rights or candidates. This does not mean that government is free to stop advertising. Freedom of speech is the rule. Censorship is the exception. In order to halt truthful speech about a legal product, the law imposes on the government the burden of showing a "substantial" interest in restricting the message, that the restriction "directly advances" that interest, and that the restriction is not more extensive than necessary to accomplish that purpose.

The government, of course, has the right to insure that products are safe and that the circumstances of marketing are scrupulously honest. Beyond this, though, it bears an extremely heavy burden because it is infringing on two very important interests: the consumers' right to information, and the producers' right to promote their products.

The problem with any restriction on speech, political or commercial, is that it infringes on the public's ability to gather information. If you want to be able to judge a candidate or an issue, you have to have access to all sides of the question. If people are to be able to judge their government effectively, they have a right to read both the glowing reports and the vicious condemnations. That same principle applies with respect to commercial speech and economic decisions. If the public is to be informed, it must hear from all speakers about a product's good and bad points, and hear from all the producers of the product. Anything less than this means that the decision-making process will be skewed and decisions will be flawed.

That is what makes censorship so undesirable. It usurps from the individual the right to know and to make his own decisions based on all the information. It is an affront to a democracy to censor political speech, and it is an affront to a consumer-oriented free market society to censor economic speech. Censorship removes from the individual the ability to conduct his life, and substitutes for his judgment the judgment of Congress, or committee or bureaucrats.

The same considerations which make restrictions on commercial speech distasteful also make them unconstitutional. The purpose of the First Amendment is to open the gates wide to all ideas, no matter how unpopular or far out, and let the individual have access to all the facts. The First Amendment "presupposes that people will perceive their own best interests if only they are well enough informed, and . . . the best means to that end is to open the channels of communication, rather than close them. If there is any danger that people cannot evaluate . . . information . . . it is a danger contemplated by the Framers of the First Amendment." Those are the words of Justice Brennan in his dissenting opinion in *Posadas*, quoting in part from previous Court decisions. So long as the information is not fraudulent or deceptive, it must be allowed.

The purpose of the First Amendment is to open the gates wide to all ideas . . . and let the individual have access to all the facts.

The other right trammeled by censorship of commercial speech is the right of a business to promote itself. Commercial enterprise cannot take place unless businesses can make others aware of the products and services they supply, and the price and quality. The economy is nothing more than millions of interlinked individuals who buy and sell to one another. The more freely information is available, the more widely it is disbursed, the more efficiently the system functions.

In view of the right to know and the right to make known, commerical speech is obviously something to be safeguarded. Restrictions on free commercial speech should not be lightly or hastily imposed. Whether a right is to be protected in a given situation depends on a balancing of that right and other interests in context. That is what the three-part test the Supreme Court uses to evaluate commerical free speech is seeking to do.

Truthful information about lawful products is entitled to First Amendment protection from censorship. "No differences between commercial and other kinds of speech justify protecting commercial speech less extensively where, as here, the government seeks to manipulate private behavior by depriving citizens of truthful information concerning lawful activities." These words are quoted from Justice Brennan's dissenting opinion in *Posadas*.

The proponents of the cigarette advertising ban act from an unacceptable motive: They want to manipulate consumers' behavior. They do not like the decision smokers have made to smoke. They want to get people to make the decision not to smoke by removing any messages about tobacco that might be positive, and bombard them with only negative information. That way, people will make the "right" decision about smoking: abstention. But getting people to make the "right" decision "for their own good," however benevolent the intention, is nothing short of Big Brother. It is right out of George Orwell's *Animal Farm*, where the pig explains to the other animals why only the pigs make all the decisions. "Sometimes you might make the wrong decisions, comrades, and then where would we be?"

The proponents of the cigarette advertising ban act from an unacceptable motive: They want to manipulate consumers' behavior. . . . Not only is such a motive unacceptable, it is sinister.

For the government to suppress information in order to influence a decision is directly contrary to the First Amendment's purpose. Censorship of the advertising of a product to decrease its use is no more acceptable than censorship of a political party to suppress its influence. Either type of censorship violates both the letter and the spirit of the First Amendment.

Not only is such a motive unacceptable, it is sinister. The proponents of the law have turned their back on the Bill of Rights. They lack confidence that they can present their position forcefully and eloquently enough to convince their audience. Rather than trying to win the debate, they want to stifle it to achieve their ends.

So long as the activity or product is lawful, the public has a right to information about it, and the supplier or producer has a right to advertise it. To argue that the power to ban the product completely includes the "lesser" power to ban advertising about it is nothing but a throwaway line to avoid any real discussion of the issue, freedom of speech. It is also incorrect. This is but one of many instances where once an activity exists, certain rights attach. For example, there is no constitutional right to government programs, but once the government begins a program, it must administer it fairly. The government could not arbitrarily cut people off or reduce some benefits, and dismiss it by saying there was no right to the program to begin with so they can run it as unfairly as they want. Similarly, if a Republican administration decides to accept political ads on a public bulletin board, it must accept the ads of all candidates. It could not exclude Democrats' ads, even if it pointed out that before its policy, there were no ads at all.

To the same end, if a product is to be legally sold, then First Amendment rights attach, and the producer has a right to advertise it and the consumer has a right to get information about it, even information that may be unpopular or does not advance some interest group's social agenda.

If a ban on cigarette advertising is permitted, it would only be the first step down a long dark road of majority tyranny. Some vocal group of activists may decide next year that another product is "dangerous" or "undesirable." Rather than add their voices to the public discussion, they will be able to stop the discussion completely by muzzling their opponents. By depriving consumers of accurate information about a legal product, they are unfairly influencing private decision making. The only acceptable course in a democracy which respects individual freedom is to permit access to as wide and varied a marketplace of ideas as possible; permit the individual to hear all sides and then allow him to choose what he believes is best for him. This is the whole point of the First Amendment's prohibition on censorship. For the government to attempt to suppress the debate and make decisions for the individual is unconstitutional, distasteful and patronizing.

Maggie Dunn
DeLand, Florida

Occupation: College Instructor
Interests: Racquetball, films, music, reading
Entered the Competition because: "I am a smoker.
The idea that my right to smoke may be in
danger is upsetting."

To America's early colonists, the promise of such freedom was worth the hazards of living, and the very real threat of dying, in a new and terrifying land.

SMOKE SIGNALS FROM THE CITY UPON A HILL

The United States of America is history's most successful experiment in liberty, its singular achievement based on the premise that the freedom to think and communicate is the wellspring of human achievement. To America's early colonists, the promise of such freedom was worth the hazards of living, and the very real threat of dying, in a new and terrifying land. Through freeze, flood and famine their vision sustained them. In the words of John Winthrop, the leader of the Massachusetts Bay Colony, they were building "a city upon a hill"—a society in which all would be free to think and act according to conscience, and a society to which the rest of the world might look as an example.

As an ideal, such freedom of expression has long been the preoccupation of great minds. John Milton, reacting to government oppression in the seventeenth century, made an impassioned plea for "the liberty to know, to utter, and to argue freely according to conscience, above all liberties." John Stuart Mill in nineteenth century Britain added eloquently, "The peculiar evil of silencing the expression of an opinion is, that it is robbing the human race." The truth of Mill's statement is as self-evident now as it was then. Every time a Solzhenitsyn or a Sakharov is silenced, thousands, even millions, of human beings are deprived of the opportunity to listen and to form their own opinions.

Freedom of speech, then, is a two-sided proposition. On one hand is the right to speak, and on the other hand is the right to hear. The makers of our Constitution and Bill of Rights profited from the wisdom of thinkers like Milton, and they envisioned an America whose guarantee of free expression would allow the interplay of individual ideas and choices advocated by Mill. Thus the First Amendment states unequivocally that "Congress shall make no law . . . abridging the freedom of speech, or of the press," guaranteeing that government shall not dictate tastes, ideas or beliefs.

The difficulty, however, comes in the very definition of "freedom." To paraphrase Abraham Lincoln, freedom to the sheep is oppression to the wolf, and vice versa. If one person's right to free expression is harmful in some way to another person, then curtailment of that freedom may be necessary. No other government in the world, of course, guarantees the full freedom of expression that America does to its news writers and editors, its artists in print and other mediums, its speakers and lecturers. Nevertheless, libel or slander must be guarded against, and if free speech breaches the peace, if a riot might occur or if a speaker urges violent action, then this poses a danger to others. In Justice Holmes' famous example, no one has the right to yell "Fire!" in a crowded movie house simply because that person is moved to do so.

All such necessary curtailments of an individual's right to free expression involve difficult questions as to rights and responsibilities. But no area is so insidiously dangerous as that involving questions of the right to express opinions and ideas which may be false or harmful. Who determines what is "false" or what may be "harmful"? In their time, the ideas of Christopher Columbus and the Wright brothers were considered false, even ludicrous. Similarly, the ideas of Darwin and Freud were, and perhaps still are by some, considered to be harmful. Does this mean that any or all should have been suppressed in the public interest? If government has a duty to protect the public from harm, it has an even more stringent duty to protect the right of individuals to speak *and* to hear.

It is not only individuals who are guaranteed free expression under the First Amendment, however, for individuals also join themselves into groups. Indeed, the complexity of our free enterprise society mandates official and unofficial affiliation with various groups. Political parties, professional organizations, labor unions and special interest groups such as Common Cause and the NAACP work to protect the freedoms of individuals and do for them what they, alone, could not possibly accomplish.

If "advertising" is defined as the truthful, accurate description of goods . . . then business has the right to speak, and consumers have the right to hear.

Other special interest groups are less obvious. In a specialized society, all self-supporting individuals are providers of goods or services. They are also, at the same time, consumers. Somehow information about available goods and services must be made available to them. And this is where the First Amendment's relationship to American business comes in. Does the right to free expression extend to businesses so that they may advertise their goods and services? Certainly it does. If "advertising" is defined as the truthful, accurate description of goods and/or services, then business has the right to speak, and consumers have the right to hear.

As with other forms of speech, certain admonitions apply. No business, through its advertising, may make slanderous statements about another product or business, or make false and possibly injurious claims for its own product. If one company claims falsely that a competing product is unsafe, for example, then that company abuses its right of free speech and should be barred from further doing so. If a business refuses to admit in its advertising that a product may cause harmful side effects, then freedom of expression is similarly abused. In instances like these, government has a duty to intervene; in fact, a clear historical trend has been toward greater governmental intervention in many areas of business. But how far may this intervention go, and upon what basis may it do so?

This question is not as easily answered as it may appear. Consider, for example, the tobacco advertising ban which is currently under consideration in Congress. Users of tobacco products readily admit that such products constitute a hazard to physical health. The medical evidence in this regard is clear, and few would be so foolish as to refute it. As evidence of their responsibility to the public in this regard, tobacco companies print the well-known Surgeon General's warnings on cigarette packages and in their advertisements.

Those who buy and use tobacco products, then, are well aware of the dangers involved, and they smoke or chew for their own particular reasons, not because tobacco companies lure them with false claims. But Congress seems now to be deliberating whether or not American citizens have the right to *hear* about tobacco products and to make up their own minds about buying and using them. This is not a question of protecting the public's health; it is a question of censorship. Smoking is not "in" at the present time. Nonsmokers have the right to smoke-free environments, and that right is justly recognized. But what about the rights of those who want to use tobacco products and those who manufacture them?

In addition, what might be the ramifications of a tobacco advertising ban if it becomes law? Ads in magazines and newspapers, as those on radio and television, would of course be eliminated. But how else might the term "advertising" be construed? Flyers and free samples sent through the mails would presumably also be banned. Posters and signs—any visual materials displaying a product's name or logo—could no longer appear in store windows or displays. A storekeeper might not even be permitted to display tobacco products; they might have to be kept, if at all, "under the counter."

More serious, though, is the question, "After tobacco, what next?" Alcohol, surely, can pose a danger to one's health. Will its advertising, perhaps its sales, and even its nonprescription availability be subject to government control? Or what about sugar? Every sugar-eating American knows that we all eat too much of the stuff. Since it, too, can be harmful, will Congress step in and ban advertising of all sugar products? The list can go on endlessly—beef, salt, caffeine, aspirin, laxatives, vitamins (mega-doses of Vitamin A can be dangerous, after all!).

Even more pernicious, this principle can be extended to other kinds of products, and to services. High-decibel stereo systems cause hearing impairment. Will any such equipment and the public performances that utilize them be immune from a ban on advertising? Contact sports such as football and hockey are physically dangerous. In the interest of protecting young people from the desire to participate in such sports, might Congress decide that televised games (certainly a form of "advertising") should be banned?

Is this carrying the argument to a logical extreme? Of course, because it is necessary to do so. The principle involved in the currently debated tobacco advertising ban is not whether Americans should smoke, or whether tobacco products can be harmful. Indeed, the principle involved is the most crucial freedom guaranteed by the Bill of Rights to all Americans—that government will not dictate tastes, ideas and beliefs. And the question is twofold: 1) whether Congress can tell any business that it does not have the right to disseminate information about its legally sold goods, and 2) whether Congress can thus implicitly tell the American people that they do not have the right to hear about products that are available. In a free market economy, to restrict in this manner the free flow of information about legally sold goods and services is clearly an infringement of the right to free expression.

We might picture John Winthrop and Benjamin Franklin, puffing contentedly on their favorite pipes, as they watch the struggle continue.

John Winthrop envisioned his "city upon a hill" when this country was but a gleam in the eye of those dauntless few who were willing to leave their English homes and heritage for the promise of freedom in a raw and untamed land. Others carried forward that vision, the framers of the Constitution and Bill of Rights accepting a monumental task that was, in the words of Benjamin Franklin, like "wrestling with a Hercules." Indeed, courage settled this land, wisdom forged its Constitution, and liberty has guided it ever since. Yet such a vision is as difficult to maintain as it was to bring into being, and those who would protect the freedoms upon which America was founded must ever fight anew. We might picture John Winthrop and Benjamin Franklin, puffing contentedly on their favorite pipes, as they watch the struggle continue.

James W. Harris
Columbus, Georgia

Occupation: Writer
Interests: Reading, playing the guitar
Entered the Competition because: "I believe very strongly in free speech and First Amendment rights, and believe that a ban on cigarette advertisements would be a blatant and ominous violation of these rights. I believe commercial speech is a critical but little understood form of speech, and hope this contest will educate the public on this important subject."

CENSORSHIP, BUSINESS AND THE FIRST AMENDMENT

Imagine for a moment that everyone in America who favors censorship of one kind or another suddenly got their wish. Imagine they could clap their hands and cause any material that they objected to, for whatever reasons, to disappear.

The result would be a country vastly different from our America today.

Virtually every film and television show would vanish; there are many who consider these mediums inherently evil and corrupting. The shelves of libraries and bookstores would be almost empty. The works of D. H. Lawrence and James Joyce would go, as would *Huckleberry Finn* ("racist"), *The Wizard of Oz* ("glorifies witchcraft") and millions of other books, classics and potboilers alike. Even the Bible would disappear; more than a few people have called for its suppression.

Many government records would never be seen by the public. School textbooks would be so watered-down as to be meaningless. Newspapers would be forbidden to run controversial stories. Advertisements for innumerable products—including alcohol, cigarettes, meat, contraceptives and feminine hygiene products—would be outlawed. Those with minority and out-of-mainstream political views would be silenced.

In short, if everyone in America who wants to limit speech were allowed to do so, the result would be a country of intolerable blandness and sterility—a country stripped of the rich diversity of viewpoints and the vigorous free exchange of ideas and products that is the hallmark of a free society.

Luckily, people cannot simply clap their hands and banish those forms of expression they find disagreeable. The rights of all Americans to free speech—even speech that is controversial and offensive to others—is protected by one of the most important political documents in the history of mankind: the First Amendment to the Constitution of the United States.

The power and beauty of the First Amendment lies in its sweep and simplicity: "Congress shall make no law . . . abridging the freedom of

117

speech, or of the press." This glorious proclamation of absolute freedom of speech makes no exceptions for speech that some find offensive. It is a declaration of free speech for each person as an innate human right.

Unfortunately, many times we as a nation have not fully lived up to the challenge and responsibility of that declaration. Throughout American history, various forms of speech have been restricted or prohibited. Books have been banned, dissidents have been jailed for speaking their views and publications have been harassed or shut down. Sadly, this sometimes happens even today. Although no one can simply clap his hands and suppress the free speech of others, it is sometimes quite possible for well-organized groups to persuade and pressure government to clamp down on forms of speech they want to eliminate.

Demands for censorship can come from all across the political spectrum—from both left and right, Republicans and Democrats, moderates and extremists. Most of those advocating censorship are not evil people; indeed, they are motivated by what they view as the best of intentions. They want to protect society from ideas they consider to be evil or dangerous or corrupting. In advocating the use of government force to suppress these ideas, however, they are gravely wrong. Not only are they violating the First Amendment rights of others, they are granting government power that may one day be used against themselves and controversial causes they might support.

One of the most attacked, least defended and least understood forms of free speech in our society today is commercial speech—the rights of businesses to advertise their products and viewpoints. There has long been a tendency by some to attempt to draw a distinction between commercial speech and other kinds of speech, and to imply that commercial speech is less important, and therefore not as strongly protected by the First Amendment. This is grievously wrong in a number of ways.

Commercial speech is, after all, *communication*.

Look again at the wording of the First Amendment. It contains no qualifiers about different forms of speech. It contains nothing to the effect that "this amendment applies to everything except business advertisements." It declares that Congress shall not interfere with speech, period. And this must include commercial speech, or else the amendment itself is meaningless.

Commercial speech is, after all, *communication*. It is an attempt by one party to communicate ideas to others. When government restricts or outlaws this communication, it is engaging in the suppression of ideas and information. This is censorship, and it is every bit as tyrannical, every bit as dangerous, as censorship of books or speeches. Saying such censorship doesn't matter because the material being banned concerns commercial products instead of political or cultural thoughts is a false and dangerous distinction.

In fact, attempts to distinguish between commercial speech and other forms of speech can run into serious and troubling difficulties. For example, when a politician runs for office, he is selling a product— himself and his beliefs—for which he expects to receive a salary. Are his ads, then, purely political speech, or do they have commercial over- tones? When booksellers advertise a book, they are clearly selling a product. Does this make them any the less deserving of protection under the First Amendment? It is difficult, if not impossible, to draw a clear line between the commercial and the political or cultural aspects of such speech.

Those who maintain that commercial speech is somehow less "important" than other forms of speech—and therefore less worthy of First Amendment protection—reveal themselves as either ignorant or uncaring. Try telling the owner of a business, whose advertising reflects his pride in his work and his efforts to meet the needs and desires of the public better than his competitors, that his right to advertise is not as important as the right of his neighbor to run for political office or publish a newspaper. The right to advertise his product might well be of far greater value to such a man than political or social speech. Indeed, his livelihood and self-pride may depend upon his advertising.

The claim that commercial speech can be regulated because it is somehow less significant is not only wrongheaded, it is frightening in its implications. For it puts the *government* in the position of determining what forms of speech are significant and insignificant—thus giving government a powerful and dangerous tool to interfere in free expression and in the economy. It is also dangerous because it moves away from the idea of speech as a basic, inalienable *right*, and instead defends speech as significant depending upon its "importance" (again, as determined by government) for society. This goes contrary to the belief of the founding fathers—clearly expressed in the Declaration of Independence and the Bill of Rights—that people have certain inalienable *rights* that govern- ment cannot legitimately interfere with. (Note that we have a Bill of *Rights*, not a Bill of Acts to Be Permitted in Some Circumstances Because They Are Useful to Society.) Free speech is one of those rights, and it belongs to businesses, publishers and advertisers as surely as it belongs to poets, politicians and journalists.

Not only is advertising protected by the First Amendment, it is the very lifeblood of a free market economy such as ours, an economic system rooted in the rights of individuals to own and exchange goods and services. Such a society depends upon advertising to provide consumers with information about the quality, price and availability of goods and services. Furthermore, advertising greatly encourages competition, price-cutting and improve products—all of which benefit consumers—since businesses must compete publicly among themselves to win the favor of the public.

Still another crucial role advertising plays in our society is funding our great diversity of newspapers, television and radio broadcasts, magazines and books. Advertising revenue literally keeps many such publications and broadcasts alive, and makes information and entertainment much cheaper and much more available than they would otherwise be. The importance of this to a free society cannot be overstated.

Given the extraordinary importance of advertising to our society, given the tremendous benefits society gains from advertising, and given that advertising is a form of speech and thus protected by the First Amendment, one would expect that commercial speech would be greatly respected in our society, and that it would be fiercely defended.

Alas, this isn't so. Many people who otherwise consider themselves staunch defenders of the First Amendment—people who would be horrified at proposals to censor books or magazines—have no hesitation in proposing to restrict advertisements for products they find disagreeable.

There is no better illustration of this than the current drive to ban advertisements for tobacco products.

Like so many others who advocate censorship of ideas they don't agree with, those who call for tobacco ad bans are spurred by what they see as good intentions. They feel that smoking is a dangerous habit, and they want to discourage it.

Good intentions do not justify bad means.

However, good intentions do not justify bad means. It is one thing to hold a view and to attempt to persuade others to accept that view. It is quite another thing to use *government force* to suppress the rights of some individuals to free speech and the exchange of lawful products in order to force a set of values on society. When tobacco opponents endorse such suppression, they have moved from being concerned citizens to being censors and moral dictators.

We have already observed that commercial speech—advertising—is a moral and constitutional right and plays a critically important role in our society. This applies to tobacco advertising as well.

A ban on tobacco advertising would set a profoundly dangerous precedent. Once we grant the principle that government can prohibit the advertising of certain products in order to "protect" us, why stop at tobacco products? Why not ban advertisements for alcohol? Why not ban the advertising of foods high in sugar, fat, salt and other potentially unhealthy ingredients?

Indeed, why stop even there? There is no question that many political writings—such as the works of, say, Karl Marx or Adolf Hitler—have caused far more misery and death than tobacco products ever possibly could. So—given the logic of those who would ban tobacco ads—why not ban the advertising of these books and other works that might create dissent or political violence? Why not prohibit minority political groups from presenting their views in an attractive, persuasive form?

Proponents of a ban on tobacco advertising frequently ignore this point, or dismiss it as an exaggerated, unrealistic objection. Yet the principle is precisely the same in all these cases—that government should protect us from exposure to advertising for lawful products deemed harmful.

And in fact, we can already see this principle being applied in America today. There are many who consider themselves good Americans who would deny speech to many of their fellow Americans for precisely the reasons given above. Furthermore, at this very moment a number of organizations are working to prohibit the advertisement of beer and wine on television and radio—again, using exactly the same rationale given for banning tobacco ads: that these products can be harmful, and therefore their advertising should be prohibited in order to "protect" us.

Indeed, the tobacco ad ban proponents themselves show us the very real danger of such precedents. When Congress outlawed tobacco advertising on television and radio several years ago, it was argued that the broadcast media were a special case. They were so omnipresent and persuasive, we were told, that an advertising ban could be justified here where media bans elsewhere could not. Yet now, just a few years later, we are now hearing calls—from many of the same people who supported the broadcast ad bans—for the suppression of *all* tobacco ads: an amazing and far-reaching (yet logical) extension of the dangerous principle that advertising for certain legitimate products can be outlawed.

Clearly, once we accept the basic principle behind tobacco ad censorship, we are opening the door to increasing government intrusion into virtually every area of our personal and economic lives. This goes sharply against the best traditions of our nation, which was founded on the idea that there are wide areas in both personal and economic life where government cannot lawfully intrude.

I believe that the moral issue—the right of all Americans, including tobacco companies, to untrammeled free speech and the right to engage in voluntary exchanges of goods and services in the marketplace—is the most important aspect of the tobacco ad ban debate. However, it is important to point out that the proposed ban would have other highly significant negative effects in addition to those already discussed.

For example, such a ban could negatively affect the health of many smokers. Many tobacco advertisements contain information on the levels of tar and nicotine in their products, thus allowing smokers the opportunity to choose cigarettes with lower levels of these substances if they wish. An ad ban would deny this information to consumers. Similarly, should a company develop a safer cigarette, a ban would make it almost impossible for them to inform consumers about their product.

An advertising ban would also deny smokers information on the prices of different brands at different locations. This would deprive smokers of the chance to spend their money most effectively. Such a ban would also lessen competition among different brands, leading to a probable increase in tobacco prices. Thus a tobacco ad ban amounts to nothing less than taking money out of the pockets of those adults who have freely chosen to smoke.

To sum up, a tobacco ad ban is a bad and tyrannical idea. It is a clear and blatant violation of the First Amendment, and an obnoxious government intrusion into private affairs. It sets a profoundly dangerous, ominous precedent, and significantly threatens our system of free enterprise. It also would negatively affect the health and finances of adults who choose to smoke.

Those who wish to discourage Americans from smoking have the same First Amendment rights as the tobacco companies. They have the same access to advertising, and they are free to issue statements, to picket, to boycott, to write articles and books and to use any other peaceful means to try to persuade others of the merits of their position. Indeed, such a lively debate—such a clash of competing viewpoints—is in the best spirit of the First Amendment.

However, when smoking opponents advocate the use of government force to restrict the speech and behavior of peaceful individuals, they are assaulting precious values that have made the United States the freest and most prosperous nation in history.

It is ironic that such a massive and precedent-setting act of censorship will be debated in Congress during the 200th anniversary of our Constitution. During this anniversary, our freedoms and the documents that preserve them, including the First Amendment, will be widely discussed. If we as a nation properly understand and respect those freedoms, there will be no ban on tobacco advertising—and no other censorship in America.

Mark C. Coleman
Honolulu, Hawaii

Occupation: Journalist
Interests: Surfing, reading, music, NFL football,
TV and movies, shooting at the handgun range
Entered the Competition because: "I wanted to
stress the connection between freedom of expression
and the right to property."

> Concede the premises for one abridgment of "freedom of speech, or of the press," and the floodgates against restrictions on that freedom will be forever opened.

Freedom of expression is a precious right that can benefit society in many ways.

By allowing for the introduction of new ideas, freedom of expression can invigorate the nation's public policy discourse, expand the boundaries of human knowledge and promote the general welfare.

A free flow of information can help consumers learn about new products, business executives learn about new markets and scientists learn more about nature.

In technologically advanced societies especially, freedom of expression is the lubricant that keeps the artistic, scientific and capital markets running smoothly, to the continuing benefit of virtually everyone involved.

Freedom of expression is also one of the greatest bulwarks against tyranny, which is primarily why America's founders sought to guarantee that freedom in the First Amendment to the U.S. Constitution.

Added to the nation's founding document in 1791, the First Amendment declared that "Congress shall make no law . . . abridging freedom of speech, or of the press. . . ."

The language was plain, with Article IV of the Constitution stipulating that as part of the Constitution it would be "the supreme law of the land, and the judges in every state shall be bound thereby, anything in the Constitution or laws of any state to the contrary notwithstanding."

Talk is cheap, however, and through the past two centuries, America has hardly been a bastion for the apostles of free expression.

From the blue laws of old to the libel laws of today, from the various "alien and sedition acts" to the many restrictions on advertising, American legislators at every civic level have sought to stop or slow the free flow of information, and thus retard the intellectual, material and spiritual growth of our nation.

Reflecting basically conservative characteristics, politicians have restricted freedom of expression to protect their political power. Business interests have urged the enactment of laws to prevent competition and secure their market dominance. And theists have approved violation of the First Amendment to repress challenges to their narrow religious concepts.

127

No doubt, many of those who would restrict freedom of expression often have had the good of society at heart, as in the case of many of those who are against pornography, slander and libel, and liquor and tobacco advertising.

Opponents of pornography, for example, often argue that such freedom of expression promotes sexual promiscuity, erodes family values, encourages profanity, leads to sexual assaults and even violates the civil rights of women.

Proponents of libel and slander laws usually believe that freedom-of-expression practitioners should be liable for the harm they may do to the reputations of others.

And opponents of liquor and tobacco advertising often want only to reduce public demand for liquor and tobacco, which they believe are the cause of much human illness and suffering.

Without passing judgment on the merits of any of these viewpoints, it should be clear that the calls for restricting freedom of expression do not come from just one quarter. And therein lies the danger of conceding to the basic premises of any of these interests.

If the government is authorized to ban pornography, why not films and publications that portray violence, divorce, infidelity, anarchism or atheism?

If freedom-of-expression practitioners should be liable for any harm they might do to another's reputation, how should they be compensated if their broadcasts or writings catapult their subjects to fame and fortune?

And if advertisements for liquor and tobacco can be banned, why not for "junkfood" products or punk rock record albums?

Concede the premise for one abridgment of "freedom of speech, or of the press," and the floodgates against restrictions on that freedom will be forever opened, subject only to the shifting, capricious norms of society.

Such a situation, indeed, is where America finds itself today. The plain language of the Constitution's First Amendment has already been overridden repeatedly, and further encroachments on freedom of expression are lurking menacingly in the wing, waiting only for legislative fiat to make them acceptable.

The proponents of further encroachments will not be swayed by arguments that the First Amendment was meant to be construed literally—that freedom of speech or of the press is absolute. Our nation's founders, they will say, did not mean to sanction absolute freedom of speech or of the press, but rather only expression that doesn't detract from the best interests of society.

It won't matter whether the motives of those opposed to free expression are good or evil. In either case the First Amendment per se will be insufficient to protect freedom of expression, should the public or its legislative representatives be inclined to ban or restrict it.

Recourse to the specific wording of the First Amendment will be useless because the absolute authority of the amendment has already repeatedly been challenged and overridden. Indeed, nineteenth-century American jurist Lysander Spooner in his 1870 tract *No Treason: The Constitution of No Authority,* reasoned that the entire Constitution is a nonbinding contract, beyond perhaps the handful of eighteenth-century Americans who drafted it some two hundred years ago.

The point must be, then, that freedom of expression goes deeper than the U.S. Constitution's First Amendment, for if not, then practitioners of every sort of public expression—from art to science, politics, religion and business—must be prepared to defend themselves in court from those who feel threatened by their actions.

The deeper principle must relate to something beyond the First Amendment per se, and that something is private property.

Freedom of expression is a corollary of the right to own property, of which the foremost form is your own body.

The reason theater patrons, for example, do not have the right to yell "Fire" during the middle of a movie presentation is that they do not own the theater premises, and their admission tickets do not entitle them to create such a commotion.

In the case of libel and slander, the issue really is "Who owns a person's reputation: the individual so regarded, or the individuals whose thoughts comprise that reputation? If a reputation is owned by the individual so regarded, at what point does gossiping over the back fence become punishable by law?

From the point of view of libelers and slanderers, it may be that everything they broadcast, write or say is false and maybe even maliciously motivated. But if you believe everything you hear over the back fence, then that's your fault.

There may be a point at which an advertisement or public statement could be considered to be a binding legal contract, but otherwise freedom of expression regulated only by whose property rights are involved could become a superb vehicle for promoting intellectual self-reliance. It also would serve its enduring function as a conduit for new ideas into the cultural, political and economic mainstream.

Professional cartels would have no power to ban advertising by upstart journeymen whose methods of practice and self-promotion might be considered unorthodox or crass. Scientific elite would not be legally able to persecute dissenting colleagues with different approaches. And entrenched politicians would not be able to restrict the efforts of "rabble rousers" by trying to "throw the rascals out."

A literal interpretation of the U.S. Constitution's First Amendment should continue to be advocated, but if it is not to be, then freedom of expression must be carved out and more clearly defined in the courts as a corollary of property rights, with takings of that right compensable under the U.S. Constitution's Fifth Amendment, which states in part that "no person shall be . . . deprived of life, liberty or property without due process of law; nor shall private property be taken for public usa without just compensation."

As in the case of many zoning law disputes, this approach in many cases may go nowhere. But it would seem to be the only other legal avenue to pursue if we are to widen the arena for free expression.

Emphasizing the link between freedom of expression and private property also will help increase appreciation of private property generally, as a convenient, simple means for resolving social disputes, and without which our materially and technologically advanced, complex, industrialized society would collapse.

There can be no turning back the clock. Without private property there can be no prices. Without prices—based on willing exchanges between sellers and buyers—there can be no accounting for profits and losses, and allocation of society's scarce resources thus become a haphazard, politicized, usually ruinous affair.

The private property-based price system itself is a prime example of freedom of expression at work. Government-imposed price controls are an abridgment of that freedom, and economists have amply demonstrated how that sort of suppression has backfired and resulted in all sorts of undesirable economic and social distortions.

So it is with suppression of other forms of free expression, as in the case again of libel laws.

Freedom of expression is . . . the vital ingredient for keeping American society in the forefront of cultural, scientific and economic development.

Libel laws are similar to price controls in that they convey a false impression to consumers about the true nature of the marketplace, causing them to behave differently than they would in the absence of such laws. Primarily they encourage people to believe that everything broadcast or published is factual, when we all should know—partly because of all the libel lawsuits that are filed every year—that such is certainly not the case.

Freedom of expression is a vital component of intellectual self-reliance, as well as the vital ingredient for keeping American society in the forefront of cultural, scientific and economic development.

The results of free expression may not always be perfect, but the freedom itself should continue to be upheld, and if the First or Fifth Amendment approach to protecting it will not work, then advocates and practitioners of free expression will have to be content with promoting the notion that society as a whole benefits more from freedom of expression than it would from its absence, and hope that reason finally prevails.

Kevin S. Wilson
Buhl, Idaho

Occupation: Student
Interests: Book collecting, fishing, travel
Entered the Competition because of: "Long-standing
interest in First Amendment issues."

For censorship robs from us all, takes piecemeal from our collective birthright, steals the freedom that lies at the core of American life.

ADVERTISING, TOBACCO AND FREE SPEECH

Americans have a tremendous capacity for disagreeing with one another, and quite often the clamor of differing voices grows deafening. But on one point we all tend to agree: the First Amendment to the Constitution protects the open exchange of information from governmental interference. Yet, though in principle we may agree, from time to time a voice is heard, warning of abuses, pointing to excesses, claiming injury. Sadly, too often the voice serves only to mask the attempts of one group to silence another.

It is precisely these attempts to silence which should most alarm us, and not necessarily the abuses to which they refer. Admittedly, shielded by the First Amendment, abuses do occur: people lie, or distort the truth, or so employ their right to free speech that harm is done. However, silencing these voices provides a corrective only for immediate damage, while wounding and undermining something far more important—the very principle which gave them their right to speak. And in nearly every instance, the harm done by silencing them far outstrips any possible injury their words might have caused. For censorship robs from us all, takes piecemeal from our collective birthright, steals the freedom that lies at the core of American life.

And however well-intentioned, censorship reaches beyond these bounds. Rarely is the exercise of free speech purely detrimental; to the contrary, any point of view, however unpopular, serves to strengthen First Amendment privileges, simply by virtue of its existence as a free expression within the ongoing exchange of ideas. Our society, our system of government grows static and enfeebled when louder, more insistent voices seek to limit that exchange, and a good portion of what keeps America moving forward is the ideas and opinions which some would have excluded. Because the First Amendment insures that they are not excluded, their presence allows for an exchange of information free from the distortion of a single, dominant voice.

Without such an exchange, social progress becomes impossible.

Or, rather, it becomes twisted, perverted from its true course. Without free speech, progress—intellectual discovery, governmental and economic strength, personal growth—deteriorates into a preordained excursion along the agenda of the majority. True progress springs from opposition, from differing ideas and conflicting opinion, from alternate points of view freely expressed. To silence the unpopular opinion is to drag this process to a halt, and to weaken the manner in which individuals strive toward common goals.

If free speech is one means by which individuals achieve common goals, then this same opportunity must exist for corporations—the framework for individuals linked by shared economic concerns. In a society based on free market notions of commerce, silencing the corporation marks a no less injurious blow to progress than does silencing the private citizen. Indeed, within a free market economy, the blow seems not only injurious, but ultimately crippling.

True progress springs from opposition, from differing ideas and conflicting opinion . . . freely expressed.

In the past, the courts have realized this, and have granted corporations many of the First Amendment privileges which private citizens enjoy, encouraging them to speak freely on matters of public concern. And even when corporate speech has commercial aims, as in the case of advertising, it still finds protection from censorship under the First Amendment. The U.S. Supreme Court has held that so long as commercial speech—advertising—meets certain conditions, then it is free from further governmental restriction. Though this does not entitle corporations to sell products through blatant misrepresentation, nor to make untruthful claims, it does provide them with substantial opportunity to speak on issues of public concern. Unfortunately, Supreme Court decisions notwithstanding, attempts at censorship continue to occur. Undertaken by private citizens, such efforts are disheartening; instigated by the government, they become truly alarming.

Last spring, the Federal Trade Commission filed a complaint against the R. J. Reynolds Company, alleging that a paid editorial entitled "Of Cigarettes and Science" was misleading to its readers. Written in the format of a newspaper editorial, the piece neither endorsed a particular brand of cigarette, nor mentioned brand names, nor encouraged buying. But it did raise some significant questions about the debate over health consequences of smoking—questions which some, holding opposing views, would as soon not have raised. In spite of the fact that the paid editorial expressed corporate opinion, and so differed from commercial speech, the FTC sought to prohibit R. J. Reynolds from distributing similar texts, in effect silencing their corporate voice on a matter of public opinion.

The danger of the FTC's actions resides in its unnecessary and intrusive limiting of free speech, for in this case government has wielded its power in order to stifle an opposing view. At least, this is the way Daniel Oliver, the FTC's chairman, seems to have viewed the situation. Dissenting in the commission's four-to-one vote, Oliver said, "I am concerned about . . . any action that may inhibit free expression of views that may not be popular with Government regulators." While the FTC claimed they acted out of the best of intentions—a concern for the public's welfare—their actions nonetheless constitute a damaging assault upon free speech. In peering past the FTC's expressions of concern, Oliver was able to see the consequences of the commission's stance, not the least of which would be a severe limiting of opinions that might not otherwise find expression.

Fortunately, his attitude was shared by administrative judge Montgomery K. Hyun, who rejected the FTC's complaint in a court of review. In doing so, Judge Hyun drew critical distinctions between commercial speech—advertising—and corporate opinion, placing the matter in perspective by noting that the Reynolds editorial did not discuss prices, indicate brand names or encourage buying. Rather, it addressed, as an expression of corporate opinion, one aspect of a public issue. Free from government regulation, corporate commentary thus expressed enjoys the same First Amendment protection afforded to any opinion—corporate, governmental or private. With his decision, Judge Hyun not only helped to distinguish between commercial speech and corporate opinion, but also helped to slow a developing political climate where all paid editorial comment would be placed at risk.

While his decision affirms that corporate speech is a free participant in the unrestricted trade of ideas, it does not guarantee immunity from other, equally disturbing, threats to free speech. If passed, congressional legislation introduced in June of 1986 would ban all cigarette advertising, including newspaper and magazine advertisements, athletic sponsorships, billboards, posters, even such peripheral advertising as matchbooks and T-shirts. Unlike the FTC complaint against R. J. Reynolds, the proposed legislation is unconcerned with factual truth in advertising, is unconcerned, in fact, with making any distinction between commercial speech and corporate opinion. Not content with an item-by-item review of commercial speech, not content with the restrictions already in place which limit what can be said in the marketplace,

137

government representatives now feel compelled to muzzle an entire industry.

Their contention is that concern for the public's welfare outweighs the rights of corporations to disseminate information without hindrance. But what they overlook is that protection of a few individuals comes at the expense of everyone's right to free speech. Staving off injury to a few with the advertising ban, legislators inflict a grave injury upon all members of the public, though of a different sort than the anticipated health injuries spurring their efforts. Focusing upon the physical, these protectors of the public ignore that public's right to spiritual and intellectual well-being, implying that the public interest is composed only of what makes for physical safety, while denying that it also incorporates spiritual and intellectual benefits realized through our most basic constitutional rights. In essence, while seeking to cure the ailments of the body, congressional doctors would allow the spiritual and intellectual patient to wither away and quietly expire.

Not content with the restrictions already in place . . . government representatives now feel compelled to muzzle an entire industry.

Once such legislation is in place, we will have moved far from the protection we now enjoy under the First Amendment, and the possibility of moving yet further astray will have grown all the more certain. Policies of this sort don't tend to reverse themselves; they tend instead to grow more powerful, more expansive, more encompassing. Already there is talk of aiming similar legislation at the alcoholic beverage industry. Will the government, concerned about the health risks associated with driving cars (a practice that kills thousands each year), next seek restrictions on the way cars are driven in television commercials? Will high-speed chases be drummed from TV programming, lest they encourage reckless driving? Will concern over environmental pollution lead to a black-out of aerosol hairspray ads? Acting in the interest of those few whose bodies react adversely to caffeine, will the government banish Mrs. Olson from the kitchen?

Many, many products available on the open market pose a health risk to users, and protection for consumers, whenever possible, is an admirable pursuit. But it is only when the buying public is well-informed, and acting consciously on a full, unbiased body of information that the individual consumer can truly be protected. And it is only a well-informed public that can be considered truly free. Some time ago,

Supreme Court Justice Oliver Wendell Holmes pointed out that "the best test of truth is the power of the thought to get itself accepted in the competition of the marketplace." By crediting consumers with wisdom and discernment enough to weigh their options and make informed choices, Justice Holmes granted them a degree of freedom which members of Congress now seek to revoke. In doing so, he upheld the key principle underlying the making of all informed choices: the right to free speech. Freedom to pick and choose, after all, is predicated on one's access to the open exchange of information, which in turn is predicated on the right to speak freely.

If restrictive measures such as the ban on tobacco advertising were to prevail, even new information about cigarettes, information beneficial to consumers about new products, recent studies, further discoveries—all would be restricted from dissemination by corporate interests. In its place would remain a single voice, dominant and overbearing, the voice of the government. In such a climate, without freedom of speech, the marketplace of ideas collapses, just as would the American system of government, commerce and social structure collapse without the support of a free and well-informed public. Legislation banning tobacco advertising is a first step toward limiting this informed and free public's ability to make choices. More importantly, and more disturbingly, it marks also a step toward the erosion of our rights to free speech.

Charles R. McGuire
Normal, Illinois

Occupation: College Professor
*Interests: Renovation of a ninety-year-old farm
house, reading, fishing, golf, spending
time with family*
*Entered the Competition because: "I sincerely
believe that we cannot compromise the absolute
language of the First Amendment."*

A QUESTION OF TRUST

The American system is based on trust. The grand experiment of the founders of our nation was only incidentally concerned with checks and balances, the three branches of government or the relationships of states and central government. Those matters were only means to the radical vision of those men. At the heart of their experiment in self-government was a revolutionary belief and confidence in the basic goodness and intelligence of humankind.

This unique and basic American trust in humanity is expressed most clearly in the two principal elements of American democracy. Both free enterprise and free speech are central to American life. Both assume that individuals are able to make choices for themselves. Both depend on the ability of individuals to discern good from bad, to educate themselves and others and to make wise decisions. And both are quite fragile.

The last decade has brought a new challenge to First Amendment freedoms and to the free enterprise system. Well-meaning citizens and legislators have begun a campaign to legally restrict the right of businesses to advertise certain products. That campaign promises to erode the trust that is so essential to our system.

The twin foundations of free speech and free enterprise both depend on a kind of "marketplace," each of which assumes that the "buyers" are intelligent, informed and honorable. The challenge to advertising, aimed initially at cigarette advertising, is based on a contrary argument that people are not capable of making intelligent choices within either of those marketplaces.

Once the wisdom and integrity of the public is called into question, the whole structure of American public life is challenged. Ultimately the ability of the nation to retain its democratic form will depend on the proper functioning of both the marketplace of ideas and the economic marketplace.

THE MARKETPLACE OF IDEAS

In the abstract, few Americans would deny that the right to speak freely is fundamental to our system of government. Justice Hugo Black

143

once wrote that "freedom to speak and write about public questions is as important to the life of our government as is the heart to the human body. In fact, this privilege is the heart of our government. If the heart is weakened, the result is debilitation; if it be stilled, the result is death." The First Amendment to the Constitution embedded those sentiments into our nation's basic law with clear and unmistakable language: "Congress shall make *no* law. . . abridging the freedom of speech."

The First Amendment is based on the concept of the "marketplace of ideas." That notion, originally conceived by John Locke and adopted by Jefferson and Madison, assumes all people to be wise and good. All ideas—no matter how bad or even dangerous—must be permitted into the marketplace. The people—the consumers of ideas—will reject bad ideas and accept good ones, in much the same way that consumers of goods reject bad products and accept good ones.

This free trade in ideas in turn assures that all viewpoints will be heard and that the democratic process will function properly. Despots cannot arise, because all are free to speak their minds, and minorities cannot be stopped from speaking by the tyranny of the majority. No one has a monopoly on wisdom or public forums. And, it is no business of government to decide what ideas shall be heard.

While the abstract notion of free speech is universally accepted, the practical application of absolute free speech has never been fully admitted. The simple and unmistakable language of the First Amendment has come under frequent attack by those who would restrict the rights of the public to speak and to learn. The history of the First Amendment has been a chronicle of the continuing battle between those who trust the will of the public and those who fear it.

The history of the First Amendment has been a chronicle of the continuing battle between those who trust the will of the public and those who fear it.

Each limitation of the First Amendment has weakened freedom of speech, in much the same manner that a wedge will weaken a log with each successive blow. Some of the limitations are perhaps necessary, such as those dealing with obscenity or slander. But, however necessary, any limitation on freedom of expression makes the next limitation easier to defend.

Those who would restrict the right of the public to speak and to obtain information have a heavy burden. They must show that somehow they are intellectually, politically or morally superior to the public. They must show that the public is unable to exercise its will or does not deserve to use the intelligence and good sense that the basic notions of democracy assume. In short, they must show that they are entitled to act as despots.

The Hitlers and Stalins of this world cannot stand the light of a free flow of information. They distrust, with good cause, the judgment of a fully informed public. It is for that reason that book-burning, censorship and government-sponsored news are the hallmarks of tyranny. Tyrants assume some kind of moral superiority and impose that "superiority" on their subjects. A common argument of tyrants is that the people do not know what is best for them, that they are stupid, or ignorant, or misled, and that they must be saved from themselves by their well-intentioned and omniscient leaders. Tyrants by definition assume that they, and not the people, know best.

Of course, as a practical matter all people are not wise and good, but democratic life must necessarily *assume* wisdom and honesty on the part of its citizens. Adoption of a different view of humankind means adopting a "government knows best" attitude. If people are not wise and good, they must be saved from themselves by those who *are* wise and good. And those who consider themselves to be "wise and good" are invariably those who are in power.

The democratic answer to an unwise citizenry does not lie in controls on the public or on what information the public may receive. The answer is instead *more* information, *greater* communication and *freer* speech. Education is the key to a public which exercises its freedoms wisely. But education depends on information. In fact, education is the purest and most noble form of free speech. But, of course, all education does not take place in the classroom. Education may come from the press, from those around us and even from advertising.

THE ECONOMIC MARKETPLACE

The political marketplace of ideas and the economic marketplace of goods work in precisely the same manner. A free enterprise system assumes that consumers know best what they want to buy. Every first-year economics student knows that consumers "vote" for products with dollars. The father of capitalism, Adam Smith, showed that these votes reward efficient production of goods and provide the optimum use of resources. Consumers receive what they want, for no more than they are willing to pay. Smith's "invisible hand," driven by consumers' dollar votes, assures the best and most efficient allocation of resources and the satisfaction of consumer desires.

Knowledge is the single essential condition to the operation of the free enterprise system. The consumer must know of the availability, price and quality of products before a purchase is made, so that intelligent decisions and comparisons can be made. Adam Smith called this condition "perfect knowledge," and argued that the more knowledge and information that sellers and buyers had, the better the market would work. Economic votes, like political votes, must be well-informed.

Some economic systems are unable or unwilling to give the public the choice in economic matters. Such systems, through extensive bureaucracies, make choices for the consuming public. Resources are diverted to industries that some government officials deem "proper," rather than to industries that produce what the public desires. The result is often widespread inefficiency, deprivation and want.

One way to make economic choices for the public is to ban certain products completely. A very small category of products are banned, including dangerous drugs and certain explosives, on the grounds that they are too dangerous to be commonly available. But at least such bans are enacted openly, through the political and legislative process.

A far more insidious way to make choices for the public is to ban advertising of certain products. Banning or limiting advertising, in an era of competition through advertising, is tantamount to crippling a product in the marketplace. Consumers often make choices between competing goods on the basis of advertisements. Without the knowledge gained through advertising, consumers cannot make informed choices about products, and the invisible hand begins to wither.

Above all, the marketplace of ideas and the economic marketplace share a similar assumption about human nature. Both assume that people are intelligent and good. Without such an assumption, decisions must be made *for* the public, by people placed in a position of superiority and power. Despotic systems fear ideas, and filter information to the public they distrust. Noncapitalist systems distrust the economic choices made by the public, and make those choices on criteria other than the wishes of the public.

TRUST AND THE RIGHT TO ADVERTISE

While the right to advertise is clearly protected under the decisions of the Supreme Court, that right is not without its critics. Chief Justice William Rehnquist has argued unsuccessfully that it is permissible to limit advertising of products which carry only a *potential* for harm. The decisions of the Supreme Court have also provided a loophole for would-be regulators, by permitting regulation of advertising if there is a substantial "governmental interest" in regulation, though the nature of such governmental interests are unclear. It seems to be only a short step from saying that regulation of advertising, and even outright banning of advertising of certain products, may be permitted if the product is somehow found "bad" or if regulation is found to be in someone's view of the "governmental interest."

The process of drawing lines between "good" and "bad" speech, or between "good" and "bad" products, is a most difficult and dangerous task. Such lines must be drawn on some notion of what is good for society. It is a despotic point of view, imposing the will of the person drawing the line on the rest of society.

In the view of the founders of our nation, it is much safer not to draw lines at all. That decision was made by the founders in the absolute language of the First Amendment by providing that *no* law "abridging the freedom of speech" may be made. It is better to suffer some "bad" speech than to restrict freedom because the speech is bad. As Oliver Wendell Holmes stated, the most essential constitutional protection is "not free thought for those who agree with us but freedom for the thought we hate."

Similarly, it is better not to draw lines between "good" and "bad" products. Certainly the government has the right to ban certain deadly products from the marketplace. But short of such bans, the marketplace cannot work effectively unless all products are allowed to compete on an equal basis.

THE THIN EDGE OF THE WEDGE

Bans on advertising are a small first step toward the destruction of First Amendment freedoms and toward despotism. They are a small first step toward the destruction of a capitalist economy and toward a planned economy. They are the thin edge of the wedge which may split our cherished and traditional freedoms in two.

Such advertising bans give credence to the fears of people like Justice Hugo Black, who argued that *any* limitation on freedom of speech was an invitation to *further* limitations on free speech, until the limitations swallowed the freedom whole. Once the absolute language of the First Amendment is breached and an exception permitted, the next exception is easier to make, and the next is even easier, *ad infinitum.*

Restrictions on the advertising of any *legal* product result in a similar first step down a slippery slope toward a controlled economy. If a product is "bad," the government may ban it entirely, as in the case of illicit drugs. But if the product is legal, it must be permitted access to the

147

market through advertising. To deprive that product of such access is to cripple it in the marketplace and to make economic choices for the public because those in power "know best."

The assumption that all people are intelligent and good, the basic assumption behind both free enterprise and free speech, also provides an explanation of the ability of the government to protect those who clearly are not able to make choices intelligently. For example, children may be protected from certain kinds of advertising. Our society assumes that children cannot make effective choices in the marketplace, for the same reason that we do not permit children to vote. But once children grow up, the assumptions of intelligence and honor descend upon them. To assume that children cannot make proper choices is merely good sense. To assume that adults cannot make proper choices is despotism.

Of course there is no proof that we will move down the slippery slope as a result of a limitation of cigarette advertising. Someone may draw a firm, bright line between advertising of cigarettes and all other advertising. Legislators, judges and administrative agencies may never use a ban on cigarette advertising as precedent for bans on advertising of other products which someone deems harmful. Someone may be able to illustrate sharply that cigarette advertising is unique and totally distinct from advertising for coffee, artificial sweeteners, firearms, certain movies, automobiles or other products which might occasionally cause harm. The problem is that slippery slope arguments cannot be proven valid until they come true. And by then it is too late.

Of course, there is no proof that we *will* move down the slippery slope as a result of a limitation of cigarette advertising. . . . The problem is that slippery slope arguments cannot be proven valid until they come true. And by then it is too late.

The proposed ban on cigarette advertising assumes that the public is incompetent to make choices. Those who would ban have a heavy burden of persuasion. They must show that the basic assumptions of both our political and economic systems are wrong. They must show that the public and the political and economic decisions made by the public cannot be trusted. And they must show that the restrictions they propose will not act as precedent for other limitations in the future. It is a burden which our law, and the underlying assumptions about our system, make even heavier—many would argue impossible—through the absolute language of the First Amendment.

148

The twin experiments of free enterprise and democracy depend at their very heart on the free trade of information. To limit that free trade, even just a little, is to demonstrate a lack of trust in the American people and to give another solid blow to the wedge in our freedoms. It is far safer, and more in keeping with the spirit of the First Amendment, to simply trust ourselves.

Herbert A. Terry
Bloomington, Indiana

Occupation: College Professor
Interests: Reading, cooking, automobile restoration,
outdoor activities like hiking
Entered the Competition because: "I believed the
U.S. Supreme Court had made some bad decisions
about how to apply the First Amendment to
advertising. I saw the contest as a way of getting my
views publicized widely."

> Advertising bans, especially if they concern perfectly accurate, truthful statements about lawful goods and services, cannot be characterized as anything other than prior restraints.

NO SALE? AN ESSAY ON ADVERTISING AND THE FIRST AMENDMENT

FOR SALE: Well-used copy of Bill of Rights. Original (pub. 1791). In family many years. Need to raise cash forces sale. Offers: Madison, 555–1234.

If descendants of former president James Madison needed to raise cash through sale of his copy of the Bill of Rights they might be surprised to find that the hypothetical ad above is not fully protected by the First Amendment's guarantee of freedom of speech and press that their ancestor fought so strongly to add to the Constitution. What the Constitution and the First Amendment mean is ultimately up to the U.S. Supreme Court. For many years that Court completely refused to extend First Amendment protection to advertising like that above—what the Court called "commercial speech." From 1975 until last summer, however, things improved. The Court seemed committed to First Amendment theories under which advertising gained substantial protection. In June 1986, however, the Court stepped backward, withdrew some First Amendment protection from advertising and coincidentally jeopardized general public rights and principles under the First Amendment. The new direction is wrong. Before it's too late to redirect course, comment on what's wrong with the new approach is essential.

For many years, the Court believed that a few types of expression contributed so little to the social or personal search for truth that they did not deserve to be called protected free speech or press. Included were such things as libel, so-called "fighting words," and, until 1975, routine forms of product or service advertising. In 1975, however, the Court overturned a ban, imposed ironically by Madison's home state of Virginia, on advertising of abortion services available in New York. Since the services were perfectly lawful, and the ads straightforward and accurate, the Court believed that Virginia could not constitutionally keep its citizens in the dark through advertising bans. The Court subsequently took essentially the same position when states tried to ban price advertising of prescription drugs, some types of advertising by lawyers and promotional advertising by an electric utility. A trend seemed to emerge. If advertising related to lawful goods or services, and was not untruthful or inaccurate, then it ought to be protected under the First Amendment. Some regulation of such advertising remained possible, under very compelling circumstances, but flat outright bans on accurate commercial speech about lawful goods and services seemed unconstitutional. If an underlying business activity was lawful, it appeared, then there was a general First Amendment right to talk about it through commercial speech.

All that changed in 1986 when the Court decided a Puerto Rico case involving advertising of casino gambling. Seeking to promote tourism, Puerto Rico authorized certain forms of gambling in 1948. Over the years, however, regulatory agencies banned advertising for casino gambling directed at Puerto Ricans. Ads aimed at potential tourists were okay, but ads aimed at residents of the island were not, even though residents were allowed to gamble.

Under the theories of the First Amendment and advertising that the Court had been developing, such a ban seemed patently unconstitutional, and challenges to it reached the Court. Surprisingly, the decision—written by now-Chief Justice William Rehnquist—allowed the ad ban to stand. The Court decided advertising could relate to two different kinds of underlying activities, goods or services. On one hand, there were a few constitutionally protected activities (for example, the right to an abortion) that the government could not ban or regulate. In that case, accurate, truthful advertising enjoyed full First Amendment protection. For all other activities, however, the rules could be different. If government could ban or regulate an activity under its general police powers, but chose to let the activity go on anyway, the Supreme Court reasoned, the government retained the power to impose "restrictions on stimulation of its demand"—including advertising bans, even though the activity was lawful and the ads truthful and accurate. As examples, the Court cited ads for cigarettes and alcoholic beverages. Use of the examples stimulated calls by some for legislative bans on advertising of those products.

Unfortunately, proposals for the kinds of advertising bans suggested by this Supreme Court decision jeopardize crucial First Amendment values and principles extending far beyond controversies over cigarette or liquor advertising. The Court's new approach is deeply flawed, but the roots of a major First Amendment problem actually trace to the Court's first major advertising decisions in the 1970s and to a tendency, in those and later decisions, to ignore basic First Amendment theories.

Figuring out what the First Amendment means is no simple task. The Court's historical reasons for not originally giving advertising full First Amendment protection aren't entirely clear. Certainly it could not have been out of any belief that it was wrong for ads to attempt to persuade, since persuasion has long been the objective of most other kinds of protected expression. To its authors in the late 1700s, its meaning seems to have been self-evident. At least they didn't talk much about what they meant, and they didn't discuss how it might apply to advertising even though advertising existed in their day. Historical records of deliberations over the First Amendment are sparse—the authors wanted to prohibit Congress from abridging "Freedom of Speech, and of the Press," and that was that. Given the sparse original understanding, jurists, legal scholars and philosophers confronted with First Amendment controversies have tried to explicate the ends and purposes of the amendment as a guide to making decisions about what it means today. They have also developed some principles of First Amendment decision making. There's much dispute about these ends, purposes and principles but they nonetheless have generally guided Supreme Court decision making. Unfortunately, some of the most basic principles seem forgotten in the Court's recent approach to First Amendment theory for advertising.

First, and best agreed upon most likely, is the proposition that if the First Amendment is intended to do anything it's designed to stop "prior restraints"—bans on expression before it occurs. Instead, when we allow restrictions on speech at all, we tend to prefer them as after-the-fact punishments. We prefer that speech take place, figuring out later whether or not it is permissible, rather than that the government have the power to stop expression in advance. For example, one may risk libeling or invading the privacy of another but does so knowing that damages may later have to be paid to the injured individual. Advertising bans, especially if they concern perfectly accurate, truthful statements about lawful goods and services, cannot be characterized as anything other than prior restraints, a point unfortunately obscured recently by the Court.

Second, the founders valued freedom of expression as crucial to self-governance. Their intent was to prohibit the government from controlling access to information necessary to keep a self-governing society working. Certainly they intended broad rights to criticize gov-

155

ernment institutions. Advertising about things other than the government also fits in here, however. Our government has turned out to be a vigorous free market economy. That outcome was not predetermined by the Constitution, but it is the way things have worked out. We chose not to have strong governmental control over the functioning of our economy. Instead, we left our economy free of government control to be largely self-determined through the interactions of vendors and consumers. It's not a perfect system, but we decided it was better than direct control by government. In a sense, then, our nongovernmental free market system can be viewed as an alternative to governmental institutions that might have regulated the economy. Had those governmental institutions for economic regulation been created, there is little doubt that speech about them would be protected by the First Amendment. Speech, like advertising, pertinent to the accurate functioning of a self-governing free market economy should be equally protected under the First Amendment. Unfortunately, unless the Supreme Court changes its theories, commercial speech will continue to have second class, minimal protection and the public may be deprived of information that could help them make better marketplace-based decisions about important things in their lives.

Third, the authors of the First Amendment were primarily interested in protecting the rights of speakers to speak, rather than concerned about the rights of listeners to listen or readers to read. They assumed that if you had many different speakers speaking freely, then the public would figure out what to believe or what to do based on comparison of often conflicting views. They assumed that the government had little business choosing speakers or guiding citizen decision making in these areas. Unfortunately, the Court's approach to First Amendment theory for advertising in the early 1970s cases was different. The virtue of those cases was that they, at least, recognized some First Amendment interests in commercial speech. The vice came through the approach. All of the 1970s and early 1980s cases approached the First Amendment issues from a consumer perspective. In each case, the state tried to prevent the public from learning about something by banning advertising about it. The Court decided that this violated the public's First Amendment right to receive information, a First Amendment theory drawn primarily from broadcasting. While the theory may have some merit in broadcasting, where it can be argued that physical principles prevent an unlimited number of channels and compel some government protection of consumer interests, it has little validity when applied to advertising, which is prolific rather than scarce.

156

Nonetheless, it was the approach the Court took. The cases did not recognize First Amendment rights of advertisers so much as they recognized public First Amendment rights to receive advertised information. While at first glance, that does not seem like a bad approach, it is in fact fundamentally contrary to the core meaning of the First Amendment. If all that is protected is a public right to receive information, then the government—ultimately in the form of the courts—remains in control of what there is a "right to receive" and what may be banned. That that's so can be seen from the Court's role in regulating Puerto Rico's casino advertising, a decision which unfortunately delegates that decision making power to legislatures. We would be far better off if we recognized, instead, the First Amendment rights of advertisers to speak commercially. Doing that would ultimately best protect the information needs of the public. We have relied upon that approach successfully in nonadvertising areas, and no sound reasons exist for doing differently when the speech involved is paid for or invites commercial, rather than intellectual, transactions.

The society at large must defend important principles of freedom of speech and press even if the Court, for the moment, has forgotten them.

In the long run, the Court must be convinced to bring advertising fully under traditional First Amendment protection. This would not mean an end to advertising regulation. Freedom of speech and press are not now absolutes. If one libels another, one can be compelled to pay damages. If one distributes obscenity, one can be punished. Knowingly or recklessly false, deceptive or misleading advertising could still be punished—just as knowing or reckless libels can be punished—but for First Amendment reasons it ought to be allowed to take place. There should be an initial right to run an ad about lawful activities, but there could be the knowledge that postpublication accountability could be demanded for certain kinds of ads. Broad governmental bans on advertising for cigarettes, liquor or other controversial but lawful activities, would be unconstitutional. Oblique efforts to control use of such products or services through regulation of speech about them would be out. Instead, government would have to face the tougher questions of how to directly regulate (or ban) those activities. While this might be a difficult approach for government to follow—it involves hard political decisions—it's preferable to one where activities continue but speech about them is restrained. It is consistent with the general First Amendment principle that it is better to regulate conduct (the production or sale of goods or services) than to regulate expression. Full First Amendment protection for advertising would not create a right to advertise. An advertiser would still have to find (or establish) a medium willing to carry the message. It would, however, provide consumers with additional information relevant to making consumer choices. It would expand the flow of information, and get the government out of paternalistically deciding when consumers can know, through advertising, about lawful goods and services. It would enable consumers to better reach decisions about their economic activities themselves.

Getting the Court to change its approach, however, is a long-range solution to the problem. Given the changing composition of the Court, it is a possibility. One member of the Court that decided the Puerto Rico case—former Chief Justice Burger—has retired and been replaced by Justice Scalia. Since the decision was a five-to-four vote, a new or reconsidered view by a new or continuing justice could result in a change in course. This can occur if consumers and business, together, forcefully and logically urge the Court in subsequent cases to reconsider its views.

The principle of free speech is not fully secure until free speech includes paid speech, too.

Until the Court changes its approach, however, other branches of government—federal and state, legislative and administrative—must be encouraged to restrain themselves from using the powers recently given them to ban or extensively regulate accurate, truthful advertising about lawful goods and services. Doing that is a matter of corporate and individual persuasion—an exercise of free expression rights at their best. When advertising bans are proposed, citizens and companies must be prepared to oppose them as bad ideas and poor public policy, even if they are for the moment constitutional. The society at large must defend important principles of freedom of speech and press even if the Court, for the moment, has forgotten them. The idea that government has any right to ban accurate truthful speech—paid or free—about perfectly lawful products, activities or services is an anathema to the First Amendment, a point that must be forcefully pressed whenever advertising bans are considered. The principle of free speech is not fully secure until free speech includes paid speech, too.

Leroy Keyt
Hartley, Iowa

Occupation: Insurance Salesman, Tax Practitioner
Interests: Golf, collecting and trading
stamps and coins
Entered the Competition because: "I strongly believe
in freedom of expression, both individually and
commercially, and this contest was an excellent
opportunity to express some of my deeply held beliefs
on this topic."

OF FREE SPEECH

Shambaugh Grade School has two rooms: kindergarten through fourth grade was in the "little" room. When my family moved into that small southwest Iowa town I was in the fifth grade, so I was placed in the "big" room. The metal urinal trough in the boys' outhouse had a tendency to rust out, so at the beginning of each school year we usually got new tin. Not much else changed during my sojourn there. The school library consisted of three old dictionaries, a government book and a book on World War II.

Each grade was generally taught separately, and the subjects covered everything from math and reading and geography to art. While the teacher was conducting classes in the other grades, you were to work on your class assignments. If you applied yourself, it usually didn't take long to complete the little tasks in spelling and addition. To while away the excess time, I would read one of the books from the "library" or listen to the other classes in progress. To my mind at least, the upper grades always got the good stuff: the seventh graders studied United States history, and the eighth graders had "government." Government class was generally oriented to the national level, but for about six weeks each year, the eighth graders got to study from a paperbound booklet which touched on highlights of Iowa history and set forth the peculiarities of Iowa civics.

The dictionaries occupied part of my idle time—the definitions with pictures, like aardvarks and medieval knights, always attracted my attention. Before I had to, I had read the Declaration of Independence and at least part of the Constitution, from the old book in the library. The short parts of the Constitution, like the Preamble and the amendments, made easier reading. Some of that stuff in the middle was pretty dry reading.

The other "source" in our library was the most fun to read, the book on World War II. If I remember correctly, the World War II book was published by the *Des Moines Register*, featuring front page headlines, cartoons and news photos of that great struggle against tyranny. The pictures of sailors lining the decks of battleships, or lines of Iowa boys who had volunteered, impressed upon me that everyone should be ready to stand up for his rights.

At Shambaugh School we had "music" once a week, usually on Friday afternoon. Unlike our other classes, the entire big room sang together, unaccompanied, and the lesson always closed with an enthusiastic but not always totally harmonious rendition of "The Star-Spangled Banner" or "America, the Beautiful." Occasionally, the closing song was "The Marine Hymn" or "The Battle Hymn of the Republic."

At least once a year there was another class that included the entire big room. That lesson dealt with "Flag Etiquette." After much instruction, we would go to the front of the room, two at a time, and practice proper handling of the flag until we had it right. Throughout the school year, each week two students were assigned the task of raising the flag in front of the school each morning (weather permitting), and lowering the flag and folding it properly at the close of each school day. At the same time that the flag was being retired for the day, another student was pounding chalk out of the blackboard erasers.

Each school day started with a Pledge of Allegiance and a moment of meditation. When you made the Pledge, you placed your right hand on your left breast in salute to the flag. Not only that—Mrs. Harris, our teacher, felt that you should raise your right elbow a bit so that the salute was "perky." "Lazy" or "sloppy" salutes received reprimands.

Thus it was in the little Shambaugh School that I first became actively aware of patriotism. It is also where I became acquainted with the Declaration of Independence and the Constitution of the United States of America, the two major documents underlying our political system. By the eighth grade, we were expected to memorize the Preamble to the Constitution, and to be thoroughly familiar with the ten amendments which constitute the Bill of Rights. We were taught that "in Order to . . . secure the Blessings of Liberty to ourselves and our Posterity" no portion of the Bill of Rights could be abridged.

Within the First Amendment to the Constitution, at the very heart of the Bill of Rights, is this provision: "Congress shall make no law. . . abridging the freedom of speech, or of the press. . . ." Without this one right, it would be difficult—perhaps impossible—to secure and defend the other important freedoms set forth in the Bill of Rights: freedom of religion, the right of the people to assemble, and trial by jury. This same right is the key to free enterprise—the right to inform the public regarding available goods and services—the right to promote one's product. The First Amendment makes no distinction between personal and commercial expression.

If one examines the circumstances surrounding the American Revolution, this lack of distinction is by no means accidental. The Whiskey Rebellion and the Boston Tea Party were in essence commercial protests. To our founding fathers, "the pursuit of happiness" included the liberty to pursue commercial enterprise freely. If one examines either the writings of those who drafted our Constitution or of succeeding leaders in the ensuing two hundred years, commercial freedom has been coupled with personal freedom as essential to our way of life.

After graduating from the Shambaugh Grade School, I went to high school in Clarinda. The library there had magazines. *Time* and *Life* had full page ads for whiskey and gin and vodka. When I watched TV, I noticed that the guys on "Gunsmoke" could drink whiskey, but that the commercials on television were always for beer. In the beer commercials someone would sing and Clydesdales would elegantly cross the screen, but never once did the singers bring the beer to their parched lips. Then, a little later, the Old Gold dancer was gone from the TV tube, and no one could "Call for Philip Morris" in a commercial.

Someone got offended by *Little Black Sambo* on a library shelf. Then the Cinderella Story. Then Mark Twain's *Huckleberry Finn*. By now, it seems, someone somewhere has attempted to ban everything from the Bible to *On the Origin of Species*.

None of this censorship reflects the spirit of the First Amendment—the concept that all of us in the United States should be free to express ourselves, our views and our products. As Thomas Jefferson pointed out, a democracy must tolerate the airing of all ideas and viewpoints—even those that are false and misleading—if we are to remain free. Jefferson also felt that, with an educated citizenry, the common man should be left free to think and choose for himself.

In promoting freedom of religion, Thomas Jefferson wrote: ". . . truth is great and will prevail if she is left to herself; that she is the proper and sufficient antagonist to error, and has nothing to fear from the conflict unless by human interposition disarmed of her natural weapons, free argument and debate. . . ." One interesting connotation is that freedom of expression is the key to our other liberties. Clearly Jefferson felt that censorship would lead free men away from the truth, whether that "human interposition" was well-intentioned or not.

Clearly Jefferson felt that censorship would lead free men away from the truth, whether that "human interposition" was well-intentioned or not.

As citizens it is easy enough to blame the lawmakers or the bureaucrats or the local school board for the various infringements upon our right to know. In fact, as yet in our society, the existence of such censorship occurs primarily because we as citizens allow it to be so. We

163

must recognize that every infringement upon the free flow of ideas and information diminishes our freedom to know. The right to know, and its correlates of free speech and a free press, are prerequisites to the exercise of all other freedoms. In a free society ideas and products should have equal opportunity to compete in the marketplace of the mind.

We allow the FCC to ban liquor and cigarette ads from the airways. Now certain interests, under the guise of protecting the public, are moving to ban all tobacco advertising and promotion. We must ask ourselves this question: If this sort of logic is applied to all commercial free speech, is any legal product free from the imposition of advertising censorship?

That is not simply a rhetorical question. Recently, when certain research indicated that bacon cooked at high temperatures might be carcinogenic when ingested in large quantities, it was seriously proposed that pork be removed from the marketplace. There have been proposals that cereals with a high sugar content be banned from advertising on programs oriented toward children. Never mind that the other carbohydrates in the cereal, the slice of toast and the breakfast hash browns all contribute to tooth decay. A steady diet consisting only of prune juice will result in diarrhea. And I have heard that you can poison yourself by ingesting huge quantities of chocolate. I am somewhat surprised that there has not been a serious move to ban all automobile advertising, considering the number of people killed and maimed by motor vehicles every year.

In a free society, companies should be allowed to promote their products and disseminate information without censorship, whether that product is Hershey's chocolate, prune juice or Kentucky bourbon. And, as a free man, I wish to be allowed, if I so choose, to eat Lucky Charms for breakfast, a McDonald's McDLT for lunch, and to smoke a good cigarette as I drink a cup of coffee. And we, as free people, should be ready to fight for the right of our children, our grandchildren and our great-grandchildren to do the same.

From the *Des Moines Register* book on World War II at Shambaugh School many years ago I learned that when tyrants seek to impose their will, whether that tyrant is a mustached Hitler or simply a neighbor who would take the B out of your BLT, free men fight back.

With the bicentennial of the Constitution of the United States upon us, how can we now best fight for our right to free speech and expression?

First, where censorship or restriction of free expression is already in place, fight it. Talk to your neighbors and friends, and appropriate government officials, expressing your opposition to any form of restriction on freedom of speech or the press already in existence. This is an idea worth repeating: *Where censorship begins, freedom ends.*

Second, when anyone attempts to ban a book or an idea, fight that attempted censorship vigorously. Whether it is the story of Cinderella or Mark Twain's *Huckleberry Finn,* both we and our children should have free access.

Third, an advertising ban on tobacco is currently under consideration in Congress. Write to your senators and your congressmen, expressing your opposition to this clear infringement on free expression in a free market economy. Whether you are a smoker or not, express your displeasure to your representatives regarding this proposed infringement on free speech and expression. When freedom begins to disappear, "No man is an island."

Write to your senators and your congressmen, expressing your opposition to this clear infringement on free expression in a free market economy.

Finally, whenever and wherever you see a threat to your freedoms, especially if that freedom is your right to free speech and free press, raise your voice loud and clear to your elected representatives. The price of freedom is eternal vigilance. The words are old, but the verity persists.

In Mrs. Harris' classes at the Shambaugh School, everyone was given an opportunity to express their opinion. Mrs. Harris occasionally opposed a viewpoint, but she never squelched your attempts to express your thoughts and ideas. The same operational concept should run free in our society.

Like the man who wrote the Declaration of Independence, and who later supported the Bill of Rights, we should, on the bicentennial of the Constitution, renew this oath: "I have sworn upon the altar of God, eternal hostility against every form of tyranny over the mind of man."

Express your support of personal and commercial free speech in our society. Even when censorship travels under the guise of social good, oppose it, whether it is the removal of *Little Men* from the school library or the proposed tobacco advertising ban now before Congress.

Then, as you salute your country's flag, you may proudly put a little "perk" in your right elbow!

Roger A. Long
Shawnee, Kansas

Occupation: Computer Programmer
Interests: Woodworking, wine making
Entered the Competition because: "I believe in the
need to preserve freedom of speech."

MY SECOND LAUGH

Many years ago, as a grade school student, I could not comprehend the significance of the famous words of Patrick Henry, " . . . give me liberty or give me death." It sounded impressive, and at the time I wondered if they would include me in history books if I could think of something clever to say. For several days, I tried to think of some adroit remark, but finally gave up. As a child, I completely missed the point.

It was many years later, as a adult, that I truly counted among my blessings the fact that I was, unlike many millions of people in the world, at liberty to express my opinion privately or publicly if I chose to do so. My opinion might be right or it might be wrong, but I didn't have to worry about being fined or going to jail if I expressed an opinion that was in opposition to someone else's line of reasoning. For many years I reveled in my masterful comprehension of most of the profound words of the founders of our nation. And frequently found occasion to laugh at the gross misunderstanding of such matters when I was a child. Little did I realize that I had one more laugh coming.

I spent most of my adult life as a patriotic citizen, jealous of my right to speak my mind. I was proud to be an American. And I was grateful that I had the constitutionally guaranteed right to " . . . life, liberty and the pursuit of happiness." If called upon, I would gladly have served my country to protect these rights. I thought reverently of the countless thousands of lives that were given to protect this government that provides freedom for me. Freedom for me. I was still missing the point.

To throw away our Bill of Rights just so people won't be tempted is absolutely ludicrous.

Sure, it's nice for me to have freedom of expression, but it now occurs to me that it is absolutely vital that everyone else have freedom of expression, even if I don't. I was looking at it from the wrong side. You see, my freedom of choice depends upon the availability of everyone else's opinion. My self-respect depends upon it. If I think of myself as intelligent enough to make my own decisions (and in a democracy, one must) it is essential to know that every side of every issue is available to me whether it is good or bad, right or wrong. And, whether I agree with it or not.

There are those who think that freedom of expression should be selective, restricting some opinions that might be bad for me. Then I wouldn't have to make a decision. God forbid. That strikes right at the heart of freedom. You see, I am wise enough now to know that freedom of expression is not for me, it is for the other fellow. Let them all make their pitch. I'll decide. Just be sure that I get all of the information from all of the sides.

If any restriction on freedom of expression is imposed on anyone, it sets a precedent. It is then more likely that a second one be imposed and perhaps a third. There is no well-defined stopping point. Let us suppose that a faction opposing tobacco advertising were successful in restricting the freedom of expression of the tobacco industry. Many would say that it is for good reason, because smoking is hazardous to your health. The door would be open to restrict advertising by beer companies also. If restriction becomes standard procedure, then what about auto manufacturers. Tens of thousands of people are killed each year by cars. Pizza, a thick juicy pizza, high in cholesterol, would probably be worse for me than any of the above. But to throw away our Bill of Rights just so people won't be tempted is absolutely ludicrous.

But now I realize that my real freedom depends upon the freedom of expression of the other fellow.

Now I look at myself as a young adult and have my second laugh. I really thought freedom of expression was important to me. But now I realize that my real freedom depends upon the freedom of expression of the other fellow. Patrick, you and your associates did a good job a couple of hundred years ago. I hope that your descendants, today's legislators, are blessed with the wisdom to continue the good work.

Bobby J. Touchton
Louisville, Kentucky

Occupation: Minister
Interests: Stamp collecting, genealogy, swimming,
reading (especially current history)
Entered the Competition because: "I deeply felt that
censorship was incongruent to the harmony of
American culture."

Yet while most people oppose censorship, in certain circumstances they also make exceptions. This is where the problem begins.

CENSORSHIP: A FAILURE FOR THE AMERICAN WAY

In Belgrade, Yugoslavia in 1937 a beloved American author had his work banned because of a supposedly antimonarchical story that pictured a plot against a young king and a conspiracy to place an imposter on the throne. At that particular time a regency was ruling Yugoslavia during the minority of the king; although there was no possible correlation, because the American author had no interest in the politics of Yugoslavia, the government was afraid that its citizens would fancy the idea of a coup d'état.

The next year in Rome, Italy, the National Conference of Juvenile Literature decided that this same author's works were unsuitable for the minds of the children, and the editors of newspapers in which these works appeared were instructed to eliminate them as counter to "Italian inspiration as to racism, and exaltation of the imperial, Fascist and Mussolinian tone in which we live." Children, they said, should be trained in the principles of "sleeping with the head on a knapsack."

Finally, in 1954, Communists raided the schools of East Berlin, Germany, in search of Western books. They found this particular author's works and banned them, because the central figure was classed as an anti-Red rebel. Surely today Mickey would not be so prone to censorship around the world. For it was America's beloved hero, Mickey Mouse, who had appeared in all kinds of comic strips, that was the object of censorship in Yugoslavia, Italy and Germany at various times in their national histories. Walt Disney could not have found it even slightly amusing to know that the works which he had spent so much time on, simply for children's amusement, were somehow making political statements around the world and therefore being banned.

It is hard to imagine a country that would be so strict as to censor comic strips, especially those comics of such simple humor as Mickey Mouse; however, once the censorship caravan begins to move, it is often hard to stop. Where must the line be drawn? By exploring and questioning censorship of expression in various sectors of American life, by defining and defending the First Amendment's application to American business and by specifically questioning the ramifications of a tobacco advertising ban on the future of free expression in a free market economy, one comes to the clear understanding that censorship is a complete failure in the beloved American way.

Among Americans, it is indeed difficult, if not impossible, to find anyone who is not opposed to censorship. The idea of censorship itself is repulsive to most Americans. They do not like the idea of certain people trying to protect the minds and morals of other individuals. They firmly believe that a majority has no right to seek to impose its views on a minority. Yet while most people oppose censorship, in certain circumstances they also make exceptions. This is where the problem begins. The decision to make exceptions begins to take hold and more and more items are censored. Once this happens, censorship becomes accepted and one's freedom of expression becomes limited.

For example, a twenty-one-year-old senior political science major at Roosevelt University in Chicago wrote an unsigned article in the school's newspaper. The article declared that the university was seething with "rumors of impending disaster," which included the possibility of the university's president being dismissed from his duties. Immediately, university officials denied that the article was true and withheld that particular issue from distribution. The subscribers to the newspaper were allowed to receive their issue; however, it contained a four-page article from university officials. In their article, the officials vehemently denied the allegations made in the article by the student. The students claimed that the university had censored their publication, and after it was discovered who the author of the article was, she was asked to reveal her sources, which she refused to do. Several weeks later the problems revealed in the article became a reality; the university president did resign. However, many people at the university felt that the damage had already been done to the freedom of speech for the students by the censoring practices that the university had put into effect. This of course is only one segment in American life where censorship has occurred; yet once the practice begins, in any part of America, it is often too hard to stop making the exceptions to the freedom instilled in the American dream.

The forefathers of America who framed the Constitution dreamed of a country where the freedom of speech was to be tremendously valued. They did not want to found a country where censorship would be tolerated, because they had experienced bans in their native lands. It was their intention that neither anyone nor anything should be allowed to prohibit the freedom of speech. Expression should not, in fact could not, be limited. In Article I of the Amendments of the Constitution, dated 1789, the patriarchs of this nation even prohibited Congress, the legislative body of the United States, to make any law to prohibit the exercise of the freedom of speech. The courts work hard to keep this treasured freedom intact.

The Supreme Court follows the direction of the Constitution and has tried to balance the freedoms of the First Amendment against local pressures and desires. The local feelings are what survive, except when someone has the time and energy to pursue a case up to the Supreme Court. Nonetheless, the high court does its very best to try to protect the freedom of speech as set forth by the framers of the Constitution.

While it is well understood what the founding fathers meant, and that the Supreme Court tries to follow it, it is also well understood that congressmen also follow their constituencies from the local, grass roots level. If the people of the nation want it, it is the duty of Congress to get it for them—or is it, when it goes against the specific instructions set out in the Bill of Rights? Imagine what would have happened if Congress had followed their constituencies concerning *The Grapes of Wrath*.

It was seven months after the publication of John Steinbeck's *The Grapes of Wrath* when three copies were ordered burned by the public library in St. Louis, Missouri because of the vulgar words used by the characters. In the same year, the book was banned in Kansas City and in towns in Oklahoma. Finally, in California the Associated Farmers of Kern County, whose policies had been attacked, mapped a state-wide ban in schools and libraries against the book as being derogatory to the state. If Congress had gone against the founding fathers' wishes and followed the fad that was sweeping America in 1939 by banning *The Grapes of Wrath*, it would have been decades, if ever, before many generations could have enjoyed this celebrated piece of literature. The nation's patriarchs had enough foresight to know what could happen when a right is taken away or when a government perverts it to the ultimate degree.

Just as it would have been an enormous tragedy to ban *The Grapes of Wrath*, so too would it be a disgrace to the heritage that America is so proud of to censor advertisements of particular businesses. It is one thing to forbid the publication of a nonfictional work because it is outright fraudulent; it is an entirely different story to ban an article in order to obstruct the flow of information so as to shape human behavior into one's notion of ideal or acceptable. Advertisers take great care not to exploit their readers by deceit. There is to be no misrepresentation or false claims in advertisements. It is highly believed that the government must protect the consumer against any written or spoken falsities in

175

advertisements. When no misrepresentation has taken place, though, then the government has no right to interfere. Nonetheless, since the Food and Drug Act of 1906 many watchdog agencies have sprung up to force advertisers to be truthful in their claims. Local prosecuters, the Federal Trade Commission, and the Securities and Exchange Commission are just three groups where there are movements toward censorship of false advertisements. No one is concerned about the unrestricted right of the individual consumer to read advertisements, nor does anyone believe that advertisers are deprived of their First Amendment rights by having their claims censored due to misrepresentation or outright fraud. Then what is the problem? Is the problem the definition of where truth ends and fraud begins? The nation's courts have ruled that the test for misrepresentation in advertising is the probable deception of the average, inexperienced buyer, not those who are experts in the field. A business may use fluffy language as much as it wishes in order to promote the actual value of the product, but if the words used mislead the average consumer about a vital fact, even if it cannot be construed as complete falsehood, then it can be rightfully banned.

As long as businesses are not spreading false advertisements they cannot be exempt from the rights set up by America's founding fathers. American businesses are not an exception to the guarantees in the First Amendment, any more than an individual citizen is. To ban any advertisement simply to coerce people to believe something else, is totally unconstitutional, whether it is an advertisement for soap, hamburgers, dishwashing liquid or baby diapers. The censoring of any advertisements, including tobacco, should never take place; for when it does, then the exceptions begin and repeated abuse, by imposing other bans, increases.

As long as businesses are not spreading false advertisements they cannot be exempt from the rights set up by America's founding fathers.

Gone are the days when tobacco companies advertised that certain brands of cigarettes encouraged "the flow of digestive fluids" or that they relieved fatigue or that they released bodily energy. No longer do tobacco companies claim that their brand of cigarettes is soothing, restful and comforting to the nerves. In America's free market economy, with all its self-regulation, any company that would promote such claims would be laughed right into oblivion by other companies.

Modern day advertisers believe that the people of the '80s are alert and well-informed. To insult the consumers' intelligence is also to inadvertently insult the name of the product. Therefore, tobacco companies are extremely careful about the wording of their advertisements so as not to mislead anyone about the virtues or problems that might arise from smoking. At worst they can be accused of creating an illusion; yet without illusion there would be no advertising at all and all forms of art and literature would be slain under the censor's bloody knife. In a free market society, if tobacco advertising is actually banned, then who is to say that other advertisements, and possibly even *all* other advertisements, will not also be banned. What then will there be? A television program without commercials or a magazine without pretty pictures?

In conclusion, censorship of expression is taboo in a society that prides itself on its freedom of speech. For the government to break that taboo is for it to break a sacred custom of American society. The First Amendment guarantees the right of free speech, both to individuals and to businesses which are owned and operated by individuals. Regardless of the type of company that it is, a ban on advertising limits the future of free expression in a free market economy. It goes without saying that all companies would be affected by such a ban, regardless of the industry at which it is aimed, and that such a ban aimed at the tobacco industry is quite prejudicial. No one has the right to coerce the public into a particular belief, whether by banning Mickey Mouse, a university newspaper article, the beloved novel *The Grapes of Wrath* or a tobacco advertisement. Even if anyone did have the right, which no one does, banning and censorship is not the most effective solution. Freedom of speech means allowing all sides to speak their minds openly. This is the best way we have to reveal truth and falseness.

Michael William Tifft

New Orleans, Louisiana

Occupation: Attorney
Interests: Amateur historian, stamp collecting,
reading, bicycling, basketball, gourmet cooking
Entered the Competition because: "The bicentennial
of our Constitution demands a reaffirmation of
rights protected by the First Amendment."

> Any suppression of speech that is in the nature of a prior restraint—such as a national tobacco advertising ban—bears a heavy presumption of unconstitutionality.

REHNQUIST RIDES AGAIN

(This Chief No Wooden Indian)

A recent United States Supreme Court decision bodes a reactionary challenge to First Amendment protection of commercial speech. In July of 1986 then-Justice Rehnquist (now Chief Justice) authored a disturbing decision in *Posadas De Puerto Rico Associates v. Tourism Company of Puerto Rico*—a decision that may provide new impetus to congressional attempts to impose a national tobacco advertising ban.

The *Posadas* decision involved a challenge to a Puerto Rican statute which forbids the advertising of casino gambling. Though casino gambling is legal in Puerto Rico, even encouraged, Rehnquist decided that an advertising ban aimed at keeping native Puerto Ricans out of the island's casinos was consistent with the First Amendment. Rehnquist reasoned that since Puerto Rico could have outlawed casino gambling, then it could take the lesser step of merely outlawing its promotion. He then intimated that his theory could be applied to other "products deemed harmful, such as cigarettes, alcoholic beverages and prostitution."

While Rehnquist appeared to rest his rationale on established commercial speech doctrine, the reality is that he relaxed the First Amendment standards used to judge governmental restrictions on advertising. By accepting Puerto Rico's argument, rather then weighing it, Rehnquist tilted the scales in the government's favor. And so the First Amendment lost.

Given Rehnquist's departure from established First Amendment principles and his traditional hostility toward the protection of commercial speech, it seems likely that the new Chief Justice would welcome and uphold a national ban on tobacco advertising.

THE FIRST AMENDMENT

Although the First Amendment literally prohibits the enactment of any law that restricts speech, some restrictions are permitted. The universal example is that one cannot yell "Fire" in a crowded theater.

181

The question in a First Amendment case is usually not whether the speech is protected, but whether or not, and by how much, government can regulate it. Early First Amendment cases sanctioned restrictions on speech only where its free exercise created a "clear and present danger" or where a "serious evil" would result. Today, any restriction on speech must be justified by a substantial governmental interest and must be no greater than necessary to further the government's end. Additionally, any suppression of speech that is in the nature of a prior restraint—such as a national tobacco advertising ban—bears a heavy presumption of unconstitutionality.

While these guidelines have long been recognized and protected, it has only been within the past fifteen years that they have been applied in the context of commercial speech. This does not detract from the development of commercial speech doctrine, however, because the Constitution is an elastic document that was designed to adapt to and function in changing times. The drafters of the Constitution left to their progeny the development and application of their governmental theories.

THE CASE LAW

While commercial speech doctrine did not take off until the 1970s, commercial speech achieved minimal First Amendment protection in *Chrestensen v. Valentine*, decided in 1941. There an entrepreneur marketing submarine tours protested New York's decision to refuse him wharfage facilities. His protest took the form of a handbill, the reverse of which advertised his submarine tours. The Supreme Court held that the protest, as political speech, was protected, and the mere fact that the handbill included some commercial promotion was not enough to "taint" the protected speech.

In *Capital Broadcasting Company v. Mitchell*, decided in 1971, a three-judge district court upheld congressional prohibition of cigarette advertising on television and radio. The court decided that commercial speech was entitled to lesser protection than other varieties of speech. It also felt, without explaining why, that Congress had the power to prohibit cigarette advertising in any media. This reasoning conflicted with the same court's later statement that "legislation concerning newspapers and magazines must take into account the fact that the printed media are privately owned." The court's real basis for decision was the fact that broadcast airwaves are publicly owned and licensed for use by the government.

The decision was not unanimous. J. Skelly Wright dissented, seeking expanded protection of commercial speech and taking issue with the purported balancing of interests by the majority. "No amount of attempted balancing of alleged state interests against freedom of the press," said Wright, "can save this Act [the ad ban] from constitutional condemnation under the First Amendment. . . . At the very core of the First Amendment is the notion that people are capable of making up their own minds about what is good for them and that they can think their own thoughts so long as they do not in some manner interfere with the rights of others."

Despite the eloquence of Wright's dissent, it was not until 1975, in *Bigelow v. Virginia*, that commercial speech was awarded First Amendment protection. The Supreme Court there held that advertising containing factual material of clear public interest could only be suppressed if the government's interest in such a ban outweighed the interests protected by the First Amendment. In that case the Supreme Court discussed a Virginia statute which made it illegal to encourage or promote abortions. The Court held that the statute, as applied to the advertisement of a New York abortion referral service, was inconsistent with the First Amendment. The Court further held that Virginia's interest in protecting its citizens from such an ad did not outweigh the interests protected by the First Amendment. The existence of commercial activity in itself, said the Court, is not a justification for narrowing the scope of protection secured by the First Amendment.

A year later, in *Virginia State Board of Pharmacy v. Virginia Citizens Consumer Council, Inc.* the Supreme Court faced a challenge to a state statute that declared it unprofessional conduct for a pharmacist to advertise the prices of prescription drugs. The Court decided that the statute could not be justified on the basis of the state's interest in maintaining the professionalism of its licensed pharmacists. It also defined commercial speech as that devoid of any content save the proposal for a commercial transaction, adding:

> So long as we preserve a predominantly free enterprise economy, the allocation of our resources in large measure will be made through numerous private economic decisions. It is a matter of public interest that these decisions, in the aggregate, be intelligent and well-informed. To this end the free flow of information is indispensable.

The Court went on to decide that the government may not suppress truthful information about an entirely lawful activity because of its feared impact on its audience. Rehnquist dissented, objecting that "the way will now be open not only for the dissemination of price information but for active promotion of prescription drugs, liquor, cigarettes, and other products the use of which it has previously been thought desirable to discourage."

The court went on to decide that the government may not suppress truthful information about an entirely lawful activity because of its feared impact on its audience.

In 1977 the Court decided *Carey* v. *Population Services International*, which struck down an ad ban on contraceptives, and *Bates* v. *State Bar of Arizona*, which lifted a ban on television advertising of routine legal services. In both cases, the court weighed the asserted interest of the state in banning the advertising, and in both instances found the interest outweighed by concerns of the First Amendment. Rehnquist dissented in both, and suggested in *Bates* that commercial speech was outside of First Amendment protection.

In *Linmark Associates* v. *Township of Willingboro*, decided in 1977, the Court addressed the constitutionality of an ordinance that made it legal to post "for sale" or "sold" signs. The ordinance was designed to prevent "white flight" from a rapidly integrating neighborhood. The Supreme Court there stated that commercial speech cannot be banned because of an unsubstantiated belief that its impact is detrimental, and further, that government cannot achieve a concededly important objective by restricting the free flow of truthful commercial information.

A major step in tpe development of commercial speech protection came in *Central Hudson Gas and Electric Corporation* v. *Public Service Commission of New York*, decided in 1980. The Court distilled earlier cases and worked out a formula to be used in balancing governmental interests in regulation with the interests protected by the First Amendment. Only when the government has a substantial interest in the regulation, the regulation directly advances that interest and is the least restrictive means to the government's end, can the government restrict protected commercial speech. Within that framework the Court decided that the challenged regulation, which banned promotional advertising of electricity, was more extensive than necessary to further the government's interest in energy conservation.

Justices Blackmun and Brennan, echoing Wright's dissent in *Mitchell* a decade earlier, argued for greater protection. Said Blackmun:

> I seriously doubt whether suppression of information concerning the availability and price of a legally offered product is ever a permissible way for the state to "dampen" demand for or the use of the product. Even

though "commercial speech" is involved, such a regulatory measure strikes at the heart of the First Amendment. This is because it is a covert attempt by the State to manipulate the choices of its citizens, not by persuasion or direct regulation, but by depriving the public of the information needed to make a free choice.

In *Bolger v. Young Drug Products Corporation*, a 1983 case, the Court considered a statute that prohibited the unsolicited mailing of literature advertising contraceptives. The Court held that the party seeking to uphold a restriction on commercial speech carries the burden of justification. The government failed to do so. Surprisingly, Rehnquist concurred with the majority, noting that narrower restrictions were available to fully serve the government's interest. "Although this restriction directly advances weighty governmental interests, it is somewhat more extensive than is necessary to serve those interests," he said. "On balance I conclude that this restriction on . . . commercial speech has not been adequately justified."

Again, in *Zauderer v. Office of Disciplinary Counsel*, a 1985 case, the Supreme Court stressed the state's burden of justification in a challenge to yet another attorney-advertising restriction. The court there stated that the burden is on the state to present a substantial governmental interest justifying the restriction and to demonstrate that the restriction vindicated that interest through the least restrictive means available.

A DANGEROUS DEPARTURE

In *Posadas*, the Court per Rehnquist upheld a ban on casino advertising. While Rehnquist appeared to apply the *Central Hudson* test, he failed to require the government to carry its end. In effect, he met the government halfway and left the First Amendment behind. At the outset, Rehnquist noted that the advertising concerned a lawful activity. Casino gambling has been legal in Puerto Rico since 1948. Nor, he found, was it inherently misleading. Therefore the advertising was entitled to First Amendment protection, subject only to the balancing test of *Central Hudson*.

Puerto Rico's purported interest in an advertising ban was to eliminate the evils of casino gambling by keeping its citizens out of the casinos. Specifically, Puerto Rico hoped to eliminate "serious harmful effects on the health, safety and welfare of the Puerto Rican citizens, such as the disruption of moral and cultural patterns, the increase in local crime, the fostering of prostitution, the development of corruption, and the infiltration of organized crime." Lofty goals indeed, surely meriting some incidental abuse of the First Amendment? Hardly. Native Puerto Ricans, while discouraged from going to the casinos, were still legally allowed to gamble on dog and horse racing, cockfights and the national lottery.

Rehnquist next addressed the question of whether the ad ban directly advanced the government's interest. He decided yes, it did, based only on the "legislature's belief" that failing to ban advertising "would serve to increase the demand for the product advertised." Rehnquist failed to require the government to prove that its regulation served their interest, preferring instead to rely on their self-serving assertion of "yes, it does." Rehnquist further decided that the ban was no more extensive than necessary merely because "the restrictions will not affect advertising of casino gambling aimed at tourists, but will apply only to such advertising aimed at the residents of Puerto Rico."

The apparent willingness to defer to unsubstantiated legislative judgment is at odds with the stance the Court took in *Central Hudson*, where the Court looked for and found a less restrictive means of securing the government's end.

When faced with the argument that in *Carey* (contraceptive ads) and *Bates* (legal services) the Court struck down similar ad bans, Rehnquist replied that in those cases, the advertising dealt with constitutionally protected activities that could not themselves be prohibited by the state. Since in *Posadas* casino gambling could have been prohibited, figured Rehnquist, the ban on casino advertising was a legitimate exercise of the government's power. "It is precisely because the government could have enacted a wholesale prohibition of the underlying conduct that it is permissible for the government to take the less intrusive step of allowing the conduct, by reducing the demand through restrictions on advertising."

While this may sound alarmist, constitutional decisions often snowball into aberrant doctrines.

Rehnquist decided the case over a vigorous dissent. Justices Brennan, Blackmun, Marshall and Stevens saw through the screen Rehnquist threw up to justify his reactionary decision. Blackmun discussed the guidelines created to protect commercial speech, then noted:

> While tipping its hat to these standards, the Court does little more than defer to what it perceives to be the determination by Puerto Rico's legislature that a ban on casino advertising aimed at residents is reasonable. The Court totally ignores the fact that commercial speech

is entitled to substantial First Amendment protection, giving the government unprecedented authority to eviscerate constitutionally protected expression.

Justice Stevens was somewhat harsher, finding that the ruling left uture determinations "as unpredictable and haphazardous as the roll of the dice in a casino."

The danger of *Posadas* is its relaxed standard of judicial review. Under the reviewed case law, government must justify restrictions on commercial speech. The job of the Supreme Court is to balance the government's justifications with the interests protected by the First Amendment. The scales are supposed to tilt in the First Amendment's favor, not the government's. When Rehnquist accepted the government's rationale in *Posadas*, he tilted the scales the wrong way. It now seems clear that Congress may enact a tobacco advertising ban, assert a substantial interest, claim the ban directly advances that interest and further pretend that a ban is the least restrictive means of serving that interest. Under *Posadas* Rehnquist need only rubber-stamp those claims to give a national ad ban constitutional authority.

One can only hope the dissenters in *Posadas* will prevail and the Supreme Court will return to the appropriate standards of review of commercial speech.

The implications go further. One day Congress may use the same reasoning to outlaw the advertising of hand guns or of Toyotas. Such bans would reach newspapers, magazines, billboards, matchbook covers, flyers, who knows—perhaps word-of-mouth promotion. While this may sound alarmist, constitutional decisions often snowball into aberrant doctrines. One can only hope the dissenters in *Posadas* will prevail and the Supreme Court will return to the appropriate standards of review for commercial speech. Freedom of speech is a national treasure worthy of vigilant protection.

Robert White
Portland, Maine

Occupation: Writer
Interests: More writing, running (NY Marathon
1983), swimming, guitar, junk movies
Entered the Competition because: "It was a great
exercise in rhetorical style."

The issue is this simple: the more information, more opinions, more people speaking their minds, the better off we all are. Curtail this flow and you court disaster.

It is by the goodness of God that in our country
we have those three unspeakably precious things:
freedom of speech, freedom of conscience, and the
prudence never to practice either of them.
—Mark Twain

Not that Mark Twain should have limited his observation to his American countrymen. Ever since human beings learned how to talk they have censored each other. It is a universal human attribute, undiminished by time or place, nation or culture. We are opinionated and derive immense satisfaction—not to mention personal gain—by imposing our opinions on others. Curtailing free speech is often prudent, as long as prudence is defined in the short run and in the narrow scope. In the long run, though, the more certain and the more heavily imposed the opinion of the day, the more foolish—or dangerous—it is often seen to be in hindsight. The Spanish Inquisition in which people were literally pulled apart limb by limb for unfashionable beliefs is unfortunately only one example.

Most essays on free speech begin with the mistaken assumption that it is a complicated issue. In America people are free to say what they will unless it's "Fire" in a crowded theater or a call to overthrow the American government. The innumerable decisions handed down by courts on both sides of the issue amount to nothing more than blunt common sense in fairly administering this fundamental right. The issue is this simple: the more information, more opinions, more people speaking their minds, the better off we all are. Curtail this flow and you court disaster.

With the suppression of freedom that drove them to war still fresh in their memories, the framers of the Constitution looked to the past, where they saw a host of examples of people repressing those who disagreed with them. They realized that such behavior was destined to be repeated in their new nation unless it was outlawed. Consequently, a goodly portion of the Constitution and its amendments—the First but the chief among them—was devoted to rendering suppression of basic freedoms impossible. The founders based their concerns not on wooly ideals but on three practical assumptions about the failure of imposed opinion.

First, the founders understood that a true democracy required an informed, independent electorate. Deprive voters of information, and they vote poorly. Deprive individuals of their ability to decide for themselves, and you end up with "a system so perfect," as T. S. Eliot said, "that no one will have to be good."

Second, they understood that "eternal truth," the absolute last word, on *any* subject is a rare commodity indeed, and the fewer people dictating such truths the greater their chances of ending up with egg on their faces. Whatever opinions appear to be irrefutably true today will, like Northeastern weather, change tomorrow. The long run can prove the majority wrong as well, which is why freedom of speech is always protected for the dissenting minority.

And, third, the founders believed, and consequent events have confirmed, that censorship rarely if ever achieves its presumed ends. The draconian measures of the McCarthy era did little to dissuade committed Communists from their cause. (If anything it affirmed their position.) But it did plenty to injure the innocent and harm faith in government, particularly after McCarthy, the "rightest" of them all, was revealed as an alcoholic incompetent.

Defenders of First Amendment rights have fought hard to save important long-term considerations over short-term and shortsighted imperatives. The First Amendment protected the NAACP from unwarranted investigation in Alabama even as it has upheld the right of the KKK to march in Skokie, Illinois.

But for some reason, many people forget all about freedom when business is involved.

Most of us are familiar with these landmark decisions and when pushed most of us will agree that even decisions in favor of hateful opinions are worth it if they preserve freedom. But for some reason, many people forget all about freedom when business is involved. Perhaps because we envy great success or because corporations seem less vulnerable than individuals, we rarely mind it when businesses are hindered from announcing or distributing their wares. As early as 1824, Thomas Babington, Lord Macaulay, observed, "Free trade, one of the greatest blessings which a government can confer on a people, is in almost every country unpopular." Time and again, with some noble goal or other in mind, the government has tried to restrict commercial activity with little of the desired effect and a lot of unexpected—and undesired—consequences. One need only to think about Prohibition and its eldest child, organized crime, to see how dismal the results can be.

192

Advertising (or "commercial speech" as lawyers call it), is generally protected by the First Amendment. And sensibly so, since free speech is the logical partner of free trade. The sale of goods depends on customers knowing of their existence, and a strong economy affords us the luxury of democracy. Look at the government of poor countries if this seems a cynical relationship.

Which brings us to the "popular" push, led by the American Medical Association, to outlaw tobacco advertising. Like mandatory seat belts and motorcycle helmets, legal injunctions of this sort get passed as the public stands by because they deliver quick satisfaction to those who know what's best for others. The most obvious problem with this approach is the first failure of imposed opinion: it diminishes people's ability to make their own decisions and it opens the way for further restrictions. Fifty thousand people die on American highways each year. Shall we ban automobile advertisements? If you ban tobacco advertising on the grounds that tobacco causes cancer then musn't you ban the advertisement of liquor, red meat, cream and eggs for similar reasons?

Defenders of the ban will say, "Well, the jury's still out on low-fiber high-fat diets but we've caught smoking red-handed." This is a perfect example of imposed opinion's second failure: the claim by a few to absolute, eternal truth. Today the evidence against tobacco is weighty, but the history of American consumption is littered with mistakes made by regulators in the name of health. In the 1940s the evidence in favor of a high protein (meat and dairy product loaded) diet was weighty and touted by government agencies including the army. Eventually, most people believed that as long as you got your protein the rest could go by the wayside. And it did. Americans dying of encrusted arteries must wonder where those protein proponents have gone. The sugar scare of the 1970s, when sweets were accused of causing everything from cancer to diabetes, resulted in the 1980s legalization of (and inundation of consumers with) a number of hastily tested artificial sweeteners now suspected of nasty side effects, while good old sugar has been found guilty of nothing beyond tooth decay.

One need only think about Prohibition and its eldest child, organized crime, to see how dismal the results can be.

Even if history confirms tobacco's current reputation once and for all, who says that banning tobacco ads will stop people from smoking? The assumption that people who smoke will forget to if they're not reminded is dubious at the very least. Banning liquor and cigarettes from television doesn't seem to have diminished America's appetite for either. I used to smoke, and I know for a fact that the absence of advertising would never have kept me from locating a cigarette machine or a variety store in minutes when I ran out. I quit smoking because of my access *to* information, not my restriction *from* it. I made up my own mind. Give people *all* the information available, and if they care to inform themselves they will come to reasonable decisions.

Proponents of a tobacco advertising ban will respond that in this case the risks are so extreme that the ends justify their means. But why won't they go further? As long as tobacco is a legal good, its manufacturers should be free to hawk it just like everybody else. So why don't antitobacco factions urge Congress to outlaw tobacco? Because they're not stupid . . . they think. At least they're smart enough to look back with horror ar Prohibition and smart enough to estimate the size of the revenue Congress enjoys from its tax on tobacco. It's so much less expensive to satisfy their moral indignation by saying "just don't advertise the stuff." The worst sort of moral self-service.

We live in health-conscious times. More power to them. As an ex-smoker who has occasionally asked someone smoking near me in close quarters to put their cigarette out, I cherish my right to free speech. But I cannot retain that right if I don't grant it to all others. The authors of the Constitution had the intelligence to take lessons from the past and apply them to the future, and their reasons for upholding free speech in *all* areas of American life are as urgent in the 1980s as when they were introduced in the 1790s. As Herbert Hoover, a man who learned the hard way, said, "Free speech does not live many hours after free industry and free commerce die."

Mary A. McAllister
Baltimore, Maryland

Occupation: Proofreader/Editor/Writer
Interests: Reading, watercolor painting,
theater, baseball
Entered the Competition because: "The topic of the
essay intrigued me. The opportunity to uphold and
defend the First Amendment is something we should
all take seriously."

But what if free economic expression is compromised under the guise of a paternalistic concern for the public good?

Several months ago, I attended a luncheon with a woman who was a reporter for a local newspaper. I could hear the slight trace of a foreign accent when she asked me questions about my life, my family and my job. When I, in turn, asked her about herself, she said, "Oh, my life has been very different from yours." She went on to tell me that she had been born in Rumania, and although she'd lived in America for more than twenty years, she still was awed by the absolute freedom we enjoy in this country. "Sometimes," she said, "I want to shake every American citizen and say, 'Do you know how precious is this freedom you have? Can you even imagine what it is like to live in a country where you are denied the basic rights you Americans seem to take for granted?'" I thought about her words for days, wondering if I could ever express what it is that makes life in the United States special for each of us . . .

On any given day, a man walks down the street and he is surrounded by color, whistling and spinning through the sounds and sights of life in a special country.

There, over to his right, is a statue, a gray chiseled monument to someone's artistic vision. Now, to his left he sees the dappled fallen leaves of trees that have shed their multicolored pieces of life for an unknown number of years. He watches the differences in light and shadow on leaves and monument, and walks on. Up ahead, there's a billboard, unique in its graphic presentation of form, colors, words, ideas. And there are sounds. His own footsteps rustle through the leaves and tap lightly on the concrete as he listens to the trill of the twelve o'clock whistle coming from the local factory. Car horns blow in the soft whisper of a light wind, and he hears pieces of human conversation mixed with the monologue of a chirping bird high on a telephone line.

Now, if this man is an artist, perhaps he'll go to his home or his studio and use those sights he's seen—that light on the leaves, that cool gray stone, that clash of color on the billboard—to create the vision of his artistic dream.

But suppose for a moment that this person is a woman. She's heard the sounds and felt the rhythm of the wind, or the splash of a fountain as a backdrop for the radio blaring from the shoulder of a teenager eating lunch by the side of a fountain. She's a musician, a composer, and the studied pattern of a symphony composition is growing inside her. She listens, carefully filtering the noises and choosing the motions and rhythms she needs to express a musical idea.

And what of the child, growing up on a farm. The child feels the cold snap of winter as he watches the warm breath of the cow his father milks early in the morning. The pace of the child's life is set by the measured needs of nature and animals. Perhaps this child will one day write about the rewards of solitude, or the absolute necessity of a respect for nature and the earth that nurtured him.

What do these people have in common? This man, woman and child live in the country where they can express the creativity that is part of every human being—a creativity born of and nurtured by freedom. Such freedom is *guaranteed* in only one special country, the United States of America, whose Constitution ensures that freedom of expression will not be infringed upon, or prohibited, in any way, by legislation. This guarantee reaches into every facet of life—individual, economic and political.

Individual freedom is part of the foundation on which our democracy is based, and democracy exists to serve and promote the rational, creative and moral capacities of the individual. But it is only through free choice that a man, woman or child can exercise and develop these capacities to their fullest extent. John Stuart Mill, in his treatise *On Liberty*, wrote:

> The human faculties of perception, judgment, discriminative feeling, mental activity, and even moral preference are exercised only in making a choice. He who does anything because it is the custom makes no choice. He gains no practice either in discerning or desiring what is best. The mental and moral . . . powers are improved only by being used.

The freedom of personal choice implies a respect for the moral significance of each person, and a recognition of his status as a choosing, autonomous being. But there is another element involved in free choice—the "filtering" of possibilities and information that leads to decision, action and the process of creative expression.

What if our artist walks down a city street in a society where everything he sees is rigidly controlled? Where the composer no longer hears the special beat of a music that has been banned? There are no billboards splashed with color, no newspapers competing for attention, and the only sounds that invade his ears are those that have been deemed acceptable. There are no choices to be made, no personal filtering of stimuli open to autonomous beings. There is only a denial of the special significance of the individual with all his rational, creative potential.

Our Constitution is a safeguard against such a society. It ensures that free choice and free expression remain strong, protected from any legislation that would try to deny these rights their prime importance in the development of the individual person. Benjamin Cardozo wrote that "Freedom of expression is the matrix, the indispensable condition of nearly every other form of freedom." The Constitution clearly outlines the function of the judicial system as one of definition and protection of individual rights. As Joel Feinberg writes, "Perhaps courts *ought* to infringe rights in desperate circumstances, but that can never be their understood legal function."

Implicit in the protection by the courts of individual rights is the extension of those rights to the political and economic spheres. A free market economy reflects and enhances individual freedom through free economic expression. The capacity for choice is exercised and enhanced by the options a supply-and-demand market provides—a sort of democratic procedure of quality determination. If we allow the government or the courts to become the quality determiners of the market, we will have sacrificed an integral aspect of our independence. Our guarantee of free choice and our capacity for filtering those choices is only of value when free economic conditions exist.

Can we allow Congress, or the courts, to take over our role as choosing beings?

But what if free economic expression is compromised under the guise of a paternalistic concern for the public good? In the case of a tobacco advertising ban, the "public good" justification is a real possibility. However, in a democracy whose strongest moral foundation rests on the primacy of the individual, paternalistic interference with individual choice or free expression can only be justified on the grounds that rationality, human dignity or individual moral capacity is in jeopardy. Tobacco advertising threatens none of these prime human values; an advertising ban would imply that individuals in our society are incapable of the filtering capacity of free choice so necessary to their status as autonomous beings. The consequences of such an infringement of individual and economic free expression represented by such a ban are frightening. Our guarantee of freedom extends to every facet of life, but an abrogation of those rights in any one area runs the risk of spreading to other aspects of guaranteed freedoms. Can we allow Congress, or the courts, to take over our role as choosing beings, undermine our free speech, choice and creativity? Will our democratic institutions survive if the free enterprise system is regulated under the justification of moral concern for the public good? If economic freedom of expression is a reflection of individual freedom, then economic institutions have the same rational, creative, moral rights and responsibilities that attain to individuals. Any infringement of these rights presents a serious threat to the conditions under which human potential can reach its fullest expression.

The First Amendment to the Constitution provides for political liberty in the right of the people to petition the government for redress of grievances. Implicit in this provision is the recognition that individuals possess the capacity to know when they have been wronged and to decide what is in their best interest. A consensus of individual opinion and desire is the determining factor under which democracy operates. Free expression and discussion provides a reasonably equitable process for the detection and correction of error. Decisions about the public good, whether for health, moral or religious reasons cannot be taken out of the hands of individuals or we risk the loss of our political freedom as well as our economic and personal freedoms. Louis Brandeis wrote, "Those who won our independence . . . believed liberty to be the secret of happiness and courage to be the secret of liberty."

Would you *choose* to live in a society where a man walks down the street and he sees no statues save those of leaders approved by the country in which he lives? As he walks on, he sees no billboards advertising tobacco or anything else that "the state" has deemed harmful or unacceptable. No graphic artist has expressed his vision in a wild splash of color; no copywriter has written a clever phrase that resonates inside the man. If this man were an artist, he might go home and try to exercise his human capacity for creativity, but he would draw no inspiration from his completely controlled environment. A woman who composes music no longer hears the rhythms of a radio (they've been banned as decadent), or the splashing fountain (the water has been declared harmful). She no longer exercises her filtering capacity in free expression of the music that is withering inside her.

And the child who lives in a rural area in that country never sees the city because he is not permitted to leave his village. He will never write about the joys of a way of life that has been imposed upon him— and the state must approve all individual writing.

The moral foundation of democracy recognizes the choice-making capabilities of each individual in all realms of society.

This society is not a democracy, where the assurance of the moral significance of each person is the prime reason for its existence. In

America, our Constitution guarantees the freedom of expression—creative, moral, economic and political—that provides the best system under which human potential can be realized. The moral foundation of democracy recognizes the choice-making capabilities of each individual in all realms of society. The Constitution provides guarantees that this recognition will not be abrogated in any way by government nor will the significance of the individual be degraded by legislative, political or economic interference. These guarantees stated in the First Amendment were not time-limited. They were valid for the revolutionaries who established our democracy, they are valid for us in the present day and, with a strong defense, will be valid for the future to ensure the continuation of free speech so basic to the larger freedom of the individual.

Robert M. Ruzzo
Boston, Massachusetts

Occupation: Attorney
Interests: Basketball, golf
Entered the Competition because: "I am interested
in First Amendment issues."

> The distinction between a justifiable exception to the First Amendment and the slippery slope of unjustifiable exceptions is obscure, and no assurances can be given as to the steepness of the slope.

COMMERCIAL SPEECH AND THE FIRST AMENDMENT

I.

[T]he ultimate good desired is better reached by free trade in ideas . . . the best test of truth is the power of the thought to get itself accepted in the competition of the market. . . .
—Mr. Justice Holmes

One irony in the history of this country's attempt to strike a balance between the need for effective governance and the desire to preserve liberty has been the languid development of First Amendment protection for speech relating to commercial affairs. As Justice Holmes noted in his famous dissent in *Abrams v. United States*, our institutions of government, most notably the Supreme Court, have continually placed the highest premium on freedom of political expression. Political ideas, according to Holmes, must compete against one another in the marketplace of public opinion. Only then can a fully informed public make rational choices between competing political "truths."

In 1991, the First Amendment, that single, simple sentence which states the fundamental principle of the relationship between the government and the governed, will mark its 200th anniversary. In anticipation of this event, historians and political scientists will assuredly undertake to reconstruct the circumstances which gave rise to its birth.

Many authorities have viewed the Constitution and the Bill of Rights as the product of a wealthy elite struggling to permit competition within its own factions, while simultaneously seeking to preserve its exclusive status. Indeed, from the point of view of Charles Beard and others, the political system created by the founding fathers represented merely a societal superstructure engineered to enhance and maintain a substructure based upon capitalism, commerce and competition. If this analysis were correct, one would expect to find a history of the utilization of this country's political machinery to protect commerce and the competitive marketplace. In the context of the First Amendment, the opposite has been true.

As new Chief Justice William Rehnquist recently observed, "commercial speech"—expression relating to the economic interests of the speaker and his audience—"was afforded no protection under the First Amendment whatsoever" prior to a 1976 Supreme Court decision. Since that time, the Supreme Court has granted commercial speech limited protection under the First Amendment. Accurate, lawful commercial speech may be "restricted" under certain circumstances, to be discussed below. In the hope of extending this doctrine of the curtailment of commercial speech to include an outright ban on certain forms of commercial advertising, antismoking interests have proposed a ban on the advertisement of all tobacco products.

The proponents this bill (H.R. 4792) have assured nonsmokers such as myself that we have nothing to fear beyond the loss of an occasional sporting event previously sponsored by tobacco advertisers. The proponents have also secured a broad spectrum of supporters for the purpose of comforting those who are given to voicing an occasional concern over the future of our constitutional freedoms.

For example, Mr. Melvin L. Wulf, the former legal director of the American Civil Liberties Union, assures the public that "our real First Amendment freedoms will be as intact as ever." Mr. Stephen Klaidman, of the Kennedy Institute of Ethics at Georgetown University sees this proposed ban as part of a "justifiable exception to the First Amendment"; he knows of no reason why it would put us on the "slippery slope leading to unjustifiable exceptions." The omnipresent conservative commentator, George F. Will, professes certainty that the ban would be neither unconstitutional nor immoral.

These authorities profess a certainty which I am unwilling to accept. I am unsure where, if anywhere, a line may be drawn between our "real" First Amendment freedoms and extraneous ones. Similarly, the distinction between a justifiable exception to the First Amendment and the slippery slope of unjustifiable exceptions is obscure, and no assurances can be given as to the steepness of the slope. Mr. Will's certitude as to the constitutionality of the proposed ban is mistaken. Moreover, he espouses an unjustifiable belief in the moral propriety of censorship.

During the war in Vietnam, one songwriter lamented that America's youth was "old enough to kill, but not for votin'." Proponents of a ban on tobacco advertising and other supporters of a distinction between commercial and political speech espouse a similar paradox: The American public is wise enough to digest competing political ideas and choose the next leader of the free world in a nuclear age. The public is not, however, capable of digesting competing messages about tobacco products and thus requires protection from tobacco advertising.

As Mr. Justice Blackmun pointed out in *Central Hudson Gas* v. *Public Service Commission*, the purported distinction between political speech and commercial speech is a false one. A cigarette advertising ban strikes at the heart of the First Amendment "because it is a covert attempt by the state to manipulate the choices of its citizens, not by persuasion or direct regulation, but by depriving the public of information needed to make a free choice."

II.

People will perceive their own best interests if only they
are well enough informed, and . . . the best means to that end
is to open the channels of communication, rather than to
close them.
—Mr. Justice Blackmun

Pro-ban forces argue that their proposal would not inhibit the public flow of information because cigarette advertising is not informative. Such advertising is, rather, merely a series of glamorized images of smokers, which unfairly induce consumers to smoke.

This proposition oversimplifies reality. First, it fails to point out that some cigarette advertising is, in fact, informative. Many ads do provide facts about a particular brand; for example, a number point out a low tar or nicotine content. Secondly, this criticism of advertising is far too broad for the blame to be placed at the feet of the tobacco industry. Exclamations about "Oh, what a feeling" consumers will have upon purchasing a Toyota offer little aid in making an informed purchase. Perfume and cologne advertisements do not inform the public about how a particular fragrance is produced. Finally, critics have long decried the uninformative nature of political advertising.

This proposition oversimplifies reality.

What the ban's proponents are attempting to do is to prohibit the advertisement of tobacco products based upon what is (in the opinion of many) an industry-wide shortcoming in the advertising trade. Their argument proves too much. No one would seriously consider banning all

207

"noninformative" advertising, even if all such ads could be identified. Moreover, even assuming that all cigarette advertising was noninformative, and that it creates a desire to consume among the public which might not otherwise exist, a ban would not be justified. In a free society, the way to combat this process is to send a countermessage to oppose the message which is found objectionable.

Antismoking groups have certainly attempted this. Indeed, while one of their principal objections is that cigarette advertising encourages smoking among children, cigarette ads, which do not feature children, have been "countered" by antismoking ads which frequently do so. Having failed to obtain the success they had hoped for with their own, more direct methods of "counterspeech," antismoking groups now seek to enlist the machinery of state censorship.

Proponents of the tobacco advertising ban have also been less than forthcoming in several respects. Despite their rhetoric about protecting those who do not yet smoke, Congressman Thomas Bliley (R.,VA) has noted: "[I]n the . . . nations that have banned tobacco advertising, there has not been a single instance in which the ban led to a change in the trend of consumption in that nation."

Antismoking interests have also derided the assertion that tobacco advertising is aimed at shifting brand preferences, claiming that too much money is spent on such advertising for this to be true. This argument ignores both the Surgeon General's 1979 finding to that effect, as well as cigarette ads which expressly address smokers. Moreover, anyone who has been semiconscious over the past several years is aware of the vast amount of advertising money which has been spent in attempting to have consumers switch to newly developed "lite" beers.

Indeed, while one of their principal objections is that cigarette advertising encourages smoking among children, cigarette ads, which do not feature children, have been "countered" by antismoking ads which frequently do so.

Furthermore, ban proponents have focused their attack on cigarette advertising. Little, if anything, has been said about the bill's inclusion of a ban on the advertisement of cigars, pipe tobacco, smokeless tobacco and other tobacco products. In sum, supporters of H.R. 4972 have been less than fully informative, while professing indignation about tobacco advertising's failure to inform the public.

The most egregious omission in the arguments of ban proponents is, however, quite understandable, since it would doom their efforts to failure. Ban proponents have never faced the American public squarely and said, "You cannot be trusted to deal responsibly with truthful information provided by conflicting points of view. We want to make up your mind for you by censoring information with which we disagree."

III.

I see no reason why commercial speech should be afforded
less protection than other types of protected speech where,
as here, the government seeks to suppress commercial speech
in order to deprive consumers of accurate information
concerning lawful activity.
—Mr. Justice Brennan

Supporters of an effort to ban tobacco advertising argue that the Supreme Court's recent decision in *Posadas de Puerto Rico Assoc.* v. *Tourism Co.* supports their proposal. In *Posadas*, the Supreme Court upheld a restriction on the advertisement of casino gambling. A Puerto Rico law legalizing casino gambling also permitted advertising of gambling which was addressed to tourists, but did not allow advertising aimed at residents of Puerto Rico. A sharply divided Supreme Court upheld the law.

The applicability of *Posadas* to a tobacco advertising ban is uncertain at best. The *Posadas* Court upheld the statute in question only after a narrowing construction had been applied to the statute by a lower court. Moreover, the *Posadas* opinion dealt with "legislative regulation of products or activities." Cigarette advertising is already the most heavily regulated form of advertising in the United States today. Congress has utilized the power sanctioned in *Posadas* to an extreme.

Furthermore, all constitutional analysis cannot end with the rendering of the *Posadas* decision. No one would argue that earlier controversies were settled by the Supreme Court's decision in the *Dred Scott* case or with its opinions in *Plessy* v. *Ferguson* ("separate but equal"). Each case, each new issue, presents a challenge within an ever evolving framework. We must not forget that Justice Holmes' theory of the "marketplace of ideas" was stated in the *dissenting* opinion in the *Abrams* case.

We must also realize that commercial speech is a relatively new constitutional doctrine. Despite Mr. Beard's view of the Constitution as essentially an economic document, the concept of protecting free speech in commerce remained unrecognized until 1976, when the Supreme Court reversed the previously held notion that commercial advertising fell wholly outside of First Amendment protection. The case which originally held that commercial speech was outside of the scope of the First Amendment, *Valentine v. Chrestensen*, was itself not decided until 1942. Justice Douglas, in retrospect, viewed the ruling in *Valentine* as "casual, almost offhand." The same may be said for the *Posadas* decision, and for attempts to apply *Posadas* to a cigarette advertising ban.

The constitutional analysis of commercial speech as propounded in the *Central Hudson Gas* case and *Posadas* permits regulation of true and lawful commercial speech *only if*: 1) The government has a substantial interest in doing so; 2) The restrictions directly advance the government's asserted interest; and 3) The restrictions are no more extensive than necessary. The proposed ban on tobacco advertising fails on all three points.

To the extent the government has a substantial interest in this area, it would be in controlling or preventing the production and distribution of the product which is complained about. Congress has chosen wisely not to do so. It has realized that a new era of "prohibition" would surely fail in the face of the wishes of 50 million smokers. Justice Rehnquist would have us believe that since Congress has the theoretical power to ban cigarettes but has declined to do so, it certainly can regulate activity relating to cigarettes. This is a correct but incomplete analysis of congressional power. The Congress may do so only if it is not otherwise prohibited from acting in this manner. The First Amendment represents just such an affirmative prohibition on total censorship.

Nor does banning cigarette advertising directly advance the government's purported interest. We have seen that similar efforts in other countries have failed to change tobacco consumption patterns. Admittedly, Congress does not need irrefutable scientific proof of advertising's effect on consumption in order to legislatively determine that an ad ban would further the government's interest, but neither can Congress simply ignore the current state of facts.

Finally, a total ban on tobacco advertising is far more extensive than necessary to advance a government interest in curtailing smoking.

The proper solution in commerce, as in politics, is the encouragement of "counterspeech"— in short, putting a point of view to the test in Justice Holmes' marketplace of ideas. The fundamental flaw in *Posadas* was the rejection of this argument. The *Posadas* Court would leave it up to the legislature to determine whether promoting "counterspeech" would be as effective as advertising restrictions in the pursuit of the government's goal. In so deciding, the Supreme Court abdicated its role as the guardian of First Amendment. Four members of the Court were convinced that this abdication was a serious error where a restriction on advertising was involved. If faced with a total ban on tobacco advertising, the Court will have the chance to redeem itself.

Charles Beard's analysis of the intent and motives of the founding fathers proved incorrect. With the expanding importance of free commerce in today's consumer society, however, the time has come to expand the protection of the First Amendment. In political affairs, Americans have long proclaimed: "I disagree with what you are saying, but I will defend to the death your right to say it." The credo of the supporters of a tobacco advertising ban appears to be: "I disagree with what you are saying, but I feel the public might agree with you anyway, therefore, I am depriving you of the right to say it." After almost two hundred years of rejecting such paternalistic censorship in the political arena, the time has come to apply the same principle of free speech to the field of commerce.

Professor James P. Hill
Shepherd, Michigan

Occupation: College Professor
Interests: Politics, coin collecting, golf
Entered the Competition because: "I teach a
university course in the regulation of the business
area of law and thus was interested in the issue."

It seems clear that significant limits imposed upon commercial speech are as constitutionally suspect as those imposed on civil liberties.

UP IN SMOKE: THE RECENT DECLINE OF ECONOMIC LIBERTY IN AMERICAN ENTERPRISE

What has been obvious to those who closely follow U.S. Supreme Court decisions is the rather cavalier way the Court dispenses with constitutional arguments raised by business against government regulation. It is as though the Court is reading from two Constitutions: one that *permits* almost any kind of economic legislation as long as it affects only business economic liberties and another that strictly *prohibits* any infringement of individual civil liberties.

The swift and unquestioned acceptance of this dual constitutional interpretation by the Court has obscured two very fundamental facts. First, the basis for the Court's distinction between corporate economic freedom and individual political freedom has no specific foundation in the U.S. Constitution. It is simply a convenient approach used by the U.S. Supreme Court to justify ignoring economic liberty arguments.

Second, the U.S. Supreme Court's decision to largely ignore constitutional arguments against government economic regulation is of relatively recent origin. Indeed, it is a total reversal of the Court's pre-1937 role as protector of business economic liberties.

These two facts are significant because they tend to weaken popular arguments that the continued decline of corporate economic freedom is inevitable, and they raise the possibility that someday the U.S. Supreme Court, in its roller coaster interpretations of economic liberties, may attempt to restore the proper balance between corporate economic and individual civil liberties.

This essay focuses upon one of the most basic corporate economic liberties: the right of business to engage in commercial speech without undue government censorship. Under the guise of what the U.S.

Supreme Court declared was the "commercial speech" doctrine, almost unlimited government infringement of business' economic speech was permitted for almost thirty years. By examining the origins and rationale for this Court-declared "doctrine," it seems clear that significant limits imposed upon commercial speech are as constitutionally suspect as those imposed on civil liberties.

Moreover, this essay explores the ramifications of further limitations of commercial speech on our free enterprise system and our democratic system of governance, highlighting the need to elevate the commercial speech issue beyond the realm of congressional politics.

THE ORIGINS OF THE DECLINE OF ECONOMIC LIBERTIES

The decline of business economic liberties in general and commercial speech in particular can be traced to three recent events: 1) A political threat to the Supreme Court, 2) A footnote in a relatively obscure U.S. Supreme Court case, and 3) The invention by the courts of a new doctrine for distinguishing free speech issues. These three events, which occurred over a period of only five years, have shaped the entire debate over corporate economic freedoms and thus merit our initial attention.

1. *The Threat*: Prior to President Franklin Roosevelt's landslide election in 1936, the U.S. Supreme Court had utilized a legal theory known as substantive due process to protect business from legislation that unduly interfered with the liberty and property rights of corporations. It was the Supreme Court's independent reading of the U.S. Constitution and the historic economic freedom of action in American life that led the Court to treat economic freedoms as the constitutional equal of other civil liberties. Accordingly, the Court became an influential check on economic legislation, overturning 44 such laws between 1900 and 1909, 111 such laws between 1910 and 1919, and 133 such laws between 1920 and 1929. *

The Great Depression of 1929 and the subsequent slow industrial recovery led the newly reelected Roosevelt to propose a series of economic restraints on business activity known as the New Deal. When the U.S. Supreme Court balked and ruled against his initial New Deal programs, Roosevelt threatened to increase the size of the U.S. Supreme Court from nine to fifteen members and pack it with justices who would uphold his programs.

The U.S. Supreme Court blinked and upheld his New Deal pro-

---

* L. Baum, The Supreme Court 176 (1985).

grams, resulting in what one wag termed "the switch in time that saved nine." As a result, between 1937 and 1983, the Court struck down only seven federal laws dealing with regulation of the economy and business enterprise, and none of these decisions affected the government's basic powers over the economy. *

2. *The Footnote*: The Court's deference to legislative judgment on economic matters was meekly conceded in a footnote in a 1937 case, *U.S. v. Carolene Products Company*. However, in the footnote the Court not only conceded the demise of the substantive due process clause to protect business economic interests, but also began the Court on its new role of constitutional liberties interpretation. Henceforth, the Court would distinguish between general economic regulatory legislation and government restrictions on fundamental constitutional values affecting individual civil rights. Only the latter would receive the Court's strict scrutiny. †

3. *The Doctrine*: Five years later, the Court would continue its slide away from protecting business economic interests and devise a new doctrine that severed business from freedom of speech protections of the First Amendment altogether. In *Valentine v. Chrestensen*, 316 U.S. 52 (1942), the Court devised the "commercial speech" doctrine and declared that the Constitution did not impose any restraints on government with respect to purely commercial advertising. Thus, government censorship of commercial speech did not violate the First Amendment.

Now the cycle was complete. In five short years, the presumption of economic liberties being the equivalent to civil liberties was quickly and unceremoniously dumped for dubious political reasons. An enormous growth in federal regulatory agencies ensued, and business economic activities became more tightly controlled by a new fourth branch of government.

But what about the commercial speech aspect of the Court's reversal? How can such a fundamental liberty be excised by one U.S. Supreme Court interpretation? It is to this issue that we must now turn our attention.

DISTINGUISHING COMMERCIAL SPEECH AND POLITICAL SPEECH

Without clearly defining what commercial speech is, but rather declaring there to be a "common sense distinction" between commercial speech and other varieties of speech, ‡ the Court embarked on a thirty-

* *Id.*, at 180.
† *U.S. v. Carolene Products Co.*, 304 U.S. 144, 152 n. 4 (1937).
‡ *Central Hudson Gas and Electric Corp. v. PSC of New York*, 100 S.CT. 2343 (1980).

year denial of First Amendment protection for commercial speech, thus inviting government censorship. The most common justifications for distinguishing commercial speech were because, unlike individual political speech, advertisers were well-suited to evaluate the accuracy and lawfulness of their activity and because commercial speech was a "hardy breed of expression that is not particularly susceptible to being crushed by overbroad regulation."* Another justification was that giving commercial speech and political speech the same First Amendment protection invited dilution of the free speech right, resulting in a leveling process that devitalized the clout of the First Amendment.†

The result was a general court deference test for legislation that affected commercial speech and a strict judicial scrutiny test for legislation affecting political liberties. The danger of this two-test approach to free speech was recognized by Justice Black who noted in 1961, "I fear that the creation of 'tests' by which speech is left unprotected under certain circumstances is a standing invitation to abridge it . . ."‡ His warning was partially heeded by the Court—twelve years later!

THE REINTERPRETATION OF THE COMMERCIAL SPEECH DOCTRINE

In 1971, the Court still seemed determined to maintain the *Chrestensen* "commercial speech" doctrine, summarily affirming a congressional ban on the advertising of cigarettes over any medium of electronic communication subject to FCC jurisdiction.§

However, the Court abruptly reversed itself in a trilogy of cases between 1973 and 1976, culminating in *Virginia Pharmacy Board* v. *Virginia Citizens Consumer Council* 96 S. Ct. 1817 (overturning a ban on advertising by pharmacies) declaring that commercial speech was not wholly outside the protection of the First Amendment.|| Then-dissenting justice and now-Chief Justice Rehnquist argued that the wavering line between commercial speech and protected speech was replaced by a line distinguishing protected truthful commercial speech from false and misleading commercial speech.¶

Two years later, in 1978, the Court moved a step further in recognizing corporate rights by declaring, "We find no support for the proposition that speech that otherwise would be within the protection of the

---

* *Posadas de Puerto Rico v. Tourism Co.*, 106 S. Ct. 2986 (1986).
† *Ohralik v. Ohio State Bar Association*, 98 S. Ct. 1912, 1918 (1978).
‡ *Konigsberg v. State Bar of California*, 366 U.S. 36, 68 (1961).
§ *Capital Broadcasting Co. v. Mitchell*, 333 F. Supp. 582 (1971).
|| *Virginia State Board of Pharmacy v. Virginia Citizens Council, Inc.*, 44 USLW 4686 (1976).
¶ *Id.*, 4697 (Rehnquist, J. dissenting).

First Amendment loses that protection simply because its source is a corporation."*

In 1980, the Court invalidated another advertising ban. This time the case involved promotional advertising by a utility (*Central Hudson Gas v. Public Service Commission of New York*). The Court, ironically by footnote again, made another significant revision of the commercial speech doctrine: "Indeed, in recent years this Court has not approved a blanket ban on commercial speech unless the expression itself was flawed in some way, either because it was deceptive or related to unlawful activity."† The Court went on to say, "If the communication is neither misleading nor related to unlawful activity, government power is more circumscribed" and then proceeded to develop a four-step approach to commercial speech issues.‡

Just when it appeared that the original commercial speech doctrine had died and commercial speech regained limited First Amendment protection, the Court dropped its 1986 bombshell. In *Posadas de Puerto Rico* the Court upheld a ban prohibiting the advertisement of legal gambling parlors to the public in Puerto Rico but permitting restricted advertising through publicity media outside Puerto Rico. Justice Rehnquist, this time writing for the majority, perfunctorily used the four-step process of the *Central Hudson Gas* case and decided that since Puerto Rico could have completely banned gambling, they also had the lesser power to ban advertising of casino gambling.§ The *Posadas* case breathed new life into the moribund "commercial speech" doctrine by allowing government censorship of truthful commercial speech about a lawful activity.

The *Posadas* case on its surface might indeed revitalize congressional efforts to completely ban tobacco promotional advertising. However, as we shall see in the next section of this essay, this type of congressional ban stands on very weak constitutional grounds.

THE ARGUMENTS AGAINST ADVERTISING BANS

Because of the special circumstances surrounding the *Posadas* case, it seems more likely that prior Court expressions of opposition to complete advertising bans would undoubtedly lead to the Court striking down a complete congressional ban on tobacco advertising on First Amendment grounds. The views of three influential justices would seem to support such a conclusion.

---

* *First National Bank of Boston v. Bellotti*, 435 U.S. 765, 784 (1978).
† *Central Hudson Gas and Electric Corp. v. PSC of New York*, 100 S. Ct. 2343, 2351 n. 9 (1980).
‡ *Id.*, at 2350.
§ 106 S. Ct. 2968 (1986).

Justice Rehnquist, dissenting in the *Virginia State Board* case, acknowledged existing restrictions on liquor and cigarette advertising and noted "apparently under the Court's holding so long as the advertisements are not deceptive they may no longer be prohibited."*

Justice Blackmun, concurring in the *Central Hudson Gas* case noted:

> I seriously doubt whether suppression of information concerning the availability and price of a legally offered product is ever a permissible way for the State to "dampen" demand for or use of the product. Even though "Commercial" speech is involved, such a regulatory measure strikes at the heart of the First Amendment.†

And Justice Stevens, concurring in the *Central Hudson Gas* case stated:

> But if the perceived harm . . . is not sufficiently serious to justify direct regulation, surely it does not constitute the kind of clear and present danger that can justify suppression of speech.‡

Indeed a ban on advertising of a legal product such as tobacco would suffer several other obvious infirmities. First, a ban on all tobacco advertising is insensitive to the informational value of commercial advertising and indeed in conflict with efforts to promote truth in advertising. Does it make sense to ban advertising that distinguishes low tar from high tar content cigarettes if the purpose of a congressional ban is based upon health grounds?

To ban advertising of a product is to encourage ignorance in consumption.

Second, such a ban ignores the importance of the exchange of information in the commercial realm. To ban advertising of a product is to encourage ignorance in consumption.

Third, such a ban is contrary to the principles of debate and free exchange of ideas. As the government has not been able to convince consumers to stop smoking through warning labels on cigarette packages, should it be able to manipulate choices by depriving the public of information needed to make a free choice?

* *Virginia State Board of Pharmacy v. Virginia Citizens Council, Inc.*, 44 USLW 4686, 4698 (1976).
† *Central Hudson Gas and Electric Corp. v. PSC of New York*, 100 S. Ct. 2343, 2356 (1980) (Blackmun, J. concurring).
‡ *Id.*, at 2359 (Stevens, J. concurring).

Fourth, is there really such a thing as pure commercial speech that can be banned without harming the free flow of ideas? Inherent in economic advertising of tobacco are ideas of capitalism and materialism. And, as Justice Stevens warned, "it is important that the commercial speech concept not be defined too broadly lest speech deserving of greater constitutional protection be inadvertently suppressed."*

Fifth, the term "commercial speech" is both unworkable and artificial. Is a political candidate selling himself entitled to First Amendment protection but not so entitled if the candidate is selling his or her autobiography?

Finally, the natural tendency of a government is to move to suppress criticism and unpopular ideas. Thus, by establishing a commercial speech exception to First Amendment protection only invites Congress to expand the exception. For that very reason the courts must not allow bans of truthful advertising of a legal product. The temptation for the exception to swallow the rule is too great.

THE MARKET IMPACT OF A RETURN TO THE ORIGINAL COMMERCIAL SPEECH DOCTRINE

At stake in the debate over advertising bans such as those being considered in Congress for the tobacco industry is an issue larger than any one industry. It strikes at the very essence of free speech in our enterprise economy.

Aside from the increased informational and transaction costs that such bans create, censorship in any form suppresses the dissemination of truthful information about lawful activity, preempting individual decision making. As the Court noted in the *Virginia Pharmacy* case:

> So long as we preserve a predominantly free economy, the allocation of our resources in large measure will be made through numerous private economic decisions. It is a matter of public interest that those decisions, in the aggregate, be intelligent and well informed. To this end, the free flow of commercial information is indispensable. †

In addition, the Court in a later *Consolidation Edison* case warned, "If the market place of ideas is to remain free and open, governments must not be allowed to choose which ideas are worth discussing or debating."‡

In the final analysis, perhaps it is the loss of confidence in American free enterprise, triggered by the Great Depression, that lies behind attempts to suppress corporate commercial speech. Perhaps, the classic

* *Central Hudson Gas and Electric Corp. v. PSC of New York*, 100 S. Ct. 2343, 2358 (1980).
† *Virginia State Board of Pharmacy v. Virginia Citizens Council, Inc.*, 44 USLW 4686, 4691 (1976).
‡ *Consolidated Edison Co. v. Public Service Commission of New York*, 447 U.S. 530, 537 (1978).

dissent of Justice Holmes in the 1919 case of *Abrams v. U.S.*, arguing, "the best test for truth is the power of the thought to get itself accepted in the competition of the market,"* rings hollow in the ears of Congress and the public in general for that very reason.

Censorship and the further weakening of constitutional protections for American enterprise is certainly not the proper vehicle for improving corporate social responsibility.

If there is a credibility or social responsibility gap, it most certainly must be addressed by American industry. The threat of suppression of commercial speech ought to be a warning sign to industry. However, it is up to the courts to protect the Constitution from this congressional assault on basic economic liberties, no matter how well-meaning it may be. Censorship and the further weakening of constitutional protections for American enterprise is certainly not the proper vehicle for improving corporate social responsibility. The market and constitutional consequences of such an approach may lead us down a slippery slope of decreased constitutional liberty from which we as a nation may never recover.

* *Abrams v. U.S.*, 250 U.S. 616 (1919) (Holmes, J. dissenting).

Timothy Hanks
St. Paul, Minnesota

Occupation: Research Chemist
Interests: Hiking, camping, biking, climbing,
stereo, computers
Entered the Competition because of: "Concern over
the erosion of the First Amendment in all areas of
American life."

THE GREAT AMERICAN SMOKE SCREEN

Once upon a time a group of men met in a central city of a tiny land to create a government. The original charter for their country was fatally flawed and ten years after gaining independence from another nation, the whole wretched mess was coming apart. After much struggle, they managed to devise a constitution and set up a government. Happily this was accomplished without bloodshed and the young nation prospered.

A typical scenario perhaps, but not so typical is the fact that the simple compromise agreed upon in Philadelphia is still more or less intact two centuries later. The amazing longevity of the document and the government founded upon it is even more astounding considering the growth and change that followed their inception. The Constitution of the United States of America has proven its versatility through the most trying of circumstances. It has held together, in remarkable harmony, the most diverse and strong-willed group of individuals ever assembled into a nation. Yet despite the strength of this Constitution, it was not perfect. Indeed, the ink was scarcely dry on the parchment when a strong movement arose to change it. Some three years after the adoption of the Constitution, ten amendments were added. These amendments are known collectively as the Bill of Rights. Together, these additions have played nearly as significant a role in the formation of our national identity as the original document. Even today we struggle with the meaning of those "simple" amendments. We seek to interpret them not only in terms of the intent of the original authors, but also in terms of what is "just."

The Bill of Rights, as the name implies, is simply a statement guaranteeing the basic rights of the citizens in our society. The first of these amendments begins with the words "Congress shall make no law abridging the freedom of speech or of the press." With this statement, the authors of the Bill of Rights sought to protect a fledgling democracy by encouraging the free exchange of ideas. The premise behind this amendment was quite simple; subterfuge and deceit are exposed in discussion, while the truth is strengthened. The authors of the Bill of Rights were political realists. They knew that without the freedom of speech, freedom of any kind was impossible. The First Amendment came first because it is the foundation on which the others depend. It is no coincidence that one of the first actions of an oppressive government is to curb the press and muzzle the opposition.

THE PROBLEM OF FREE SPEECH

We owe the continued health of our political system to the freedom of speech. Without it, it is certain that the melding of our diverse ethnic and cultural groups into one people would have been (and would still be) a much more violent and much less enriching process. Yet there are serious difficulties with unrestricted speech. Consider the classic example of the sadist who cries "Fire" in a crowded theater in order to see people trampled; consider the traitor who divulges battle plans on the eve of war; consider the political candidate who mercilessly slanders his or her opponent. Are these people criminals or are they simply exercising their rights? Most of us would agree that in order for society to function, there must be some restrictions on speech. Yet the First Amendment reads "Congress shall make *no* law abridging the freedom of speech."

It quickly becomes obvious that the First Amendment cannot and is not taken literally. Laws restricting the freedom of speech are on the books at every level of the government. The First Amendment, which is so obvious and reasonable on the surface, has resulted in literally thousands of volumes of interpretation. The question is not if freedom of speech should be permitted, but how much freedom.

The writings of the founding fathers do not offer much help in interpreting this amendment. Alexander Hamilton, who opposed the Bill of Rights, did not dispute the sentiments, but thought they were "impractical." He realized that whatever was written in the Constitution would be interpreted by the courts according to the opinions of the day. The major promoters of the Bill of Rights are also strangely silent on the matter of speech. Both Madison and Jefferson expressed the idea that the Bill of Rights was important, but not crucial. Apparently the problem of checks and balances within the political system were far more important to these gentlemen than a statement of human rights.

For the next hundred and thirty years, the freedom of speech issue was not seriously raised before the Supreme Court. It was not until comparatively recently that the limits of the freedom of speech have been explored by the judiciary. The legal challenges to laws involving speech were originally in areas such as libel and slander, but more recently have extended into such areas as pornography and corporate advertising.

There are several arguments by which laws restricting the freedom of speech have been enacted and upheld by the courts. For example, the First Amendment reads *"Congress* shall make . . ." It may then be reasonable to assume that laws restricting speech are the priority of state and local governments. While this interpretation makes some sense, it is not the historical approach to the problem. The federal government has chosen to retain the power to restrict speech in most areas.

A more common, but perhaps less easily justified approach is to define some types of speech (shouting "Fire" in a crowded theater) as outside the "freedom of speech." This type of speech may then be restricted without violating the Constitution. In general, speech that results in great harm is more likely to be restricted than speech that does not. Speech can also be categorized. Speech involving political, social or religious matters, for example, traditionally enjoys more protection than speech involving criminal matters.

This scheme has served us well, but is not without problems. There are several ways in which speech may be unjustly restricted. A serious difficulty arises from the system of categorizing speech. A particular statement may cross several of the artificial boundaries that have been established. An example of this is the advocation of the violent over-throw of the government. Is this a political statement or a criminal one? Similarly, religious or social messages are often nearly indistinguishable from economic ones. If different rules are to be applied to different classes of speech, then care must be taken in the definition of these classes and in the categorization of a given statement.

The First Amendment was not written to protect popular speech, but to protect controversial or even distasteful speech. As popular opinion and the opinion of the courts swing to a particular point of view, radically different points of view may be labeled as "criminal." The most obvious candidates for this type of activity are in the political or religious arenas. When an extreme idea grabs the attention of the majority (or a vocal minority), contrary opinions may be dismissed with vehemence. The more fevered the belief, the more intolerant of dissension the majority becomes. It is easy to find graphic examples of this intolerance in the Nazi era in Germany or the McCarthy era in the United States. Perhaps more important, however, are the more subtle occasions of intolerance. The First Amendment violations in situations often go unnoticed in the mass media, either because those suffering from the resulting censorship are so powerless that their opinions are insignificant, or because they have been painted as such villians that the public delights in their harassment. Unimportant though these in-fringements may seem, they diminish the freedom of all of us and ultimately cheapen the value of our governing principles.

FREE SPEECH AND THE TOBACCO INDUSTRY

An interesting example of a "subtle" violation of the freedom of speech is in the area of tobacco advertising. Tobacco has been a popular recreation for hundreds of years. The early European explorers of this continent took the leaves back with them and started a craze in their homelands. Since that time, the use of tobacco has been very popular among all segments of the population. The last few years, however, have seen a dramatic decline in this popularity. Evidence of this change in public perception can be obtained through the kaleidoscope of film and television. Until very recently, the smoking of tobacco was portrayed as an activity of the wealthy and sophisticated by these media. Today however, the image of the tobacco user is suffering. Filmmakers do not yet portray the smoker as a criminal, but the lighting of a cigarette no longer occurs during moments of suave satisfaction. Celluloid smokers now tend to be rather weak-willed individuals who only light up during periods of great stress. The public is seemingly being programmed to see tobacco as a mild sedative and a rather distasteful one at that.

What prompted this fall from grace? The first, and perhaps the most important reason, was the discovery that tobacco contains a variety of potent carcinogens. Researchers have demonstrated a strong correlation between tobacco smoke and various lung ailments. These facts combined with the addictive nature of nicotine resulted in an all-out war on tobacco by the medical community.

Americans are continuously reprimanded for unhealthy lifestyles. The medical ministrations on smoking probably would have had little impact if other events had not conspired to magnify their dire prophecies. In the early 1980s, America's fascination with eternal youth exploded into a fitness craze. Smoking did not jibe with the picture of a healthy body and the bandwagon knew it. At this same time, a ban on tobacco advertising in the broadcast media was in effect. Not only did it become "cool" to be a nonsmoker, but the advertising dollars which might have tempered the "smokers are diseased" movement were by necessity channeled elsewhere.

Seeing the shift in public opinion, the tobacco industry developed new products. Low tar and nicotine cigarettes began to appear. While not eliminating the risks associated with tobacco smoking, these products offered the consumer the opportunity to minimize his or her risks. This sincere effort by the tobacco industry was hampered by the condemnation of the new products by the medical community on one hand and the limitations of advertising on the other.

It seems strange that the antismoking lobby would not endorse this effort. It may be that they feel they have the prosmoking faction on the run, at least politically. There is no question that they would prefer a tobacco-free America.

The current ban on tobacco advertising is a clear infringement on the speech of the tobacco industry. It is not at all obvious, however, whether or not this infringement is justified. This question is especially significant in view of proposals to ban tobacco advertising in all media. The medical community has been able to prove that smoking is harmful both to the individual (increased risk of disease) and to the society (lost work time, increased medical costs). From the point of view of the medical community, the infringement on the tobacco industry's freedom of speech is fully justified by the resulting benefits to society. They see tobacco advertising as the same as shouting "Fire" in a crowded theater. The motive is profit instead of sadistic thrills, but the damages are just as certain.

I share a certain empathy with this position. I am a nonsmoker who does not permit tobacco use in either my home or vehicle. I don't listen to tobacco advertisements and their disappearance would have almost no effect on my life. Indeed, I would have little reason to write this essay except for one small point: the ban on tobacco advertising deprives me of my right to choose *not* to smoke.

I am a nonsmoker. . . . Indeed, I would have little reason to write this essay except for one small point: the ban on tobacco advertising deprives me of my right to choose *not* to smoke.

The Price of Freedom

There are important differences between tobacco advertising and shouting "Fire" in a theater. Unlike the latter example, the decision to smoke need not be hastily made nor is it irrevocable. Another difference is the availability of data. The views of the antismoking lobby are available for consideration by the potential smoker. Society has insured this by requiring broadcasters to make periodic public service announcements. Qualified organizations such as the American Lung Association provide the stations with messages which are broadcast free of charge. In addition, tobacco products, and even advertisements, are required to carry warnings concerning the health risk of tobacco consumption.

These provisions are more than sufficient to insure that tobacco users are aware of the risks they take, yet millions continue to smoke. This action seems almost inexplicable to nonsmokers. Medical researchers tend to pass off such incomprehensible actions with terms such as ignorance or addiction, but I would suggest something else is occurring. Smokers receive intangible benefits from smoking. These benefits (pleasure, a sense of security, a calming feeling) cannot be measured and are therefore nonexistent to the scientific method. Nonsmokers do not experience these phenomena and cannot comprehend their absence. Yet though these benefits are intangible, they are very real and very important.

In every major controversy, there are "gurus" who believe they hold all the answers. These gurus may have credentials ranging from medical degrees to divine inspiration to a good TV presence, but they all tend to belittle other viewpoints. The opinions of the gurus are important and need to be heard, but they are only opinions. No matter how well-qualified the individual or organization may be, no matter how well-intentioned their actions, it is the individual who must make the final decisions concerning his or her existence. As long as we differ from one another, the right lifestyle for each of us will vary.

It is intriguing that in a democracy, where information is available for the asking, the dogma pushers have so much influence. The problem is a serious one, perhaps the most crucial facing our democracy today. It seems that when we are handed the rights that our ancestors struggled for, they become unimportant. Citizens in a democracy have an obligation (and it is a difficult one) to think for themselves. Thinking is not a trivial exercise and people will go to great lengths to avoid it, but without careful thought, a democracy cannot function. In order to think, a citizen must have all the data, even that which is unpopular with a portion of society. For every person who follows a guru without thinking, the health of our country is diminished. For every law enacted which enforces the dogma of one of society's factions, a step away from our traditions of freedom and tolerance is taken.

The consequences of free thought and free choice can be expensive. Individuals may make "wrong" choices, some may even die, but this is the price of freedom. In much of the world, this price is thought to be too high. The rulers do the thinking while the "huddled masses" can only dream. The authors of the Bill of Rights rejected this vision of life for the intangible rewards of freedom. In rejecting the secure and the thoughtless, they permitted us our humanity. Censorship is acceptable only in situations where the exercise of free speech for a few unavoidably results in great harm for many. It is not acceptable as a means of eliminating life's risks, especially when the risk takers have all of the necessary data at hand. If we must err in restricting speech, we must err on the side of free speech, not censorship. This is the true meaning of the First Amendment.

Gus G. Sermos
McComb, Mississippi

Occupation: Health Advisor
Interests: Reading, bicycling, entertaining
my children
Entered the Competition because: "I do not want to
see the erosion of our First Amendment."

> **Our laws do not require that we relinquish constitutionally protected rights in order to be allowed to engage in commerce or enterprise.**

THE SUPREMACY OF THE CONSTITUTION AND THE BILL OF RIGHTS

The Declaration of Independence, the Constitution of the United States and the first ten amendments to the Constitution, popularly known as the Bill of Rights, purposefully committed our country to be a nation in which the unalienable rights of all persons were equal before any authority. Ordained and established by the American people, our Constitution is the fundamental enunciation of the laws of these United States. Our Constitution created the basic institutions of government and delineated their powers. Even more important, the Bill of Rights specifically limited the areas into which our government, or any other authority, may intrude.

No doubt, the founding fathers had faith in the carefully worded Constitution. Nevertheless, they were too intelligent and cognizant of past abuses to entertain the notions of blind faith. To prevent the erosion of the rights of the American people, the drafters of the first ten amendments knew they would have to declare that certain substantive values must remain forever beyond the grasp of temporary political majorities or other governing coalitions. The Bill of Rights is their strident declaration of the particular values and rights that would have to transcend the decades and centuries to come for our democratic republic to thrive and prosper.

Abridging the freedom of speech or expression in any sector of American life is a violation of the First Amendment. Without the right to free speech none of us would be permitted to describe or even discuss any violation of our other constitutional rights. For that reason, the drafters of the Bill of Rights placed the right to free speech and uncensored expression in the most logical position—FIRST—among the other amendments. Our liberties would flee from us like a retreating tide were there no First Amendment.

Obviously, there are circumstances when unbridled speech is considered irresponsible and inappropriate. An old analogy serves two purposes in delineating our right to free speech and uncensored expression. It is irresponsible behavior for someone to shout "Fire" in a crowded theater when no such danger exists. Ironically, the two most salient elements of this analogy are rarely, if ever, pointed out. First: the actors, producers and exhibitors of the performance had the First Amendment right to offer their presentation to the audience. Second: the audience had the First Amendment right to assemble peaceably in the theater for the express purpose of viewing the performance. Each group, exhibitors and audience, is protected by concisely phrased First Amendment guarantees.

A business enterprise is an individual or a group of individuals engaged in providing a product or service to a customer or customers for a profit. Our laws do not require that we relinquish constitutionally protected rights in order to be allowed to engage in commerce or enterprise. Whether or not we are working together as partners, stockholders, employees or any combination thereof is of no consequence. Our protected rights do not fall away from us like unraveled garments the moment we begin to perform our chosen work. We must be free and unencumbered from the pressures of temporary political majorities, or minorities, if we are to promote our enterprise effectively and succeed in our business. We must be free to enjoy the unalienable rights endowed by our Creator. Liberty is nothing more than a catchword if we, the American people, are restricted from seeking sustenance via our labor, enterprise or our pursuit of business opportunities.

Our well-articulated rights to free speech and expression will be diminished . . . if temporal authorities are allowed to divide constitutional guarantees into those currently acceptable and those that do not qualify according to today's enlightened standards.

American business is protected and covered by the same First Amendment umbrella that shields our free speech, uncensored expression and peaceable assembly. No provision exists which permits either our elected officials or appointed bureaucrats to tailor our First Amendment protections to the whims of prevailing public opinion regardless of whether or not the purported opinion represents the majority or minority view. Our well-articulated rights to free speech and expression will be diminished, or perhaps even eradicated, if temporal authorities are allowed to divide constitutional guarantees into those currently acceptable and those that do not qualify according to today's enlightened standards.

Today we are faced with the possibility that our Congress will approve a ban on tobacco advertising. Congress is considering the banning of all tobacco advertising because of the unrelenting pressures it is feeling from the antismoking lobbies and "health-oriented" action groups. Such a ban would have disastrous ramifications for the future of uncensored expression and free speech in a free market economy. In fact, a tobacco advertising prohibition would nullify the term "free market economy." Two salient ramifications come to mind. First, if the proposed ban is enacted, business will lose its right to offer or exhibit its products and services to the American audience. Second, the American audience simultaneously will be stripped of its rights to peaceably assemble, either in front of a magazine or billboard or other medium of advertisement, so that it may "view" the exhibition of a particular product or service. If business is denied the right to advertise a legal product by the United States Congress, a viable merchandising avenue will disappear.

In addition to trampling on the First Amendment rights of the tobacco industry and the customer, I believe a ban on tobacco advertising will tangentially violate the Fourth Amendment rights of each of those parties. In my opinion, a concomitant of the proposed advertising ban will be the illegal "seizure" of the tobacco product from the potential customer before the customer has the opportunity to choose freely for himself whether or not he desires to purchase the product. Under the cloud of an advertising ban, we will be disengaged from our right to be a "member of the audience." The exhibition of the product will have been seized from us before we see the curtain rise. As the exhibitors, the tobacco companies will have been thrown off the stage, seized and removed from the theater before the show could begin. Our ability to exercise free will, our freedom of choice and our right to reject or accept a tobacco product will be destroyed if the advertising ban becomes the law.

The tobacco industry will suffer an almost identical violation of its Fourth Amendment rights because it will have its potential customers illegally and unreasonably "seized" from the theater of advertisement before they are allowed to view the product the company is offering to them for their use or consumption. In essence, potential customers will be isolated from the theater of advertising and the tobacco company will be denied the right to exhibit its legal product. In its zeal to "protect" us, our government has forgotten that it exists to enhance our opportunity for life, liberty and the pursuit of happiness. The Constitution and the Bill of Rights were drafted and ratified to proscribe the behavior and actions of the government, not the legal actions of the American people. The Bill of Rights exists to guard us from illegal, unwarranted governmental intrusion.

If the Congress enacts the tobacco advertising ban, what product will be next on the list? Perhaps the authorities will then attempt to save us from those "dangerous" three-wheeled, all-terrain cycles by deciding to ban or restrict their advertisements. Maybe tampon advertisements will be curtailed because the use of tampons has been associated with the illness described as toxic shock syndrome. Alcoholic beverages are widely consumed in this country. Since their use is evidently a primary factor in a large percentage of traffic accidents and deaths, they may be next on the list of unacceptable, but legal, products. These examples clearly illustrate how quickly and easily our First Amendment rights can be eroded and flushed down the drain if our umbrella of constitutional protection is pierced by constricting governmental intrusions.

President Franklin D. Roosevelt, in a speech to the United States Congress on January 6, 1941, proclaimed the "Four Freedoms" he believed were of special significance and value to the American people. President Roosevelt declared the "Four Freedoms" that were intrinsic to American democracy to be: "freedom of speech and expression," "freedom of every person to worship God in his own way," "freedom from want . . . ensured by economic understandings which will secure a healthy peacetime life," and "freedom from fear."

Economic health and viability will suffer in direct proportion to the decline in our nation's constitutional health if the proposed tobacco advertising ban becomes law.

The "Four Freedoms" linked together by President Roosevelt received particular attention from him because he understood the correlation of freedom of speech and expression and freedom from want. I believe that any dilution of our First Amendment rights will debilitate the free market economy of the United States. Economic health and viability will suffer in direct proportion to the decline in our nation's constitutional health if the proposed tobacco advertising ban becomes law. All aspects of our social, legal and business fabric are meticulously intertwined. If our constitutional protections are removed a slice at a time, our free market economy and our democracy will die a slow,

238

wasting death. If Congress intrudes into the protected area of freedom of speech and uncensored expression, the free market economy of this country will rapidly fade and then disappear as silently as a sinking ship slips beneath the swirling ocean.

As government insinuates itself more deeply into the areas of our private and professional lives that were once considered to be protected or private, there is an even greater urgency to make sure that individual rights are not undercut and disparaged in the interest of what becomes temporarily defined as the "public good." Governmental power and authority are expanding to the detriment of First Amendment protections. If our society and a cohesive, responsive free market economy are to prosper we must maintain constant vigilance and rally against all incursions on the right to free speech and uncensored expression. Those who govern must recognize and accept the enforcement of constitutional limitations on their power and authority.

Keltner W. Locke
Olivette, Missouri

Occupation: Attorney
Interests: Photography
Entered the Competition because: "I believe the First Amendment issue is extremely important and should be discussed."

Advertising has evolved in the past eighty years into a potent *truthful* force maximizing both consumer choice and fair, vigorous competition.

A LIBERTY AT RISK: THE PEOPLE'S RIGHT TO CHOOSE

Two centuries ago, Americans proclaimed a truth which then seemed outrageous: Individuals, not government, should make the choices which affect their lives.

We weren't kidding! After winning independence, we created a Constitution uniquely preserving the sanctity of individual choice, by protecting everyone's right to receive information needed to make intelligent decisions.

Often historians view this precious right in terms of political and religious choice. Yet the authors of our liberty also drew on the wisdom of economic thinkers, whose philosophical revolution was mirroring the coming Industrial Revolution. They rejected the government-enforced economic monopolies of the Old World, and found equally repugnant state-imposed monopolies of thought.

These thinkers embraced competition—in Adam Smith's marketplace of products as well as Thomas Jefferson's marketplace of ideas—to guarantee the people's right to life, liberty and, significantly, the pursuit of happiness.

Freedom of information has always been essential to this competition. Without consumer knowledge of the choices, there can be no competition, and restricting the flow of information chokes off competition as well. Today, in totalitarian countries which stifle competition and the flow of information, modern mass production alone has not been enough to create the plentiful life taken for granted in America.

Sadly, as we prepare to celebrate the bicentennial of our Constitution, the United States Supreme Court has issued a decision which jeopardizes the rights of consumers to receive truthful information from a very important source: advertising. The legal reasoning of this decision could imperil other free speech, as well, and threaten the very values which make the United States unique.

In rendering this dangerous precedent, the Court not only ignored its previous findings about the value of advertising, but also failed to consider how advertising has evolved in the past eighty years into a potent *truthful* force maximizing both consumer choice and fair, vigorous competition.

TRUTHFULNESS NOT AN ISSUE

A century ago, some advertisers earned the public's suspicion by justifying extravagant claims under the principle "Let the buyer beware." However, beginning with the Food and Drug Act of 1906, Congress has imposed increasingly stringent standards to assure truthfulness in advertising.

In 1938, Congress empowered the Federal Trade Commission to eliminate not only false advertising, but also ads which are unfair or deceptive even if the words themselves don't lie. For instance, a television spot showing actors in white coats could be deceptive by silently implying that the actors were physicians. Instead, we now see commercials beginning, "I'm not a doctor, but I play one on TV."

The FTC wields powerful weapons to assure that consumers are not deceived. It ordered one mouthwash maker to include in its commercials a clear statement the product would not help prevent colds or sore throats or lessen their severity. Even though the mouthwash had been making this claim for almost a century, it had to publicize the corrective message in its advertising.

Other federal and state agencies also enforce laws assuring the truthfulness of advertising. Today, advertisers must meet an even higher standard of truthfulness than journalists. As one Supreme Court justice reasoned, advertisers have a thorough knowledge of their products, while reporters must rely on outside sources for their information.

THE CONSUMER'S RIGHT TO KNOW

A citizen's right to receive *all* kinds of information, including that contained in advertising, lies at the heart of a modern free society. As the Supreme Court noted in a landmark 1940 decision, "Freedom of discussion, if it would fulfill its historic function in this nation, must embrace all issues about which information is needed or appropriate to enable the members of society to cope with the exigencies of their period."

Even more today than in 1940, advertising provides an essential source of the information needed to cope with the exigencies of daily life. Anyone who reads a newspaper's grocery ads rather than driving from store to store, relies on advertising to save both time and money, and as a guarantee that area-wide competition will remain intense, keeping prices low.

In 1976, the Supreme Court recognized the importance of advertising as a truthful source of information which consumers needed to have, by finding unconstitutional a Virginia law prohibiting pharmacies from advertising the prices of prescription drugs. A consumer group had sued, asserting that the Virginia law deprived patients of important information regarding the cost of the medicine they had to buy.

The Court noted that in one study the price of a particular prescription varied up to 1,200 percent just among drug stores in the Chicago area. The patients who buy prescription drugs, frequently the old and poor, have a great need for price information presented in its most readily available form, through advertising.

Most significantly, the Court held that these consumers had a First Amendment right to receive the information: The protection afforded by the First Amendment "is to the communication, to its source and to its recipients both." The consumer's interest in the free flow of commercial information, the Court found, "may be as keen, if not keener by far, than his interest in the day's most urgent political debate."

A year later, the Supreme Court found unconstitutional an Arizona prohibition on lawyer advertising. Many states then tried to restrict the content of lawyers' advertisements, not just to ensure truthfulness, but also to protect the "dignity" of the legal profession. Ohio, for example, prohibited lawyers from including an illustration or drawing in advertising.

However, a Columbus attorney ran an advertisement aimed at women who had used a dangerous IUD contraceptive. The ad included a drawing of the device. When the Ohio Supreme Court disciplined the lawyer, he appealed to the United States Supreme Court, which held that Ohio could not prevent the lawyer from including a truthful drawing merely because Ohio authorities considered it "undignified." Consumers had a right to know, through advertising, the appearance of the dangerous device.

Thus, during the past decade, the Court recognized the public's interest in receiving truthful information about lawful products and services through advertising. Surprisingly, in the summer of 1986, the Supreme Court issued a decision which seriously threatens consumer rights. This case involved a Puerto Rico law making casino gambling legal, but prohibiting casinos from advertising to Puerto Rico's citizens.

A DANGEROUS DECISION

As interpreted by the Puerto Rico courts, a casino could advertise in newspapers outside the island, for example, in *The New York Times*, but *not* in Puerto Rican newspapers. A combination hotel and casino

245

could advertise the hotel part of its services in Puerto Rican media, but could not mention gambling. In fact, the law, as applied, prohibited the advertisement from using the word "casino," except as part of the hotel's name. The Puerto Rico law uniquely discriminated against certain advertisements because of the ideas expressed, namely, that legal casino gambling was available to Puerto Rico's citizens.

Justice (now Chief Justice) Rehnquist, who had been the sole dissenter in the Virginia pharmacy advertising case, wrote the majority opinion upholding the Puerto Rican advertising ban. Justice Rehnquist narrowly—and incorrectly—viewed the primary purpose of advertising as stimulating demand for a product. Since the legislature could have prohibited casino gambling entirely, he reasoned, it would "be a strange constitutional doctrine which would concede to the legislature the authority to totally ban a product . . . but deny . . . the authority to forbid the stimulation of demand for the product. . . ."

However, Justice Rehnquist's reasoning disregarded a 1980 Supreme Court precedent expressly rejecting the idea that government could prohibit advertising to reduce consumer demand. In that case, involving electric utility advertising, the Supreme Court noted, "Commercial expression not only serves the economic interests of the speaker, but also assists consumers and furthers the societal interest in the fullest possible dissemination of information." Since the "First Amendment's concern for commercial speech is based on the informational function of advertising," the Court held, even "in monopoly markets, the suppression of advertising reduces the information available for consumer decisions and thereby defeats the purpose of the First Amendment."

A WRONG ASSUMPTION

Not only was the casino advertising decision legally questionable, it also made the incorrect factual assumption that advertising's only purpose was stimulation of demand. To be sure, one function of advertising is to stimulate demand, particularly for new products, ranging from home computers to Kiwi fruit, not yet familiar to the public. For the great majority of products, such as prescription drugs, demand already is present, and advertising stimulates competition by allowing consumers conveniently to compare truthful information about product features and price. For example, the demand for personal transportation already is present, but advertising lets consumers compare prices, fuel economy and important but less quantifiable benefits such as automobile comfort and handling.

Advertising also rewards manufacturers who respond to consumer demand for healthier products by giving these entrepreneurs a competitive advantage. Thus, when medical studies suggested a health risk in eating red meat, a large number of consumers decided not to avoid beef and pork entirely, but to demand leaner cuts. Pork producers satisfied this demand by developing a healthier product, which they publicized through advertising. Public concerns about saccharin and caffeine have prompted similar product improvements.

Among consumers who choose to smoke, the demand for improved choice already is present, and growing. Cigarette advertising provides more than 60 million American smokers truthful, convenient information about the tar and nicotine content of each brand, and thus allows these consumers to choose the product each considers best.

Among 207 brands of domestic cigarettes, nicotine content of one brand can be more than twenty-one times that of another. Tar content can be more than twenty-eight times greater in one brand than another. Consumers who choose to smoke need this information, readily available only through advertising which, in fact, must include it.

Cigarette advertising also prompts competition among manufacturers to develop better products, which lower the tar and nicotine while preserving the flavor. Prohibiting cigarette advertising would eliminate the incentive to develop a healthier product for consumers who choose to smoke. Why would a manufacturer expend the time and money to create a safer product than its competitor, if the manufacturer can't proclaim the advantage through advertising?

CENSORSHIP FOR ECONOMIC ENDS

The Supreme Court's casino advertising case is also troubling because it condones government control of information as a tool of economic regulation. The dissenting justices noted that Puerto Rico's reason for prohibiting casino advertising aimed at its residents may have been, in part, to minimize a casino's competitive threat to the state-operated lottery. Certainly, advertising spurs such competition, but competition is essential to progress.

If *any* state interest, even the meager one of lessening competition to the state lottery, is sufficient to justify censorship, then lawmakers across the country will be tempted to impose advertising censorship at the drop of a hat. After all, proposing a ban on advertising a certain product is a cheap way to satisfy a special interest group, and it costs no tax dollars. For example, although states cannot prevent the entry of imported products, such as cars and textiles, state lawmakers reading the Puerto Rico case will be tempted to ban the advertising of imports. Such censorship, in the service of politics, is precisely the evil which the First Amendment is designed to prevent.

Seemingly, there are few products on which government cannot impose advertising censorship. (One exception, the Court noted, involved advertising for abortion services, which were "constitutionally protected." Regardless of one's views on abortion, it must seem at least unexpected that the Court should give favored treatment to the advertising of abortion, yet find other advertising unprotected by the specific language of the First Amendment that Congress shall make no law regarding freedom of speech or of the press.)

THE EVIL CANNOT BE LIMITED

Once the Court permits lawmakers to censor the advertising of one legal product, there is simply no legal way to draw the line. For example, in 1967 the Federal Communications Commission decided to apply its Fairness Doctrine (encouraging on-air discussion of controversial public issues) to one particular type of advertising—cigarette advertising—but cautioned that this product was unique and justified unique treatment. Later, however, a court of appeals held that the FCC could *not* treat cigarette advertising as unique, and if it applied the Fairness Doctrine to cigarette commercials, it would also have to apply it to other product advertising, such as gasoline commercials.

In a still later case, a federal court of appeals noted that if the Fairness Doctrine were applied to commercials for one particular product, such as cigarettes, "there may be no practical stopping place. . . ." Similarly, once government officials are allowed to prohibit advertising for one lawful product, there may be no practical stopping place to prevent censorship of ads for *any* product displeasing officials at a given moment.

There may be no practical stopping place to prevent censorship of ads for *any* product displeasing officials at a given moment.

The casino advertising case therefore opens the frightening possibility that legislatures across the country will indulge in advertising censorship, harming both the free enterprise system of competition and the rights of consumers to receive product information. However, the consequences of this case cannot even be limited to product advertising.

In labor/management disputes, unions frequently urge consumers to boycott the products of a company which, the union believes, has violated employee rights. Unions publicize their dispute both through media advertising and through handbilling. In 1985, the National

Labor Relations Board issued an order prohibiting a union from peacefully distributing a truthful handbill asking consumers not to shop at a mall where a store was being built by nonunion labor.

The court of appeals in Atlanta reversed the NLRB by interpreting the labor law narrowly. The court did not decide, however, whether a union handbill truthfully advising consumers of the labor dispute is protected by the First Amendment.

Legally, the question remains in doubt. If government can prohibit advertising because it "stimulates demand," can it not also censor union advertising seeking to reduce demand?

At its heart, the issue is profound. Do we desire to live in a society where condescending government officials, at their whim, can censor or suppress truthful speech to further some social or economic policy? Or do we want to continue to live in a nation where the debate is robust, and open to all, and where consumers are free to make choices based upon their unrestricted access to the truth?

Or do we want to continue to live in a nation where the debate is robust, and open to all, and where consumers are free to make choices based upon their unrestricted access to the truth?

BIBLIOGRAPHY
(Listed in order of reference in text.)

Posadas de Puerto Rico Associates v. *Tourism Company of Puerto Rico,* U.S., 13 Med. L. Rptr. 1033 (July 1, 1986).

Warner-Lambert Co. v. *Federal Trade Commission,* 562 F. 2d 749 (D.C. Cir. 1977), cert. denied 435 U.S. 950 (1978).

Thornhill v. *Alabama,* 310 U.S. 88 (1940).

Virginia State Board of Pharmacy v. *Virginia Citizens Consumer Council, Inc.,* 425 U.S. 748 (1976).

Bates v. *State Bar of Arizona,* 433 U.S. 350 (1977).

Zaunderer v. *Office of Disciplinary Counsel,* U.S., 85 L. Ed. 2d 652 (1985).

Central Hudson Gas & Electric Corporation v. *Public Service Commission,* 447 U.S. 557 (1980).

Federal Trade Commission Report: " 'Tar,' Nicotine and Carbon Monoxide of the Smoke of 207 Varieties of Domestic Cigarettes," (August 1985).

WCBS-TV, 8 FCC 2d 381, *stay and reconsideration denied,* 9 FCC 2d 921 (1967).

Fairness Report, 48 FCC 2d 1 (1974).

Friends of the Earth v. *FCC,* 449 F. 2d 1164 (D.C. Cir. 1971).

Public Interest Research Group v. *FCC*, 522 F.2d, 1060 (1st Cir. 1975), cert. denied 424 U.S. 965 (1976).

Florida Gulf Coast Building & Construction Trades Council (Edward J. DeBartolo Corp.), 273 NLRB 1431 (1985).

Building & Construction Trades Council v. *NLRB*, F.2d, 123 LRRM 2001 (11th Cir. 1986).

Jacqueline McCartney
Billings, Montana

Occupation: Writer
Interests: Writing, travel, pets (two dogs
and three cats)
Entered the Competition because of: "Concern
about growing trend of censorship, especially
government's involvement."

IN ORDER TO FORM A MORE PERFECT UNION

Two centuries ago, one of the most brilliant and certainly one of the boldest documents known to humankind was penned. "We the people of the United States, in order to form a more perfect union. . . [to] secure the blessings of liberty for ourselves and our posterity, do ordain and establish this Constitution for the United States of America." This collection of phrases was not destined to become mere rhetoric; the ramifications of this document known as our Constitution were felt across oceans. The complexion of history was forever changed.

A few years later, amendments were added that spelled out these "blessings of liberty," the first ten known as the Bill of Rights. Among the rights our forefathers placed at the top of the list is the right of the people to have freedom of speech.

Two hundred years later, the media and libraries are included with those continuing to wage the battle to keep this most basic right outlined in our most basic of laws—and among those fighting to retain this right of free speech is the tobacco industry. The tobacco industry? Americans accustomed to thinking of free speech in terms of the individual or groups of citizens, may cast a suspicious eye upon a business' claim that its constitutional rights are in danger of violation by a proposal to ban all advertising of its products.

The stark and simple reality is that the portion of the First Amendment that guarantees freedom of speech does not specify a select few, but all American people, including men and women in business. Another unadorned—and alarming—fact is that if lawmakers are allowed to deny the freedom of commercial speech to tobacco businesses, the individual American citizen will indeed suffer. Censorship by the hand of the government threatens to sever "We the people" from the right of free speech guaranteed by the Constitution, the very right the same government has sworn to protect.

In order to form a more perfect union?

The fight for free speech and against censorship is nothing new to the media, dedicated to bringing the facts and the truth to their readers despite the ever-growing constraints placed upon them by lawmakers. No strangers to the conflict are our libraries and schools, where some would banish from the shelves classical works of literature by the likes of Mark Twain and William Shakespeare.

And the battle is a familiar one to the tobacco industry, to whom the government has extended its silencing hand in the attempt to deny it the right freely granted to other businesses, the right to advertise and dispense information about its products.

Americans pride themselves on their championing of human rights. The seven-year exile of dissident Andrei Sakharov in the Soviet Union drew the outrage and sympathy of the American public. We applauded for his release in late 1986 from the closed Soviet city of Gorky. That anyone would be jailed or otherwise suppressed for freely expressing themselves is appalling to the people of the United States, who enjoy such a freedom under the law.

Yet, a quieter war is being waged in our own backyard, one that does not garner front-page headlines or top-story coverage, but one that is more dangerous to our democratic way of life. Factions in our own government seek to stifle the tobacco industry's right to provide information to the American people about its products in the form of paid advertising.

This is not merely a fight of words and posturings for lawyers, nor a battle of wits for philosophers, nor even an issue of importance for only one segment of the business population, although some of our government's leaders would like you, the American public, to believe so. Those legislators who seek unfairly to impose such a ban on tobacco companies would love for you to focus exclusively on the Sakharovs, the repressed individuals of the world, instead of sharing that outrage with similar issues in the U.S. Nothing would please them more than for you to view corporations as faceless inhuman things, instead of seeing the businessmen and businesswomen behind the company logo, instead of seeing the individuals who make up the corporations struggling to hold on to the last remnants of their First Amendment rights.

Those factions of government couldn't be happier if you drew boundaries between "free speech" and "free commercial speech" as if they were not one and the same under the First Amendment. In their wisdom, however, our country's first leaders made no such distinctions nor created no such qualifiers when they approved the Bill of Rights. The portion of the First Amendment regarding free speech states only that "Congress shall make no law . . . abridging the freedom of speech."

Within the text of the First Amendment, there are neither "except fors" nor "but not includings." Freedom of speech is a privilege granted to all. Period. Any segment of government that would insinuate otherwise would do well to remember the firm words of renowned jurist Hugo L. Black: "I am for the First Amendment from the first word to the last. I believe it means what it says."

Proposed bans on tobacco advertising raise more than ethical or moral issues. If the government takes it upon itself to forbid tobacco advertising, the consequences will be felt not only by tobacco corporations. The ripples will extend to rock each American home.

Under our country's free enterprise system, industries are allowed to contend in the marketplace for consumer favor, and one of their chief means of competing as such is through advertising. Advertisements allow businesses to let consumers know that their products are available, to give consumers data and details about their products. The information provided by advertisements is paramount to consumer choice and decision.

The government has already invaded advertising departments of broadcast media to prohibit advertisement of tobacco products on radio and television. Some legislators now want to enter advertising departments of the print media, to deny tobacco companies any form of paid advertisement, to barricade the main avenue of economic success while granting other legal products free access.

Our newspapers, magazines, etc., are privately owned businesses, not branches of the government. Yet, the government asks the American public to sanction a proposal that would order these private businesses not to accept advertisement of legal products from other private businesses. The government asks the American public to close its eyes, and to ignore those words, "We the people of the United States, in order to form a more perfect union. . . ."

Little wonder that the press, which also enjoys freedom under the First Amendment, is concerned. The possibility of censorship in any area of the media is distressful to journalists. The steps from advertising departments to newsrooms are frighteningly few. As American citizens who rely on unfettered journalists to report fairly and accurately the news events, however these reports may reflect on our government, you, too, have a stake in keeping government out of the media's affairs.

Little wonder that this continued persecution—for how else can it be viewed?—of the tobacco industry dismays leaders of every business. Under such a dangerous precedent, who next will fall victim to the government's disfavor? As employees, how will it affect the existence of your jobs if the government chokes off your companies' lifeblood, the ability to advertise?

Business aside, what other segment of American society would be next to lose the freedom of speech and expression if the public keeps silent on this issue, and thereby sending the government an inadvertent message of approval?

Little wonder that this continued persecution—for how else can it be viewed?—of the tobacco industry dismays leaders of every business.

Very quickly, the battle being waged by such businesses as Philip Morris Companies, Inc. to retain the precious right of free speech is not only crucial to a corporation's right to contend freely in the marketplace, as do other industries, but the battle becomes imperative to each American citizen. Those who advocate whisking away those rights would love for you to be blinded as to how the consequences trickle down to your doorstep.

Have some of our country's leaders perhaps forgotten those words forged with bravery and defended with life's blood, "We the people of the United States, in order to form a more perfect union. . ."? Do they view the words "freedom" and "democracy" as dispensable principles? Do these legislators wink at the convictions and warnings of some of our country's most important statesmen?

> If men are to be precluded from offering their sentiments on a matter . . .
> the freedom of speech may be taken away, and dumb and silent we may be
> led, like sheep to the slaughter.
> —George Washington

> In the future days, which we seek to make secure, we look forward to a
> world founded upon four essential human freedoms. The first is freedom
> of speech and expression—everywhere in the world.
> —Franklin Delano Roosevelt

> Imperative is the need to preserve inviolate the constitutional rights of
> free speech. . . . Therein lies the security of the Republic, the very
> foundation of constitutional government.
> —Charles E. Hughes, former U.S. Supreme Court Chief Justice

Indeed, if this "foundation" Hughes spoke of is destroyed, if the cornerstone of free speech is snatched out from under the American public, how quickly will the remainder of our constitutional rights topple without its support. Few of our rights and freedoms exist without the critical right to free speech and expression.

The American people have another right, one which these presumptuous lawmakers would be wise to remember. The public has the right to vote for their representation in government, and the right to hold those representatives accountable for their actions. We the people can put a halt to the proposed ban on tobacco advertising by writing our congressmen and women, and airing our concerns regarding casual dismissal of our rights. Many newspapers and reference departments of libraries, which have an interest in preserving the freedom of speech, will be happy to provide you with your lawmakers' addresses.

We the people can put a halt to the proposed ban on tobacco advertising by writing our congressmen and women, and airing our concerns regarding casual dismissal of our rights.

This crucial issue crosses political lines and affiliations. It is one of concern to every business leader. It is of importance to every individual, smoker and nonsmoker alike. But the issue will not resolve itself in your favor without your support.

We the people must express to lawmakers our displeasure regarding attempts of censorship by the government. We the people must say no to any tampering with or suspension of our constitutional rights. In order to form a more perfect union.

Professor John R. Snowden
Lincoln, Nebraska

Occupation: Law Professor
Interests: Reading, walking, music
Entered the Competition because: "I have taught about the First Amendment and government regulation of speech for fifteen years. A colleague saw the announcement and I could not pass up the challenge to speak for freedom of expression in the face of righteous repression."

> In America, a free marketplace of ideas has been at the foundation of our free market economy and a free and democratic society.

TOBACCO ADVERTISING AND THE FIRST AMENDMENT: WILL THE PROMISE GO UP IN SMOKE?

There is a clear and present danger to freedom of expression in the recent congressional consideration of a further ban on tobacco advertising. Already the promise of the First Amendment is tarnished by the legal prohibition of tobacco advertising on television and the second-class status given to truthful commercial advertising. Now some voices in Congress and the press are asking for a total ban of tobacco advertising in all media.

Of course, the journalists and politicians who clamor for this infringement of speech and press are patriots and believers in freedom of expression. I imagine they would all agree with John Milton's famous lines: "And though all the winds of doctrine were let loose to play upon the earth, so Truth be in the field, we do injuriously by licensing and prohibiting to misdoubt her strength." But the similarity to Milton is also clear when they seek to ban tobacco ads. Milton, a Puritan, would not give free expression to Catholicism or atheism. Like Milton, those advocating a tobacco ad ban stop their concern for free expression when it threatens a consequence to which they are opposed or committed.

This is the crux of the problem of free expression: though freedom of expression seems right it may lead to bad consequences. Those who would ban tobacco advertising claim to act for my good, but the censorship of expression is a wrong. My cigarette pack carries a message imposed by government censors, "Quitting smoking now greatly reduces serious risks to your health." Unfortunately, my health is always at risk and the greatest danger is not tobacco, or even alcohol and drugs, but ideas. Ideas are the world's number one killer. But every new idea that rises from the ashes of death promises an even greater life than that which was lived or imagined. A "Dangerous to Your Health" warning is not needed on books and schools; a people raised in freedom know this.

I believe that freedom of expression in every oral and written form is crucial to self-fulfillment in all aspects of society. From the beginning to the end of life a human being creates and defines both self and world by the giving and taking of stories. A person may be given stories that, if affirmed, threaten life itself by determining political, social, economic and religious outlooks. In America, a free marketplace of ideas has been at the foundation of our free market economy and a free and democratic society.

A free market of ideas is the intellectual corollary to the sea of possibilities that is the human personality. Freedom of expression, the free exchange of stories of ways of existence, is to serve individual, not collective goals. We do not structure our economy to produce at government demand and we have tried to hold steadfast to the promise of free expression. In this effort we have asked the help of the law. In our supreme law of the land, the Constitution of the United States, government has promised in the First Amendment to ". . . make no law . . . abridging the Freedom of Speech, or of the press. . . ."

Freedom of speech and press is placed at the heart of the social contract because freedom of expression is central to the striving for human potential. It is the foundation of personality and the source from which all other actions spring. Freedom of expression is never at an end, but it is rather a process. As so well told by Professor Thomas Emerson in *The System of Freedom of Expression* (1970), the advancement of knowledge and the discovery of truth does not end at a stage of history to be measured and maintained. Participation in democratic decision making occurs in the choice of toothpaste as well as in the voting booth. And, the free exchange of stories is a way to stabilize a community with a healthy balance of individual freedom and group solidarity.

Participation in democratic decision making occurs in the choice of toothpaste as well as in the voting booth.

Among the stories of our society are the law stories; the Constitution, the statutes of the legislatures, and the opinions of the courts. These stories not only carry all the power of a story to define and create the world, but they also legitimize the power of the state to enforce their reality with guns. The story of the First Amendment is part of our culture creating and defending a society of freedom and human rights. The discussion of a complete tobacco advertising ban aims at a translation into a law story. If Congress bans tobacco advertising the full force of the state will see that the ban is observed. The Supreme Court of the United States may well be asked to consider whether a tobacco advertising ban is coherent with the story of the First Amendment. Hopefully, the wisdom of Congress will reject a further ban of tobacco advertising, for freedom of advertising expression has been the victim of oppressive legal stories in the courts.

American business is at the core of work and family, its messages are a vital part of the free exchange of stories to which one must have access. Today the law stories of the courts subject the messages of the business world, advertising, to a discriminatory and weakened legal standard. Advertising is given only second-class protection in First Amendment jurisprudence, and the most recent law story concerning advertising emasculates even that protection with a chilling twist.

In *Posadas de Puerto Rico Associates* v. *Tourism Company of Puerto Rico*, 106 S. Ct. 2968 (1986), Justice Rehnquist writing for the majority of the United States Supreme Court retold the law story of First Amendment protection for truthful advertising. In the *Posadas de Puerto Rico* story the reader learns that commercial speech, advertising, is thought to be distinct from other types of speech since it is said to do no more than propose a commercial transaction. For that reason it was held not to be protected by the First Amendment in a 1942 case, *Valentine v. Chrestensen*. It was not until 1976 in *Virginia Pharmacy*, that the Court, still believing in the earlier characterization, nevertheless found advertising not so removed from any exposition of ideas that it lacked any First Amendment protection.

In a 1980 case, *Central Hudson Gas*, the Court articulated exactly what kind of protection advertising was to get. In *Posadas de Puerto Rico*, the Court applied that test to an advertiser that wanted to tell residents of Puerto Rico about their opportunity to engage in legal casino gambling on the island. First, for the advertising to be protected it must be neither misleading nor related to unlawful activity. Here the advertisement met this test; casino gambling was legal for residents and tourists. In fact, Puerto Rican law allowed advertisement *if* it was directed to tourists. Second, the state must assert a substantial state interest to be achieved by the censorship of the truthful ad. This standard gives truthful advertising a second-class position. Other truthful speech may be censored only if the state demonstrates a compelling interest. Though the scales of "compelling" and "substantial" are vague and subjective, a believer in the law story believes that there is a distinction in the protective power in these symbols for thought and judgment. Third, the censoring regulation must directly advance the state interest. And, fourth, if the government interest may be served as well by a more limited restriction on speech, the excessive restriction may not stand.

The Court found that the reduction in demand for casino gambling by residents of Puerto Rico was a substantial interest, and that the regulation directly advanced the interest by keeping residents uninformed of their legally allowed choice, thereby reducing the demand. Finally, the Court said that the regulation was no more extensive than necessary.

Justice Rehnquist added a chilling twist in response to the advertiser's argument that a more limited approach, the promulgation by the government of speech to discourage gambling by residents, would serve the state interest as well as censorship. Justice Rehnquist said that unless the activity advertised is itself protected by the Constitution it could be entirely prohibited by the state. (There are very few activities that are constitutionally protected.) Thus, since the state could entirely prohibit the gambling activity it could certainly take the lesser step of censoring truthful advertising about the activity.

Such a twist stands the First Amendment on its head. It comes initially from the Court's discriminatory treatment of advertising as being a lesser form of speech, and winds a serpentine coil around the protective promise of the First Amendment. It is the very promise of the First Amendment that though activity may be made illegal, the people may discuss the stories that would change, as well as continue, that state of affairs. Surely, if tobacco products were made illegal the people could speak and publish urging an end to the prohibition. Yet, the Court has seemed to say that while tobacco is legally sold the government might ban its advertisement.

What else might the government and its wise advisors wish to discourage? This returns to the stories told in the school civics class to help adolescents learn the value of free expression. There students are asked whether we should ban advertisements of high-fat foods, fast cars and wasteful vacation trips. It is all too clear that the value of free expression, like all stories of value, has not been completely told. For all the stories of freedom in the marketplace of ideas and the free market of goods and services there are always competing stories. These are stories not of choices of goods or actions, but stories of choice and authority in a way of life.

The law story which attempts to relate truthful advertising to the liberating promise of the First Amendment is weak and pathetic. If accepted by a people they will reflect its nature. The story of *Posadas de*

Puerto Rico and the stories of those who seek to use it to censor tobacco advertising do not uplift the hearer. They do not mark honor in the storyteller. The *Posadas de Puerto Rico* story seems a sad and silly rationalization of a broken promise. Justice Rehnquist legitimizes censorship of truthful advertising as a little child would excuse stinginess.

In the end, whether or not I am able to enjoy a good smoke is not the issue in the discussion of the tobacco advertising ban. I am sure I will be able to do that even if those who know best what to order others not to do prohibit the sale of tobacco products. At stake is the story of my people about the freedom to exchange the stories that create the world. The promise of the First Amendment that government shall maintain a free marketplace of ideas has always been at risk. It places a notion of right action, freedom of expression, prior to the calculation of consequences of good or bad that might flow from a free exchange of ideas.

In the end, whether or not I am able to enjoy a good smoke is not the issue. . . . At stake is the story of my people about the freedom to exchange the stories that create the world.

Like all stories, the legal story of the First Amendment cannot in itself tell all that is to be told. Freedom of expression is not exhausted in the First Amendment, and the stories of the Court are not all the law. As the American people discuss the censorship of tobacco ads, I will hope for the law's promise despite the frail hearts of the legal storytellers who interpret it. But my trust will be in the stories of the people, of families, of workers of American business; stories of courage, fortitude, generosity and honesty.

Robert Sagan
Reno, Nevada

Occupation: Public Relations
Interests: Music, reading, tennis, writing
Entered the Competition because: "It is a good topic to write about, and one I believe in. I am concerned about the fact that there are a disproportionately few people out there who are quite willing, and able, to try and legislate the way the rest of us should live our lives."

WHO'S RESPONSIBLE HERE?

Congress shall make no law respecting an
establishment of religion, or prohibiting
the free exercise thereof; or abridging
the freedom of speech, or of the press;
or the right of the people to assemble,
and to petition the government for a redress
of grievances.
—First Amendment to the
Constitution of the
United States of America

It's no accident that the freedoms of religion, speech, press and assembly
are included in the First Amendment. In identifying those rights and
assigning them the place of prominence they did, the framers of our
Constitution recognized not only their primacy, but actually anticipated
the never-ending tests such freedoms would be put to over the years—
including those dealing with commercial free speech.

Two major considerations cry out for attention in any discussion of
the First Amendment and how it should affect commercial speech.

First, should each of us ultimately be the best judge of his or her
own interests? Or is it to be left to government to make such decisions
for us through censorship and other restrictive regulations?

And second, if the sales of an industry's products or services are
legal under the law, can there be any justification for restraining the
truthful advertising necessary to sell those products or services?

Addressing the first question, Supreme Court justices and experts
in constitutional law, over the years, have interpreted a First Amendment stressing individual rights and responsibilities over governmental
restraints—including those imposed on commercial free speech.

Supreme Court Justice John Marshall Harlan recognized that freedom contains within itself the possibility that we may not always make

the right decision, that we may at times act "irresponsibly"; but that, in fact, no person is truly free who is not permitted occasionally to be . . . irresponsible.

More to the point, *New York Times* columnist Tom Wicker has written, "The highest freedom of all may well be the freedom to conduct one's life and affairs responsibly—*but by one's own standards of responsibility*" (author's emphasis).

Wicker insisted that it was no freedom at all if the standards of responsibility were uniform, designed to *prevent* rather than to *punish* "failures"—and all established by some higher authority.

Although some people are more mature, more intelligent or better educated than their fellows, each informed person must finally be considered the best judge of his or her own interests.

In fact, the whole philosophy of free speech presumes the existence of our freedom to accept or reject the alternatives offered us. Communication which does not allow for this individual decision making violates the integrity of those to whom it is addressed and, in the process, injures them.

Conversely, exposure to the widest possible range of communication could well be the most effective growth-producing experience. Reliance is placed on the free marketplace of ideas which trusts that even if our decisions do not always turn out to be the wisest ones, the idea of free communication is more likely to come closer to the "truth" than will the restriction of communication.

Even if our decisions do not always turn out to be the wisest ones, the idea of free communication is more likely to come closer to the "truth" than will the restriction of communication.

Franklyn S. Haiman, a professor of communications at Northwestern University, wrote in his *Speech and Law in a Free Society*, that even if we were not the best judges of our own interests, "It is infinitely more dangerous to try and determine *who is* best equipped to make decisions for themselves."

Haiman recognized that a government such as ours, one governing a large and technologically advanced nation, develops inclinations to subvert the free marketplace of communication—even at the same time that its stated intent may be to bring about the self-fulfillment of its citizens. Thus, the "servant" of the people acquires an appetite for power which, if left unchecked, transforms the servant into the master.

Finally, Haiman believes that, unless the harm done by an act of communication is "direct, immediate, irreparable, and of a serious nature, the remedy in a free society should be more speech rather than enforced silence."

In addressing the second question (Can there be any justification for restraining truthful advertising of a legally sold product, when that advertising is part of the selling process?), we cut more to the quick of tobacco industry concerns.

Again, no less a judicial body than the U.S. Supreme Court has made its opinions clear on this issue more than once. A few years ago, the Public Service Commission of New York sought to enjoin Central Hudson Gas and Electric from advertising in a manner that would sell its customers more electricity. The Commission's position was that the utility should instead be encouraging energy conservation.

Justice Harry Blackmun, in his opinion wrote, ". . . I do not agree that the Court's test is the proper one to be applied when a 'State' seeks to suppress information about a product in order to manipulate a private economic decision that the State cannot or has not regulated or outlawed directly."

In an opinion concurring with Justice Blackmun, Justice John Paul Stevens noted, "The justification for the [commission's] regulation is nothing more than the expressed fear that the audience may find the utility's message persuasive. Without the aid of any coercion, deception or misinformation, truthful communication may persuade some citizens to consume more electricity than they would otherwise. . . ."

The Court went on to say that it doubted whether suppression of information concerning the availability and price of a legally offered product is ever a permissible way for the state to "dampen" demand for, or use of, that product.

Justice Stevens further recognized that even though commercial speech is involved, such regulatory measures "strike at the very heart of the First Amendment," because they represent a covert attempt by the state to manipulate the choices of its citizens—not by persuasion or direct regulation, but by *depriving the public of the information needed to make a free choice.*

If the First Amendment guarantees mean anything, the Court observed, they mean that, without clear and present danger, the government has no power to restrict expression because of the effect its message is likely to have on the public. In publishing its opinion in this case, the Supreme Court emphasized that the First Amendment guarantees apply "even to commercial speech."

271

A similar application of these opinions is seen in the case of the *Virginia State Board of Pharmacy* v. *Virginia Citizens Consumer Council, Inc.* In this case, Virginia statute sought to prohibit pharmacists from advertising the prices at which they would sell prescription drugs to the public.

Justice Warren Burger's Court overturned this law, with a majority holding the existing statute unconstitutional. In his concurring opinion, Justice Blackmun said that the advertiser's interest in publicizing his wares and prices was primarily economic; but that this fact did not "render his interest insignificant for the purposes of the First Amendment." Blackmun's main concern was that such limiting statutes would interfere with the free operation of the marketplace.

Electric utilities, pharmaceuticals or tobacco, the potential for constitutional abuse seems the same among those who would impose their own standards on the rest of us.

Franklyn Haiman contends that if it is society's judgment that smoking is sufficiently harmful to require a ban on the advertising of cigarettes, then cigarette sales should be prohibited. However, if we are not willing to make the sale of cigarettes illegal, Haiman could not see how we can justify restraints on any truthful advertising which is part of that selling process.

"Okay, have it your way," the antismoking groups well may say. "Let's indeed ban the sale of cigarettes and other related tobacco products."

An article appearing on the front page of a November 1986 *Wall Street Journal* ("The Tobacco Institute Loses Political Power as Attitudes Change") seemed to portend that very intent. "Not only are a growing number of tobacco's [congressional] backers wavering, but an increasing number of senior-level, more powerfully situated members of Congress have become anti-tobacco spokesmen," according to an antismoking lobbyist quoted in the *Journal.*

The article went on to state that, "Opponents of tobacco are becoming more numerous and certainly more vocal." It further noted the plans of one antismoking leader to "portray politicians who are pro-cigarette as pro-drug dealers."

Apparently "dirty tricks" are justifiable as long as the dirty trickster is also a crusader.

Apparently "dirty tricks" are justifiable as long as the dirty trickster is also a crusader.

272

Is it reasonable to assume there are those—including some in "high places"—who would opt for the depression, if not the ultimate and outright suppression, of a tobacco industry in this country without giving due consideration to the serious social, economic and political consequences which most certainly would follow?

Of course it is.

And, if such harsh action would seem anachronistic in these enlightened and permissive times, consider this "litany of legislations and leanings" which has taken place in our recent history:

- Cigarette advertising banned from the electronic media
- Cigarette manufacturers forced to put health warnings on packaging and print ads
- Medical/health care community steps up its unceasing bombardment of public information alleging the harmful effects of smoking—first on the smoker, then on the nonsmoker
- Government, military and private industry introduce restrictive smoking measures into their operations
- Stronger health warnings mandated for cigarette packaging and print advertising
- Health warning labeling ordered for smokeless tobacco products
- High cigarette excise taxes extended
- Legislation introduced to disallow business deductions for cigarette advertising
- Antismoking interests begin a drive for elimination of cigarette advertising in the print media
- U.S. Surgeon General calls for a "smokeless society" by the turn of the century.

Such restrictive measures feed on themselves—a juggernaut gaining strength and momentum—particularly when they go unchallenged. The erosion of the industry's rights is clearly evident, and the prevailing climate seems to promise more of the same for the future.

But is it possible to suppress a $32-billion-a-year industry, employing more than 65,000 people in manufacturing alone; and many thousands more who help support the economies of the fifty states through farming, warehousing, distribution and sales?

Is such suppression possible without doing serious harm to an entire economy?

Consider an industry whose products were responsible in 1984 (last year for available statistics) for $10.1 billion in excise and sales taxes to federal, state and local governments. . . and one which *exported* nearly $3 billion of leaf and tobacco products for that same year. Those

273

exports mean a positive contribution of more than $2 billion to the U.S. balance of payments.

More ominously, does the erosion of one industry's commercial freedoms, perhaps leading to its ultimate suppression, serve as a harbinger for others?

The National Rifle Association still clings to its bromidic "Guns don't kill, people kill." Yet, they cannot dispute that the incidence of murder by handguns in Great Britain is far less, by any measurement, than it is in the United States. The British, of course, have enacted stringent gun control laws. So Great Britain does indeed have people. . . but it does not have guns. . . and it does not have gun-related murders.

Will the gun industry be the next to be hobbled by an onslaught of restrictive legislation, enacted by those who would impose their own standards on others—because they perceive those others as being incapable of deciding their own best interests?

What about beer, wine and liquor industries, and the lives reportedly ruined as a result of alcohol abuse? And carrying the premise to its logical (albeit *ad absurdum*) conclusion, why should the automobile industry be excluded? After all, more than 40,000 Americans are killed each year on our highways. Or does it become a case of "Cars don't kill, people kill"? Perhaps we should legislate people out of existence.

Given one's particular axe to grind, and in a climate of regulatory abuse, the potential for censorship and eventual suppression is boundless.

The last time America experimented with a national Prohibition, it failed miserably under the Eighteenth Amendment and the Volstead Act. Much worse, it opened a Pandora's box of new social ills—a foothold for organized crime being only one of them—for which we are still paying.

We have seen time and again that people's mores and manners are not readily decided by fiat—that, in fact, they cannot be. There is a particular something in the American character that rails against the attempt.

Why some of us, through the suffocating overlegislation of our fellow citizens, would chance inviting a renascence of the same abuses we suffered as a people in the 1920s and '30s is difficult to comprehend.

Clarence Darrow and George Santayana were of the same mind when they spoke and wrote about history. Darrow said, "History repeats itself. That's one of the things that's wrong with history."

And it was Santayana whose perhaps most famous quote has been erroneously attributed to so many others—from Mark Twain to Winston Churchill: "Those who will not learn from the past, are condemned to repeat it."

Vera Josephine Green
Exeter, New Hampshire

Occupation: Retired, currently completing an M.A. degree in English

Interests: Reading, swimming, writing, studying at the university

Entered the Competition because: "The theme of the contest, 'If liberty is worth fighting for . . . It's worth writing for,' holds a powerful appeal for me, as it must for anyone of my generation who has seen liberty threatened in war and peace."

FREEDOM AT RISK

It is the great pride and privilege of Americans to live in a "nation
conceived in liberty and dedicated to the proposition that all men are
created equal." On the battlefield and in the polling booth we have
tested "whether that nation or any nation so conceived and so dedicated
can long endure."

Our Liberty was first won by men and women who dared to leave
the comfort and security of familiar surroundings and venture to a far-
off, unknown and hostile land, where only the strongest, or the luckiest,
survived disease, hunger and exposure, or murderous attacks by under-
standably belligerent savages. The colonists' right to enjoy the freedom
so dearly wrested from the soil of their new country had to be won anew
by the sword of Revolution, and over a century and a half later, the
Nation's liberty had to be defended, again by the sword, in a war against
an axis of totalitarian powers.

Is that freedom won and rewon by heroic struggle and the sacrifice
of life itself to be yielded bit by bit through a lack of vigilance? The
answer has resounded repeatedly in our history. On a national level,
within a few years after adoption of the Constitution, the Alien and
Sedition Act, aimed at freedom of speech and of the press, was defeated
by a party revolution, by public opinion, by the people. Advocates of
sedition the people were not, but they recognized and repulsed an attack
on their fundamental right of free speech. Again on the national level,
the Volstead Act, the Noble Experiment, lasted just thirteen years
before it was repealed in expensively belated recognition of its un-
enforceability among a free people. On the state level, very recently, the
people of Massachusetts, one of the thirteen original colonies, rejected a
mandatory seat belt law. Among the majority voting against this well-
intentioned but dictatorial law were many who believe in seat belts but
not in government curtailment of individual liberty.

Similarly, the issue of whether the government is to be allowed to
forbid advertising to the tobacco industry is not to be considered on the
basis of the desirability of the use of tobacco. The use of tobacco is, and
should remain, a matter of free, individual and private choice. The issue
is whether government of the people, by the people and for the people is
threatening our freedom and overstepping its constitutionally limited
powers by attempting to control the use of tobacco, or any other legal

277

product, through denying the privilege of advertising—of free speech—to an industry of its selection on whatever ground.

To deny free speech to an industry is not different from denying it to a person. A corporation is an artificial person created by state or federal law. It represents the collective interests of individual persons. As such it has the obligations and responsibilities and therefore the privileges and rights of an individual person.

The suppression of advertising by an industry carries an even more threatening implication of dictatorship than lies in the basic infringement on liberty involved in the denial of free speech. In a free market economy, advertising is an essential tool of marketing, and marketing and production together determine the viability of a business enterprise. In denying an industry the right to advertise, the government is denying it access to its market and potentially destroying it. Are we ready to accord to government, or special interest groups that may influence it, the power to do that? Do we really agree to accord to Congress arbitrary life-and-death power over any person, or any group of persons, or the legally established person that is a corporation? Does the Constitution confer any such power? It does not. The powers of Congress are specific and enumerated. This awesome authority is not among them.

The tobacco industry has not challenged the government's right to inform the public regarding its findings of potential harm to users of its products. It asks only to be allowed to reach the market among those who have different comparative values for the pleasure and risks of smoking. The right to make such free choices is basic to democracy. The government's censorship of an industry's advertising, not monitoring for truth but absolute prohibition, amounts to the assumption by Congress of a supreme judicial function, antithetical to freedom and democracy. Such suppression implies a paternalistic authority that is the essence of dictatorship, with all the related dangers of the abuse of power by special interest groups.

The tobacco industry. . . asks only to be allowed to reach the market among those who have different comparative values for the pleasures and risks of smoking.

When freedom of speech, the cornerstone of liberty, is denied to anyone, everyone's freedom of speech is endangered. There are no little defeats in the struggle to maintain our liberty. None is ever isolated; any defeat is the forerunner of others. "The price of liberty is eternal vigilance."

278

"Congress shall make no law. . . abridging the freedom of speech or of the press." That restraint on Congress is contained in Article I, the very first amendment to the Constitution of the United States. That amendment came first because it incorporates what were conceived to be the most urgent rights of a free people. It is the first of ten articles of the Bill of Rights, adopted almost two hundred years ago, in 1791, by a Nation whose citizens had laid their lives on the line for freedom.

The Bill of Rights, a declaration of the fundamental rights of human beings, like other treasures of our priceless heritage, did not come into being without a struggle. And this time it was the people, not the members of the Constitutional Convention, who spoke. The "masses" with their intimate knowledge of the many faces of tyranny were heard from. When the proposed Constitution was published in the newspapers, Catherine Drinker Bowen tells us in *Miracle at Philadelphia,* "Nothing created such an uproar as the lack of a bill of rights. What had the Convention been thinking of to neglect a matter so elementary, so much a part of the heritage of free people?"

Her explanation of the omission by the convention is illuminating. In Alexander Hamilton's words: "Why declare that things shall not be done which there is no power [in Congress] to do?" Other champions of freedom echoed that thought. The Magna Carta wrested powers from a monarch, and it was therefore necessary to list those gains. The Constitution, in contrast, was adopted by a free people in whom fundamental human rights already resided and did not need to be specified.

There is nothing in the Constitution . . . that accords *discretion* to Congress for selective denial . . . of any of the rights and privileges that the Constitution expressly guarantees. . . .

But others, more alert to freedom's many perils, thought differently. Patrick Henry, to whom death was preferable to the loss of liberty, named the lack of a bill of rights as first and foremost of what he did not like in the proposed Constitution.

We know now that such specification of the rights of a free people was indeed necessary and could not be taken for granted. Fortunately the will of a watchful people prevailed. The restraints on Government that some of the best minds considered implicit were made explicit. And Article I of the Bill of Rights importantly included, as we have mentioned before: "Congress shall make no law. . . abridging the freedom of speech or of the press."

But that victory for freedom was not won, it cannot be won, once and for all. It is a victory that only ceaselessly alert public opinion can safeguard. Congress in gagging the tobacco industry is clearly violating that First Amendment guarantee of free speech. There is nothing in the Constitution, or in the concept of an elected government of free people, that accords *discretion* to Congress for selective denial to some citizens, individually or organized as a business, of any of the rights and privileges that the Constitution expressly guarantees to all citizens of this Republic. To grant government such discretionary power, or passively to permit to arrogate such power unto itself, is to open the door to tyranny and to supinely yield the blessings of liberty won for us at untold cost and received by us in sacred trust.

NEW JERSEY STATE PRIZE WINNER

G. T. Lenard
Somers Point, New Jersey

Occupation: College Instructor
Interests: Reading, gardening, music
Entered the Competition because: "The issue is one that is important to me."

1984 in 1987

In his novel *1984*, George Orwell presents a bleak look at a future society where all power and all decisions have been surrendered to state control, to a mythical Big Brother. During the Orwellian Year itself, when I questioned my students about Orwell's vision, they agreed that "it could never happen here." Some of them jokingly conceded that the IRS may be the closest we come to Big Brother, but they were adamant that the press could never be censored in this country, that human rights would prevail, and that Americans would continue to have freedom of choice as guaranteed by the Constitution. Two years later, there was a series of meetings at school; a committee was to decide which areas of the college would be "smoke free" and which would prohibit cigarette smoking. We are a state college in New Jersey, and a tough antismoking law was going on the books statewide, particularly aimed at public buildings. In 1987, we will celebrate an important anniversary of the national Constitution, the First Amendment of which guarantees our rights as citizens. It seems somewhat ironic that New Jersey should put together such stiff antismoking legislation on the eve of that anniversary—and so close to the passing of the Orwellian Year. Granted, taking away smoking privileges in certain areas of the college may seem small potatoes in the general arena of "censorship," but the new state legislation is a tiny part of a more disturbing national trend that deserves a closer look.

We do not have (in this country or any other) the "right" to smoke. There is far too much talk about "rights" these days, and precious little talk about responsibilities. We do, however, have the right to choose our pleasures and our personal habits, provided these pleasures and habits do not infringe on others. Those who would put antismoking legislation packages into effect would argue that cigarette smoking can be harmful to nonsmokers as well as smokers—the "passive smoker" argument that comes up so frequently. But I would argue that I live in New Jersey—a state with a very high cancer rate, a state brimming with toxic waste, a polluted pocket of the Northeast. Smokers are not responsible for these problems in this state, and yet we fight and fight every year for "Superfund" money and grants for "cleanup" programs to reduce the risks and dangers of living here. The "pollution" cigarette smokers add to this already disabled state is nothing compared to what we deal with in industrial fumes and waste. Also, I do not order buses off the road, though their fumes make me cough and choke when I have to drive behind them. I do not request an Act of Congress to ban people from wearing strong perfumes and after-shaves that "invade my air." When smokers obey the laws regarding smoking, and do not smoke in "prohibited" areas, no "harm" is done to nonsmokers. Responsible smokers deserve some peace and quiet in their "pursuit of happiness."

The tobacco industry deserves the same kind of peace and quiet that responsible smokers are entitled to. If we are guaranteed the freedom of speech by the First Amendment, then the tobacco industry is certainly acting within its rights to advertise without fear of censorship. As far as TV advertising goes, though, it is already too late, since cigarette advertising has long been banned from the TV screen. Big Brother has banished tobacco advertising from TV, as he may perhaps do to beer and wine advertising in the future. Print and billboard ads still make their way into the American culture for tobacco products, but always accompanied by the Surgeon General's warning (which also appears on every pack of cigarettes). If the tobacco industry is willing to act responsibly, presenting this warning in each ad and on every pack of cigarettes, then it has earned the "right" to advertise at will, without fear of censorship. Anyone over the age of five who does not know about the Surgeon General's warning quite possibly lives in a cave. How much more responsibly can any industry behave?

The argument runs that advertising affects and influences people, and indeed it does; therefore, people should not be "influenced" to indulge in a potentially dangerous practice (cigarette smoking). That same argument is being applied to beer and wine advertisements on TV. In fact, that argument is often applied to TV in general, which has become the scapegoat for every personal and social problem our country faces. There are those who have lobbied (successfully) for a ban on cigarette ads on TV; there are those who are now lobbying for a ban on beer and wine commercials. And there have long been those who have lobbied for different kinds of TV programming. These people are the self-appointed "protectors" of others. I see these people as disciples of a Big Brother mentality, people who talk, talk, talk about "rights" and "protection" when in actuality they are potential censors. Who are these people to impose their values and their brand of "morality" on others? Who are these self-righteous tastemakers of the market economy?

To try to stop any lawful business from advertising their products in the media is a dangerous form of censorship. Where does it end? We already have the "Smoke Police" who would ban all cigarette smoking everywhere in the name of "health" and "rights of nonsmokers," when they do not consider the rights of American business. For better or worse, our economy is based in capitalism. I have never been the champion of capitalism, nor have I been known to defend the interests of business. However, I realize and I understand that the culture and the society we live in condones and encourages capitalistic exchange. And I certainly shudder at the thought of an Orwellian future, which may be where we are heading if we don't stop the censorship now.

Who are these people to impose their values and their brand of "morality" on others?

Potentially, any product seen "unfit" by any person with a gift for dealing in loaded words and sweeping generalizations could be a target for censorship. The "Smoke Police" have already won a number of battles. Will the "Beer Police," "Wine Police," and "Programming Police" emerge victorious, too? Of course I will grant that any American has the right to voice his own opinion on any given subject, but he should keep his mouth shut until he has carefully thought out not only his position, but the reasons he holds that position. What does one have to gain by trying to ban any form of advertising? No one is forced to buy any advertised product. And if we are "victims" of any kind of advertising, then we are victims of our own making—we may think through the "message" of any ad, we may discern the techniques used by advertisers to get our business—if (and only if) we are willing to take the time and the trouble to do so. Those who would argue that the advertising of "harmful" products may influence children are using an argument that I cannot accept. Children have parents and teachers to explain the effects of certain products on them—no stranger has the "right" (or the responsibility) to usurp the responsibilities of the parents, just as no Big Brother has the "right" (or responsibility) to tell adults how to live and what to do when it comes to advertising or buying products.

The "public watchdogs" who would ban advertising of any product because of its potential influence on children are using an argument that has been applied time and time again to TV programming; and I'm not sure that argument holds water. I grew up on TV, as did my friends. I watched (and still watch) hours and hours of "Three Stooges" reels; somehow, though, I never had the urge to hit my sisters over the head with lead pipes, stuff a turkey with a live parrot, or pretend to be a plumber when I wasn't. Children can separate fantasy from reality, and children can separate TV programs from commercials. Besides, children are much more influenced by the example of their parents than they are by anything they see or read in the media. How many studies have been funded, for example, to prove the truism that children who see their parents read will read more than children who do not? Will potential Big Brothers next try to censor the actions of parents? Actually, to accomplish their goals, they may want to try that suggestion, since it certainly would be more effective than banning advertising for certain products.

Children have parents and teachers to explain the effects of certain products to them—no stranger has the "right" (or the responsibility) to usurp the responsibilities of the parents. . . .

There are many advertisements in print and electronic media that I find much more offensive than I ever found cigarette ads to be. I am frankly embarrassed by ads for douche, tampons, mini-pads, and all the other paraphernalia of so-called "feminine hygiene" than I am by tobacco ads. And I feel that if the potential censors are looking for a real area to explore, they may want to try the nonprescription drug advertisements. And I do not like the current explosion of "Televangelism" on the airwaves, either. However, just because I do not like (or approve of, or endorse) such areas does not mean I want to censor or ban them. I believe that in a culture such as ours, those products or services that do not fill some need tend to disappear on their own. As long as people are buying and using such products and services, they will continue to appear in the media—as long as self-appointed civic "guardians" of public taste do not lobby to take them away. No one has the "right" to take away whatever fills some need to some people—provided it is not proven harmful to others, and provided the advertisers or the suppliers are acting legally.

A tobacco advertising ban would not really hurt the tobacco industry, as far as I can see, since there are people who smoke, and since there will continue to be people who smoke. I am not worried about the tobacco industry itself, since it fulfills a need in our culture. My worry goes much deeper than the tobacco industry. I worry that if the "Smoke Police" gain any more victories, they will not stop with tobacco, or beer, or wine. Perhaps they will then turn to the nonprescription drug industry, and I won't be able to get aspirin without a costly visit to a doctor. Perhaps they will turn to the coffee industry, and become the "Caffeine Police." Once any product faces a ban on advertising, the works are set in motion, and a certain inertia takes over. The public may begin to accept the idea of censorship, convinced by "public spirited" and "health conscious" propaganda that it is being done "for their own good." People may begin to feel that it is not so bad to let others do their "thinking" for them. Therefore, my concern is not for the tobacco industry itself, or any particular business, or even for American business, but for the idea that Americans may begin to accept the idea of censorship—and even approve of it (or at least not object to it).

We are indeed fortunate that we live in a culture where we are not only allowed, but expected, to make choices every day of our lives. And although we do not have any particular "right" to our choices, we certainly have every "right" to make them. We also have many responsibilities, though, since there are no rights without responsibilities. And one priority we must keep in mind is that we cannot afford to let others do our thinking for us. The Orwellian nightmare is a vision we should keep in front of us, so that we can ensure it stays in the province of literature. Self-appointed (and self-important) Big Brothers are everywhere around us. We see those who would censor rock and pop music and music videos right now; those who have banned the advertising of condoms from network TV (and this in the teeth of record cases of sexually transmitted diseases); those who have banned the advertising of tobacco products on TV.

Although my students thought that the Orwellian vision could never happen here, I think parts of it have, in small ways, already come to pass. We are nearing the celebration of two hundred years of the American Constitution, so this seems to be an appropriate time to identify the Big Brothers among us, and censure them—so that they will not be able to censor anything more.

Philip C. Jackson
Albuquerque, New Mexico

*Occupation: Retired Jockey, Control Clerk—Social
Security*
*Interests: Reading, writing, horse racing, study of
thoroughbred racehorse pedigrees, acting as an agent
in the buying and selling of quality bloodstock*
*Entered the Competiton because: "I really believe
that government regulation has gone too far, and it is
time to let the marketplace express the will of the
people."*

In 1798, barely seven years after the Bill of Rights was adopted as part of the Constitution, the Alien and Sedition Acts were passed as law. This law made political dissent against government policy as dangerous as if there were no First Amendment.

FREEDOM FALLING: DECLINE OF THE FIRST AMENDMENT

"Like fire. . . . A dangerous servant . . . a fearful master." George Washington used those words to describe government when this nation was founded. Two hundred years later a tiny spark has become a roaring inferno; protecting and preserving has expanded to regulating and restraining. And the questions are: Do we survive because of government regulations, or in spite of them? Shall we extinguish or contain the blaze, or be consumed by it? And shall we allow the government to control the advertising medium, or shall we stand behind the First Amendment?

The First Amendment is the guaranteed right we all share to have freedom of religion, freedom of speech or of the press, and the right of the people peaceably to assemble and to petition the government for a redress of grievances.

The Bill of Rights is what Thomas Jefferson and James Madison worked so hard to include in this declaration of the rights of man. They include what John Adams called "rights derived from the Great Legislator of the Universe." Thomas Jefferson said many times, "A Bill of Rights is what the people are entitled to, against every government on earth, general or particular, and what no just government should refuse or rest on inference."

Censorship of expression by the government has been a problem to individuals and businesses from almost the inception of the Bill of Rights. In 1798, barely seven years after the Bill of Rights was adopted as part of the Constitution, the Alien and Sedition Acts were passed as law. This law made political dissent against government policy as dangerous as if there were no First Amendment. The Act punished, by fine and imprisonment, anyone who uttered, wrote, or published "any false scandalous and malicious [speech] against the government of the United States."

Thomas Jefferson was elected president in 1800 and upon the expiration of the Sedition Act on March 3, 1801, he immediately pardoned everyone who had been convicted under it and Congress soon repaid most of the fines levied by it. Jefferson had earlier called the Sedition Act an unconstitutional "reign of terror." James Madison, in reference to the passing of the Alien and Sedition Acts, said it "ought to produce universal alarm because it is levelled against the right of freely examining public characters and measures, and of free communication among the people thereon, which has ever been justly deemed the only effectual guardian of every other right."

Madison went on to ask a basic question: "Is then the federal government destitute of every authority for restraining the licentiousness of the press, and for shielding itself against the libellous attacks which may be made on those who administer it?"

Madison answered his own question by saying, "The answer must be that the federal government *is* destitute of all such authority. The censorial power is in the people over the government, not in the government over the people."

One hundred and thirty-two years later, in 1931, the state of Minnesota came down against Mr. Jay M. Near, publisher. At the core of this case was the so-called Minnesota Gag Law (1925), which allowed the state to temporarily or permanently shut down a publication held to be "a public nuisance."

Jay M. Near, after having been beaten twice by lower courts, was awarded a favorable decision by the Supreme Court. "It is difficult to see," said Supreme Court Justice Louis Brandeis, "how one is to have a free press. . . without the [First Amendment] privilege this Minnesota Act seems to limit. You are dealing here with a scandal that ought to be a matter of prime interest to every citizen."

Oliver Wendell Holmes, in 1919, said, "Congress certainly cannot forbid *all* effort to change the mind of the country." Holmes went on,

> The best test of truth is the power of the thought to get itself accepted in the competition of the market. . . . That at any rate is the theory of our Constitution. [italics added]
>
> It is an experiment, as all life is an experiment. . . . While that experiment is part of our system, I think that we should be eternally vigilant against attempts to check the expression of opinions that we loathe and believe to be fraught with death, unless they so imminently threaten immediate interference with the lawful and pressing purpose of the law that an immediate check is required to save the country.

In 1971 *The New York Times* published the first of a series of articles based on a secret Defense Department history of America's involvement in Vietnam.

On June 15, 1971, an assistant United States attorney in New York asked in court that a temporary restraining order be issued barring the *Times* from going on with the series. Federal District Judge Murray Gurfein granted the order, the first time in American history that a federal judge had prohibited a newspaper from publishing a specific article or series of articles.

On June 30, 1971—only fifteen days after the government had first moved to censor the *Times*—the Supreme Court gave its decision.

Noting that censorship, in any form, is directly opposed to the First Amendment and is therefore unlawful, the Supreme Court instructed the *Times* (and the *Washington Post*) to go ahead and print the rest of the material.

Justice Hugo Black, in 1978, regarding the First Amendment said:

Since the earliest days, philosophers have dreamed of a country where the mind and spirit of man would be free; where there would be no limits to inquiry; where men would be free to explore the unknown and to challenge the most deeply rooted beliefs and principles.

Our First Amendment was a bold effort to adopt this principle—to establish a country with no legal restrictions of any kind upon the subjects people could investigate, discuss, and deny. The Framers knew, better perhaps than we do today, the risks they were taking. With this knowledge they still believed that the ultimate happiness and security of a nation lies in its ability to explore, to change, to grow, and ceaselessly to adapt itself to new knowledge born of inquiry, free from any kind of governmental control over the mind and spirit of man.

Attempts by various governmental agencies have continued through two centuries to censure either individual or corporate interests. All such attempts have either been ruled unconstitutional or are unresolved.

Government intervention into the area of private business operating in a seeming free market economy is frightening to say the least. Regulation upon regulation, many even contradictory, are the enemy of the American businessman rather than his protector.

Regulations, or the threat of regulations, have the businessman scared of his own shadow. In 1975 the National Cancer Institute reported that the solvent trichloroethylene, known as TCE, might be a cancer-causing substance. At that time TCE was used in decaffeinated coffee. The government agency doing the testing used an exorbitant dose of TCE on the test animals. The prescription called for the mice in the laboratory to drink the equivalent of a human drinking 50 million cups of decaffeinated coffee every day for an entire lifetime. As extreme as these "research" parameters were, the coffee industry did not fight the validity of the results. Word of the "cancer-causing" ingredient caused a panic among coffee drinkers, and the industry responded by immediately changing ingredients. A tobacco company, R.J. Reynolds, fought for the right to have both sides of the story told when they questioned the "scientific" evidence presented against tobacco use. They wanted to use newspaper advertising challenging the scientific validity of the studies. The Federal Trade Commission, however, shot them down when it ruled that such ads should be banned because they mislead and defraud consumers. They have decided for us; we will not be able to hear both sides and decide for ourselves. The "protector" is restraining our freedom of choice.

What will happen in America when the American Medical Association gets its way and tobacco advertising is banned? Smokers will continue to smoke and nonsmokers will continue to scream foul. If by some miracle the AMA decides to play the game fairly, without the help of Uncle Sam, it might have a chance to win through the use of tough competition. America is the home of very tough people who respect a good fight. If the medicine men want to win this game of life or death let them get their word out into the marketplace and COMPETE.

The AMA may have a completely legitimate position, but the only way to find out is by testing their product in the field, without the help of government regulations. Americans by and large are very intelligent people who can make their own decisions concerning health. This is not to say that they should not be made aware of both sides of an issue. They indeed should.

America is the greatest land on earth and she has achieved that recognition by being a land of a total free market economy. Is it not time to back away from excessive government control and return to that free market?

An advertising ban on tobacco would not alone save lives. If it would, then an advertising ban on automobiles would have to be the next item for lawmakers to consider. Some thirty-nine percent of deaths to persons between the ages of fifteen and twenty-four were caused by automobiles in the years between 1960 and 1980. Whereas deaths in the same age group caused by cancer totaled five percent during those same years ('60 to '80). It would appear that the young people of America have more to fear than smoke.

294

If an advertising ban is passed, a precedent would be established. This opens the door for all special interest groups to limit commercial press. When an individual or group felt threatened by any product or service, this precedent would encourage further censure. The costs to industry and eventually to the public could be astounding. Fear of censure and the costs to fight it for the right to market a product could in time limit the risks both large and small businesses are willing to take. For us the consumers that will mean a dwindling number of choices in products and services at higher costs.

Let us stand and fight here, no matter how we feel about tobacco use; for it is we, each citizen, who ultimately pay the excessive cost of government intervention.

This article was begun with questions. The answers to those questions lie within each of us. Let's extinguish the blaze of regulation before it damages the First Amendment.

Self-restraint, not regulation, is the key, whether it be driving too fast, smoking too much or eating too much. Excessive amounts of any of these things can cause harm or even death but when handled with caution they can be good.

Ours is the greatest government in the world and will continue to be the greatest, as long as we let it do the job of governing and not try to force it to listen without question to the many special interest groups, like the AMA. Let us stand and fight here, no matter how we feel about tobacco use; for it is we, each citizen, who ultimately pay the excessive cost of government intervention.

Susan Marie Szasz
Ithaca, New York

Occupation: Librarian
Interests: Swimming, knitting, cooking
Entered the Competition because of: "A fervent
interest in defending and protecting individual
liberties in the face of government intervention."

> There is bitter irony in the targeted product, tobacco—a plant of American origin and one of the mainstays of the American economy from colonial days to the present.

ADVERTISING TOBACCO: FREE EXPRESSION IN A FREE SOCIETY

The ban on advertising tobacco products currently being considered in Congress violates our ideal of freedom—political, economic and personal. It is an attempt to interfere not only with the free flow of goods, but also with the free flow of ideas. In addition, there is bitter irony in the targeted product, tobacco—a plant of American origin and one of the mainstays of the American economy from colonial days to the present.

The hypocrisy inherent in the proposal to ban advertising tobacco runs deep and wide, and reflects ambivalent attitudes toward the conflicts between freedom and health, prosperity and security. The production of tobacco is thus considered to be healthy for the American economy, but its use unhealthy for the American people. Such conflicts are, of course, not unusual in human affairs. In a country founded on individual liberty, the founding fathers tried to reconcile the economic advantages of slavery with its ethical evils. Today, our lawmakers are trying to reconcile price supports for tobacco growers and tax receipts from tobacco products with warnings about the health risks of smoking.

How is it possible, despite the clear language of the First Amendment, that many important individuals and institutions—former President Jimmy Carter and the American Medical Association among them—now agitate for the prohibition of advertising tobacco products? A brief review of the major controversies surrounding the American love/hate relationship with free expression may help to answer this question.

The men who framed the Constitution of the United States were keenly aware of the irresistible temptation of rulers to oppress those over whom they rule. History had shown that the powerful tend to seek glory by tyrannizing the weak, while the powerless tend to seek security by submitting to the strong. Possessed by a noble vision of human beings

299

endowed by their Creator with inalienable rights and responsibilities, the founding fathers set themselves the formidable task of fashioning a new political order: that is, a system of government expressly designed to safeguard both individual liberty, by protecting people from the ruler's despotism, and personal responsibility, by protecting them from the ruler's paternalism. While much of the original Constitution addresses this lofty ideal of minimal government and maximal individual liberty, nowhere is this more clearly stated than in the First Amendment.

The First Amendment begins with the command that "Congress shall make no law" against the inviolable rights of freedom of speech, press, religion and assembly. Although this may sound straightforward, the fact is that ever since its inception the First Amendment has been so expanded and contracted that it is a wonder there is any meaning left to it at all. Fortunately, the sentiments it enshrines are so highly valued that the principle of free expression has endured innumerable attacks. Among the latest of these is the proposal in Congress to prohibit advertising tobacco products, known as its Health Protection Act of 1986.

Let us recall that the freedoms specified in the First Amendment were added to the Constitution not so much in order to secure the views shared by the majority, but rather in order to safeguard the unpopular beliefs of a minority or, potentially, of a single person. Such seemingly undue attention to odd or peculiar ideas became necessary once men began to take seriously the revolutionary notion that neither church nor state could be looked upon as a guarantor of what constitutes truth or falsehood. In a free society, as John Stuart Mill stated, "We can never be sure that the opinion we are endeavoring to stifle is a false opinion; and if we were sure, stifling it would be an evil still."* Freedom of speech must then include what some are bound to regard as the abuse of speech. A modern joke, revealingly of Russian origin, captures this point perfectly: An American is trying to explain to a Russian one of the most important differences between the two countries. "We have freedom of speech," he says; "you don't." Replies the Russian: "I don't think you understand the differences between our countries at all. You see, we have freedom *of* speech too; but you also have freedom *after* speech."

Although governmental restraints on free expression appear to be absolutely prohibited by the First Amendment, limitations on its umbrella of protection began to emerge soon after its enactment in 1789. Less than a decade later, in 1798, Congress passed the first law

* John Stuart Mill, *On Liberty*. (London: John W. Parker and Son, 1859), Chapter II, "Of the liberty of thought and discussion," p. 34.

against seditious libel, forbidding the writing, printing or uttering of any false or malicious words against the government. While it would be hard to imagine a law more inimical to both the spirit and letter of the First Amendment, the Supreme Court waited more than a century to address the constitutional issues involved. In thus temporizing, the Court exhibited behavior emblematic of our collective ambivalence: We want individual liberty to think and speak freely *and* governmental protection from the burden of having to sort out, for ourselves, truth from falsehood, good advice from bad. Such indecision has resulted in confusion: Some of our laws and social practices uphold the value of free speech, others, the value of suppressing it. Again suppressing it, Congress passed the first obscenity law in 1842, thereby commencing attempts to carve out another category of unprotected expression. Mushrooming in the late 1800s with the passage of the Comstock Act, this wave of hysteria continued into the twentieth century, and led to the banning of many literary works now considered to be classics.

In its focus on sedition, obscenity and libel, the Supreme Court identified types of speech unworthy of First Amendment protection. Paradoxically, at the same time, the Court also began to expand what might, to the founding fathers, have seemed the proper boundaries of the First Amendment: By categorizing certain types of *conduct* as *symbolic speech*, the Court placed under the umbrella of the First Amendment nonverbal behaviors such as refusal to salute the flag, wearing black armbands to protest the war in Vietnam, and certain types of picketing. Apparently responding to popular fashions, the Supreme Court increases personal self-determination in one area and diminishes it in another. For example, while the Court extended First Amendment protection to symbolic speech on the one hand, it found another form of expression to constrain: "purely commercial advertising." Thus, in 1942, the Court found no First Amendment protection for an entrepreneur, one F. J. Chrestensen, distributing handbills on the street to advertise admission to an old submarine, or, in 1951, for the door-to-door sales of magazines.

The history of attempts to restrict First Amendment rights is replete with examples of the difficulties—nay, the absurdities—that such efforts inevitably entail. Unable to define obscenity, the justices nonetheless went forth claiming to "know it when they see it." Not surprisingly, the Supreme Court has found the problem of what constitutes commercial speech no less challenging than the problem of what constitutes sexual speech—especially when the two go together. The result has been a series of unprincipled, ad hoc decisions. Thus, since the 1970s, the Court has accorded First Amendment protection to

301

advertisements not only for contraceptives but also for abortions (a procedure that, only a few years earlier, was a criminal offense). On the other hand, and despite the brazen state-sponsored encouragement of gambling via state-sponsored lotteries, the Court, in July of 1986, upheld the right of the government of Puerto Rico to severely restrict advertising for privately-sponsored casino gambling. It seems the justices have overlooked the core of the First Amendment, indeed of our system of representative government as a whole: that is, the presumption of personal autonomy. Thomas Jefferson made this premise explicit when he observed that "it is an insult to our citizens to question whether they are rational beings or not. . . ."* Today's advocates of prohibiting tobacco advertising insist on insulting us in precisely this way.

Thomas Jefferson observed that "it is an insult to our citizens to question whether they are rational beings or not. . . ." Today's advocates of prohibiting tobacco advertising insist on insulting us in precisely this way.

The mischief of the Supreme Court's ruling restricting advertising for casino gambling is magnified by the realization that the justices' selection of which cases to hear panders to prevailing prejudices: There are countless products and activities as distasteful or dangerous as gambling—escort services, public bath houses, X-rated movies, motorcycles and hunting rifles—which continue to be advertised. Indeed, we are even treated to advertisements for products intended solely to obstruct the enforcement of criminal laws, such as radar detectors and samples of "clean urine."

Time and again our politicians profess to know not only what is best for themselves, but what is best for the rest of us—rather than, as the founders intended, the other way around. Once we accept the principle that it is the government's duty to protect us from health risks, we must also accept the consequences of this paternalistic expansion of state authority at the expense of personal autonomy: In the name of health, any self-regarding act of even questionable harm could be regulated. We have, in fact, already started down this slippery slope. Moreover, as the justices of the Supreme Court choose which forms of expression to exclude from First Amendment protection, so do our lawmakers choose which forms of conduct to regulate, prohibit or

---

* Thomas Jefferson, "Letter to Monsieur N. G. Dufief," April 19, 1814, in *The Writings of Thomas Jefferson,* edited by Andrew A. Lipscomb and Albert Ellery Bergh. (Washington, D.C.: The Thomas Jefferson Memorial Association, 1903), v. 14, p. 127.

ignore. Thus we have "drug laws" and laws mandating the use of seat belts and motorcycle helmets, but we are free to engage in dangerous sports such as boxing, hang gliding, or race car driving, or in dangerous habits such as consuming junk foods or saccharin-laced soft drinks.

While all concessions to political authority are clear encroachments on personal freedom and responsibility, the outright regulation or prohibition of a particular activity or product at least can be plainly recognized for what it is—namely, overt behavior control. It would seem then that *if*, as citizens in a free society, we decide to grant paternalistic power to our government to determine whether tobacco is good or bad for us, and *if* our government decides that protection of public health requires a tobacco-free society, then the "democratically" honest solution would be a total ban on the production, sale and use of tobacco. But the logical answer is not necessarily politically correct. We thought otherwise with alcohol, and need not be reminded of the failure of that "noble experiment."

Obviously, the pleasures of smoking tobacco and the profits of cultivating it are too dear to us all, citizens and legislators alike. "Nothing so needs reforming," remarked Mark Twain, "as other people's habits."[*] Recognizing this situation, but nonetheless insistent on meddling in matters where it has no business, Congress has proposed a seemingly less intrusive means for controlling the use of tobacco—that is, banning its advertising. This raises two important questions: First, will such a ban achieve its avowed goal of reducing tobacco consumption? Second, is a ban on tobacco advertising less dangerous for our personal liberties than a ban on tobacco products?

Our own experience with a limited ban on advertising tobacco on broadcast media, and experiments in other countries with more extensive bans, afford ample evidence for a negative answer to the first question. In the United States, cigarette advertising has been banned from television and radio since 1971; during the same period, and despite a large price increase, the per capita consumption of cigarettes has remained nearly constant. The evidence from Western Europe is similar: With advertising banned, Norway has seen little change in the per capita consumption of cigarettes, while Italy has witnessed a large rise. In the United Kingdom, where cigarette advertising is permitted, consumption has fallen steadily since the 1960s. Finally, in the Communist-bloc nations—hardly appropriate models for us to follow in matters respecting economics or freedom—where tobacco advertising has been banned for decades, consumption has risen steadily and dra-

[*] Mark Twain, *Pudd'nhead Wilson*. (Hartford, Ct.,: American Publishing Company, 1894), p. 197.

matically. Surely it is relevant also to note that lack of advertising has not hampered the widespread use of illegal drugs in the United States.

But what about the second question: Can we afford, in a free society, to accept the political paternalism underlying a ban on tobacco advertising? Those who now argue that such a ban is justified to discourage smoking and to shield the American people from false or misleading advertising have apparently forgotten that "it is error alone which needs the support of the government. Truth can stand by itself."* It is important to keep in mind that this memorable phrase of Jefferson's refers to "truth" and "error"—notions relevant only with respect to *verifiable propositions*. For example, the assertion that "a glass pitcher is less fragile than a plastic one" may be said to be true or false. But the recommendation, "buy glass pitchers. . ." —followed by justifications ranging from appearance to price—cannot be said to be either true or false; it can—depending on the content of the message and perhaps the charisma of the person proclaiming it—only be said to be persuasive or unpersuasive. In short, while descriptive propositions can be said to be true or false, prescriptive propositions can only be said to be convincing or unconvincing. This is why, especially in a pluralistic society such as ours, it is inconceivable that anyone could advance a recommendation for a particular action without evoking some objection by someone else. In sum, although the proposed ban on tobacco advertising may, at first glance, appear to be a subtle, inoffensive form of behavior control, more careful scrutiny reveals it to be an offensive form of mind control.

Although the proposed ban on tobacco advertising may, at first glance, appear to be a subtle, inoffensive form of behavior control, more careful scrutiny reveals it to be an offensive form of mind control.

Compromises between individual liberty and state authority are of course necessary, even in the freest of societies. Well aware of the need to make such choices, Jefferson once remarked: ". . . and were it left to me to decide whether we should have a government without newspapers, or newspapers without a government, I should not hesitate a moment to prefer the latter."† Paraphrasing Jefferson, we must now choose between the perils of advertising and the perils of government—or, more simply, between balancing the risks of freedom to advertise

* Thomas Jefferson, *Notes on Virginia*, in *op. cit.*, v. 2, p. 222.
† Thomas Jefferson, "Letter to Colonel Edward Carrington," January 16, 1787, in *op. cit.*, v. 6, pp. 57–58.

against the risks of government censorship. The struggle for permitting or prohibiting advertising tobacco must thus be seen for what it is as well as for what it is not. It is not a struggle for truth or health; instead it is a struggle for free participation in the marketplace of goods, services—and ideas.

William A. Bake

Boone, North Carolina

Occupation: Photographer
Interests: Travel
Entered the Competition because of: "Concern
about erosion of constitutional freedoms."

The Appalachian farmers who market their tobacco at Big Burley in Boone are only doing what they've always done, what their fathers and grandfathers did. . . . Yet in the name of public safety, the whole chain is threatened.

FIRST AMENDMENT FREEDOMS AND BUSINESS

Frost lies heavily on the hills, looking almost like snow, but the battered pickups are already lining up at the huge door of the Big Burley Warehouse. It is November—the 19th to be exact—and a way of life, an annual ritual, is underway in Boone, North Carolina. From Dark Hollow, Vilas, Sands, Foscoe and dozens of other Appalachian communities, farmers are bringing the tobacco in.

These are people for whom raising tobacco has been a family tradition for generations. It isn't just the money they'll get that matters to them—you can see that from the way the tobacco has been dried, sorted and arranged for display. They are as proud of their product as a stonemason, a fence builder or any craftsman might be. Whole families come, and when the tobacco is finally stacked on the dirt floor of the cavernous warehouse, the men await the buyers and the women wander over to Smithey's Department Store to look at overalls and shoes.

America doesn't say much about these quiet people—those who keep to themselves, producing what others of us consume—so you might not notice what happens at the Big Burley or thousands of other huge old wooden tobacco warehouses like it, but without these ageless rituals and the people who live them, the rest of us would falter. Because they are the foundation of America, rock-solid, and taken too much for granted.

The Appalachian farmers who market their tobacco at Big Burley in Boone are only doing what they've always done, what their fathers and grandfathers did. They would seldom describe themselves as unsung heroes, but they are as much a part of America as the newsmakers—including the well-intentioned professional public guardians whose goals might be safety and security rather than community and continuity.

From farm to warehouse, from factory to consumer, tobacco depends as much on marketing as it does on the soil that nurtures it. Yet

309

in the name of public safety, the whole chain is threatened. Government would restrict the advertising of tobacco, believing in the justice of its actions as much as the mountain farmers believe in what they have always done.

Such a small nation; such a huge nation. We can cross it in four hours, but we fail to understand and tolerate the diversity that gives us a collective strength matched by no other nation. And through this lack of understanding, those with education and influence strive to create and enforce regulations which they believe will make this a better, stronger land. But in doing so they weaken the foundation—the unseen America—which few of them have ever seen firsthand.

Wisdom, the kind not swayed by short-term political goals and well-intentioned miscalculation, is needed. We look for clear and careful thinking in government, find it in the Constitution, and then must sometimes depend on our judiciary system to protect it from officials who are convinced that their objectives outrank the Constitution. So in the final analysis tobacco farmers from Dark Hollow and Foscoe are linked with Supreme Court justices in Washington. It is an alliance upon which each depends, and it must be preserved.

The issue is basic. Advertising is information, and when it is restricted, the chance to be right or wrong, to succeed or fail, to remain ignorant when offered information or to grow through knowledge, is denied us. Realizing the importance of information, the founders of our nation dealt with it in the First Amendment to the Constitution:

> Congress shall make no law respecting an establishment of religion, or prohibiting the free exercise thereof; or abridging the freedom of speech, or of the press; or of the right of the people peaceably to assemble, and to petition the Government for a redress of grievances.

Like many parts of the Constitution, the First Amendment is open to interpretation. One person's free speech may be another's subversion, blasphemy, or obscenity. Almost as soon as the ink was dry on the First Amendment, laws were passed by Congress and the states that restricted freedom of expression. Sedition acts limited political dissent. Other laws dealt with blasphemy—speaking out against Christianity—and though little suppression was actually attempted in this area, a related area—obscenity—has been the object of many laws and court decisions.

Seen across the years, there has been a trend beginning with relatively less freedom and then, in this century, an awakening of the idea that protection should be given to freedom of expression. But within the trend there are uneven developments. In brief, some forms of expression have received less protection than others. "Commercial speech," or advertising, is one of them.

Legally, advertising was long treated as if it were unimportant to the functioning of our system of government. To generations of Americans there were no constitutional principles involved when someone was banned from advertising a product or service. Probably some of this was pure bias—a reaction to preposterous claims once made for patent medicines and miracle machines.

But government is not unbiased. It heeds the popular mood and reads the daily mail. . . . These days it hears the echoes of its own loud campaign to limit tobacco advertising.

In any event, advertising was not considered to be a First Amendment subject and was quickly subjected to regulation as a part of the social reform movement called "muckraking" at the turn of this century. From the beginning of federal control in 1914, only the amount of regulation was questioned. Truth in advertising was the accepted goal, and eradicating the misleading was the continual challenge. Gradually, false advertising ceased to be a major problem.

Once truth became the accepted standard, attention focused on a new question: Can truthful advertising be regulated? If you believe that advertising used cars or over-the-counter pain killers should be protected by the Constitution, this could be an important issue. If you think these are commercial matters deserving less protection, you may be less concerned about regulation of advertising.

The courts—principally the United States Supreme Court—took the latter position until the 1960s, allowing laws that restricted advertising to remain in effect. Then, in 1976, the Court reversed its historic stance, declaring that advertising should receive First Amendment protection. This was the reasoning as stated in *Virginia State Board of Pharmacy v. Virginia Citizens Council* (1976):

So long as we preserve a predominantly free enterprise economy, the allocation of our resources in large measure will be made through numerous private economic decisions. It is a matter of public interest that those decisions, in the aggregate, be intelligent and well informed. To this end, the free flow of commercial information is indispensable.

Of course, as the Court observed, this was not meant to allow all kinds of advertising. Government still has the right to regulate advertising to insure that it "flows cleanly as well as freely." In other words, deception was—and is—prohibited and so is the advertising of illegal products and services. Expanding its decision to let the marketplace serve as the control, the Court has recently extended First Amendment guarantees to corporations as well as individuals.

Advertisers now have a basic right—a First Amendment right—and can be restricted by government only if 1) the government can show the commercial message to be untruthful and related to an illegal activity, 2) the government can show that it has a substantial interest in regulation, 3) the government's proposed regulation will advance its interest, and 4) the regulation is no more extensive than is necessary to accomplish the goals of the government.

Under such circumstances would state or federal government dare restrict truthful advertising displayed in a normally acceptable manner? Could the courts be convinced that any or all of these tests might be met? Certainly not under most conditions. But government is not unbiased. It heeds the popular mood and reads the daily mail—and sometimes even manufactures its own "news." These days it hears the echoes of its own loud campaign to limit tobacco advertising.

America, some fear, may go out wearing seat belts and breathing clean air. And if this happens, the rest of the world will scarcely know it is gone.

Armed with federal reports on smoking and health—including recent studies on the effects of "passive" smoking—government may well feel confident enough to attempt a ban on tobacco advertising that extends beyond the current restriction of ads in the electronic media. But in doing so, it would injure as well as heal.

The point is this: Ours is a society based on information, and so it is crucial that we continue to have the advantage of deciding from an informed viewpoint. In the case of tobacco, as long as the public has access to information about any disadvantages using tobacco might have, it should have equal access to positive information about tobacco products. The right to choose therefore would remain open—and this is very much the essence of being American. Information is a source of strength; without it we would grow lame.

And what about economic effects? In America we tend to buy that which is advertised, in the process creating demands where none existed. Denied access to the marketplace, the tobacco industry would lose its lifeblood, taking with it the pride and independence of farmers,

312

processors and marketers. A way of life that has spanned the generations would vanish. America might be one increment safer to live in, but it would also be a weaker America. Tobacco might eventually follow steel toward foreign shores, and we could find ourselves one step farther along the road toward regulating ourselves into ineffectuality.

Life is to be lived, whether individually or collectively. Ours is a nation that succeeded on taking chances, not in hoarding security. Each time that changes because we are "protected" from our own actions by benevolent government, something in the spirit dies. America, some fear, may go out wearing seat belts and breathing clean air. And if this happens, the rest of the world will scarcely know it is gone.

Judith A. Cummings
Fargo, North Dakota

Occupation: Attorney
Interests: Reading, walking, watching her husband
race his motorcycle
Entered the Competition because: "I had recently
gotten a new computer for my office and wanted an
opportunity to practice using it."

> The health of our system of self-government. . . depends upon the widest possible dissemination of information from diverse and even antagonistic sources.

BAN ON TOBACCO ADVERTISING: ATTEMPT TO GUARD OUR MINDS

A proposal has been made that the advertising of tobacco be banned by the Congress of the United States. Arguments regarding the proposed advertising ban have frequently focused on whether the public interest is served by such a move. To those engaged in debating the public interest, the issue is framed in terms of whether the people want a ban on this particular kind of advertising. The underlying assumption is made that the will of the people can or should determine the issue.

The difficulty with this proposition begins with the fact that the freedom of expression is a right secured by the protections of the First Amendment to the United States Constitution. Freedom of speech and freedom of the press are a part of the network of rights which form the foundation of the American system of self-government. These freedoms are not mere privileges enjoyable only through the grace of a government—not even when that government is a self-government. They are rights which were carefully and deliberately reserved to the people individually at the creation of our system of government.

The framers of the Constitution recognized the inherent rights of free expression and sought to guarantee them by prohibiting interference with these rights by the government. The First Amendment to the Constitution declares the guarantee very clearly: "Congress shall make no law. . . abridging the freedom of speech, or of the press. . . ."

We must remember that the fundamental rights of free expression were not created by the founders of this nation or by the authors of the Constitution. The rights preexisted the protections granted by the Constitution. In recognizing and guaranteeing the existing rights of free expression, the framers sought to protect the point of view of the minority from the tyranny of the will of the majority. The Constitution does this by prohibiting censorship even when the censorship is desired by the majority.

The government is foreclosed from imposing a guardianship of the public mind through regulation or censorship of expression. The rationale is that the health of our system of self-government, and therefore the welfare of the public, depends upon the widest possible dissemination of information from diverse and even antagonistic sources. The late William O. Douglas, as Justice of the United States Supreme Court, analyzed the close relationship between the freedom of expression and the continuation of American self-government. He stated in this regard:

> [E]ffective self-government cannot succeed unless the people are immersed in a steady, robust, unimpeded, and uncensored flow of opinion and reporting which are continuously subjected to critique, rebuttal, and re-examination.

The protection from censorship is not so much for the benefit of the speaker or writer as for the benefit of the listener or reader. The listener or reader takes the information provided and evaluates it. The information becomes a factor in the individual's decision making process. The unimpeded flow of information helps assure the independent decision making that is necessary to the functioning of a government of the people.

Censorship of expression in any sector of American life is unacceptable under the Constitution. The constitutional protection guards equally the impassioned oration of a political candidate and the publication of a grocery store circular. The constitutional guarantee of freedom of expression cannot be disregarded merely because the expression does not appear to be of political importance or of material impact upon the community. Freedom of expression is a right existing without regard to the message expressed.

Commercial speech is entitled to the same protection . . . as other forms of communication, without regard to whether dissemination of the information is under the auspices of an advertising budget.

Since the inherent worth of the expression is in its capacity for informing the public, businesses are entitled to enjoy freedom of expression. This inherent worth is not dependent upon the identity of the source. The free market system requires informed consumers. In order for the widest range of goods and services to be available at the least possible cost, the consumer must have access to the greatest possible amount of information regarding the choices available.

The First Amendment means that the government has no power to restrict expression due to its subject matter or its context. Advertisements by businesses are intended to persuade the reader. The constitutional guarantee does not draw a line between informing the people and seeking to persuade them. Commercial speech is entitled to the same protection from censorship as other forms of communication, without regard to whether dissemination of the information is under the auspices of an advertising budget.

There do exist some controls against specific abuses of the right to free expression. The law can provide redress for those whose privacy has been invaded by someone else's speech. There are laws against libel and slander. In addition, the courts of this nation have found that freedom of expression does not limit the regulation of what is defined as obscenity.

However, the First Amendment does not permit the government to restrict the speech of some elements of society in order to enhance the relative voice of others.

The proposal to ban the advertising of tobacco goes far beyond the narrow confines of these few carefully articulated exceptions to the right of free expression. Tobacco advertising does not invade the privacy of any citizen. It does not libel anyone. It does not meet any definition expounded for obscenity. The ban on tobacco advertising is sought on the basis that the use of tobacco is unhealthy and therefore the use and purchase of tobacco should not be encouraged. The idea is that it is not in the public interest to persuade people, through advertising, to use or purchase tobacco.

Those who wish to limit the use of tobacco in the nation would have an easier burden convincing people of their mission if advertising was banned. However, the First Amendment does not permit the government to restrict the speech of some elements of society in order to enhance the relative voice of others. Congress is not permitted to withhold the rights of the First Amendment merely because it believes the group seeking to exercise those rights is less worthy than another group.

The proposal to censor tobacco advertising is founded on the position that the public must be protected from the message contained in the advertising. The proposal asks that Congress become a guardian of the public mind and protect the public from information that might persuade it. It is difficult to imagine a more direct attack upon the rights of free expression.

William L. Shanklin
Kent, Ohio

Occupation: College Professor
Interests: Jogging, running, spending time with
family
Entered the Competition because: "I feel strongly
that different points of view on any subject—
controversial or otherwise—need to be protected in a
free society. In order to do that, people and
institutions must have freedom of expression of their
viewpoints."

> The legal/illegal dichotomy is an important one. It provides a logical context or way of thinking about business' rights in a free society.

PRESERVING FREEDOMS IN A FREE SOCIETY

According to Penton Publications, the United States, as of 1986, had 35 million laws trying, in Penton's words, "to enforce the Ten Commandments." In 1985, some 3,100 federal regulations were proposed, down from a peak of 5,800 in 1979. But this decline in the federal growth rate was made up for multifold by the state and local governments. In 1986 alone, there were 200,000 state, city and local regulations proposed, which is more than double the number in 1983.

This plethora of legislative activity points to an escalating government involvement in the everyday affairs of the U.S. citizenry and in commerce. It also suggests that many elected officials have little faith in their constituencies to live and let live without a healthy list of *dos* and *don't*s to guide them and circumscribe their behavior. Or to function without extensive protection. This "we know what is best for you" mentality is evident in attempts in the Congress, some federal agencies and certain citizens' groups to totally ban tobacco advertising. Regardless of one's personal opinions about tobacco smoking, and these opinions may be strongly held and streaked with emotion, the tobacco advertising ban issue can be looked at on more objective lines pertaining to government's role in industry regulation, First Amendment rights of business and consumer sovereignty in a free society. That kind of reasoned analysis is the purpose and goal of this essay.

LEGAL VS. ILLEGAL INDUSTRIES

The term "an industry" means the commercial manufacture and/or sale of a specific genre of good or service, such as a computer, television or banking industry. Additionally, an industry can be legal or illegal under the laws enacted by a society. In the United States, for example, most industries operate legally, but a few illegal industries run by organized crime are significant in terms of size, revenues and profits generated.

Which industries in a democratic society are legally sanctioned and which ones are not is determined by the people through their elected representatives and the courts. Across nations, the distinction between what is legal and illegal is often culturally based and subject to change over time. In Moslem countries, many industries legal in other parts of the world are illegal. Even in the more homogenous "Westernized" and industrialized countries there are differences. Professional boxing is now outlawed in Norway and Sweden, but not in most of the rest of Western Europe and the United States, notwithstanding that the American Medical Association and others have repeatedly called for professional boxing's abolition. Whaling is legal in Japan, but widely condemned elsewhere as barbaric.

It is unnecessary to look globally for divergent societal views about whether an industry should be legal or illegal. For instance, in the United States, there are many differences of opinion among the various states, due largely to subcultural diversity. Lotteries and parimutuel betting are big tax revenue producers for some states, but banned entirely in sister states. Alabama recently legalized racetrack gambling, yet Texas turned it down. Nevada alone sanctions prostitution. In some jurisdictions, not wearing an automobile seat belt is illegal, while in others it is lawful. As for changes in the legal versus illegal distinction over time, there are numerous examples. In 1919, the Eighteenth Amendment to the U.S. Constitution prohibited "the manufacture, sale, or transportation of intoxicating liquors. . . for beverage purposes," only to be repealed fourteen years later by the Twenty-first Amendment. In the 1970s, the controversial act of abortion was interpreted by the U.S. Supreme Court to be legal under the Constitution. More currently, the laws and regulations pertaining to the incipient biotechnology industry and new forms of life are in a state of flux.

Over time and between and among cultures, then, the definitions of legal and illegal industries evolve. Sometimes the underlying issues and potential ramifications are so divisive, as in the cases, say, of nuclear power, marijuana, pornography and abortion, that a consensus regarding legality or illegality is unlikely in a pluralistic society, let alone across societies and nations with their vastly different religious, moral and ethical precepts.

The legal/illegal industry dichotomy is an important one. It provides a logical context or way of thinking about business rights in a free society.

CONSTITUTIONAL RIGHTS AND PROTECTIONS

Once a democratic society speaks collectively, via its elective actions and judicial renderings, and determines or reaffirms that a particular industry is legal, then that industry is entitled to all the rights, protections, privileges and responsibilities afforded to and required of other legal industries. Indeed, under the Fourteenth Amendment to the U.S. Constitution, a corporation within an industry sanctioned by society is a "legal person," albeit not a citizen who is, for example, entitled to vote. Two of these fundamental rights, protections and privileges—which both flesh-and-blood and legal persons are entitled to enjoy—are clearly identified by Article I of the Bill of Rights: freedom of speech and of press.

Under the Constitution, all corporations and their respective industries are afforded equal protection. More pointedly, all these legal persons are meant to have equal access to First Amendment privileges and protections. Just as a real-life person does not have partial First Amendment protection, while his or her neighbor has full protection, neither does an artificial person in the form of a corporation have partial rights. For anyone to attempt to establish legally that Corporation X has more protection under the First Amendment than Corporation Y is tantamount to working for the recognition of first- and lesser-class entities.

It is undeniably a prerogative of society through representative government to decide if an industry is legal or illegal. However, imagine a system that would allow elected officials, regulatory agencies and the courts to go further in classifying legal industries into categories of acceptability, varying according to each industry's "perceived" value to society. In turn, the industries with the most perceived value to society would have greater constitutional rights than those with less perceived value. Consider what a partial industry listing might look like:

- First Class. Education, medicine and health and fitness.
- Second Class. Computers (very beneficial, but they can be used for abridging citizens' rights as in the Soviet Union), automobiles and airlines (necessary, but they pollute and are involved in many transportation-related deaths) and defense (an essential industry, yet is inherently destructive in purpose).
- Third Class. So-called hedonistic goods and services, alcohol, tobacco and television and other forms of entertainment with potentially deleterious effects. (Television, for instance, has been linked to a growing American illiteracy problem and there have been unsuccessful efforts in the Congress and the relevant regulatory agencies to ban all commercial advertising from children's programming.)
- Fourth Class. Emotionally-charged legal industries, such as nuclear power, pornography, abortion clinics and prostitution in Nevada.

The preponderance of people in a free society would find this kind of formal classification schema to be repugnant. A legally sanctioned caste system for corporations is undesirable for the same philosophical and legal reasons that a legally sanctioned caste system for individuals is antithetical to a free society's ideas about fairness, equity and even-handedness. In the nineteenth century, the War Between the States was fought over Supreme Court decisions like the one rendered in the famous *Dred Scott* case, that slaves were "not intended to be included under the word 'citizen' in the Constitution." Similarly, the hard- and long-fought Nineteenth Amendment enfranchised women to vote and thereby corrected an obvious inequity.

A legally sanctioned caste system for corporations is undesirable for the same ... reasons that a legally sanctioned caste system is antithetical to a free society's ideas. ...

CONSTITUTIONAL RESPONSIBILITIES

As a democratic society of people grants rights, privileges and protections to itself, so too does it expect and require responsible actions from its citizenry and institutions. Freedoms granted to persons by the United States Constitution were not intended to be licenses to engage in unfettered behavior. The Courts have been clear that the First Amendment does not allow one to "yell 'Fire' in a crowded theater." The Federal Trade Commission has the delegated power to challenge commercial advertising claims that may mislead or deceive or are outright untruthful. The U.S. Postal Service has the authority to exclude certain materials from the mails without abridging freedom of expression. Freedom of speech does not allow one to libel another.

In return for the rights and protections of living and working in a free society, both people and institutions are subject to regulation in the public interest. What is in the public interest, of course, is debated and debatable. Consequently, concepts about the public interest and how it is best served evolve with the philosophical composition of elected bodies and the courts, and usually approximate the tenor of the times. Periods of conservatism and liberalism tend to ebb and flow. Still, there are eternal verities that do not change much with the times, notably a pervasive and adamant societal attitude that respects and insists on equal access to First Amendment rights and the protection of dissenting minority opinion from a tyranny by majority thinking and actions.

To take one especially noteworthy example, under the Constitution it is not possible for a government at any level to establish a religion

326

and force it on all citizens. Our forefathers who wrote the Constitution were cognizant of historical abuses of this kind, such as when Charles II and the English Parliament of 1665 passed the Conventicle Act for the purpose of compelling all persons to attend the "established" Church.

Almost all industries are regulated to some degree in the interests of the public and the individual. No one but an anarchist would seriously argue that regulations are not needed at all. However, regulation requires fine tuning between too much and too little. Overregulation in any society stifles entrepreneurship and innovation, and ultimately eviscerates the job-producing and goods/service capabilities of business. It ends up lowering the standard of living. The stagnation of the Soviet economy is a prime example. Yet, underregulation in antitrust, consumer protection and other areas can be risky in a number of important ways, such as monopolization by large business concerns and labor unions and potential harm from products and services to the physical and emotional health of consumers and the public. Certainly, government has the right and responsibility to protect the public interest so long as constitutional rights are not infringed upon in the process.

In the case of goods and services with arguable health consequences, government walks a narrow line between protecting the public and suppressing the constitutional rights of both companies and people. Few would argue against a minimum drinking age for purchasing alcoholic beverages; however, whether that age should be eighteen or twenty-one is hotly debated. Does a federally mandated drinking age of twenty-one protect eighteen-to-twenty-year-old adults or infringe on their rights?

By law, cigarette companies doing business in the United States are prohibited from advertising on television. These firms also must label their products' packages with an unmistakable health warning about the hazards of smoking and prominently place the same caveat in their print advertisements. In addition, numerous restaurants, office buildings, airlines and other public facilities, often per local ordinance, have smoker and nonsmoker sections available. This system is not perfect, but it strikes a democratic balance between accommodating the majority of people who do not smoke and protecting the minority rights of those people who do. It alleviates nonsmokers' concerns about passively inhaling smoke, yet does not abrogate the rights of smokers.

CONSUMER SOVEREIGNTY

Citizens in the United States inherently have had the prerogative of thinking and doing for themselves. They make up their own minds about what books to read, which movies and advertisements to view,

327

what candidates to elect to office and which products and services to purchase.

Their federal government is obligated to perform such tasks as protecting citizens from domestic and foreign belligerents and collecting taxes; on that virtually everyone agrees. It is in the area of "personal choice" and "behavior" that government's interference in matters of the citizenry and institutions becomes far more arguable.

Suppose that the federal government proposed to form review boards to decide what advertisements to permit to be run in the various media. What would be the criteria used to judge each advertisement's redeeming qualities (or lack thereof) and, more importantly, who should sit on the review boards? If an elected or regulatory official proposes censorship of advertising, he or she is often suggesting, at least obliquely, that people are not sufficiently informed and intelligent to evaluate for themselves. Many of the same people who would rail at a literacy criterion as a prerequisite to vote—the basic right in a democracy—have no problem whatsoever in accepting regulative or legislative decisions on the grounds that there are consumers who are not literate enough or bright enough to make up their own minds. Naturally, the Federal Trade Commission and other protective agencies should proceed with vigor and dispatch against deceptive advertising. Moreover, appropriate government officials and bodies should, where the evidence warrants it, require additional information be supplied to the public so that more informed and better quality decisions can be made. The lucid cigarette warning label is a prominent example.

Government cannot legislate morality, ethics, happiness or similar denouements.

After these types of protections are afforded to the public, then it is government's obligation to let people decide for themselves. It is not 35 million laws and countless attorneys, courts and regulatory bodies that make for a continually improved American society. Government cannot legislate morality, ethics, happiness or similar denouements. In fact, government should not try because that is precisely the first step toward the paternalistic approach which inevitably impedes rather than improves human welfare. A host of historical and current global examples in governance stand as ignominious cases in point.

Peter Edwards
Tulsa, Oklahoma

Occupation: Writer

A concept that would otherwise be summarily rejected if presented in its full form and content can be—and often is— sold in smaller, sugarcoated and more digestible portions.

A RECIPE FOR EATING AN ELEPHANT

Among the fondest memories I have of my father was his penchant for using quotations. He was convinced that the great orators, writers and philosophers were far more articulate than he could ever be with his limited immigrant's education. As a result, he would habitually draw on his memory of what he had read of their works, or thought he had read, to prove a point.

Of all the brief excursions into fractured Shakespeare, slightly inaccurate Thomas Paine and bended Lincolnisms he used to focus my attention, one left a lasting impression. I never learned its origin, but it should be engraved in stone in each voting booth of every precinct throughout this country. It went:

Nobody can eat an elephant at one dinner.

If my memory serves me well, he used the expression at the time to impress me with the principle of being patient. Within those few short words, he taught me that a concept that would otherwise be summarily rejected if presented in its full form and content, can be—and often is— sold in smaller, sugarcoated and more digestible portions.

That must be among the very first items that are brought to the attention of any new congressional freshman when he or she arrives in Washington, at least based on the congressional record for following such a formula.

We Americans have eaten elephants throughout our history, but never so much as in the twentieth century.

Anyone old enough to remember the passage of the first income tax law will recall how Congress promised that the rate would never exceed two percent. It was obscene to think that Americans would ever be required to pay more than that figure, or so the headlines read. Furthermore, ". . . only the wealthy would have to pay such a rate," or such was the conventional wisdom then.

When the Sixteenth Amendment was finally passed, the Congress of 1913 must have quietly celebrated. A massive source of revenue had just been made available. All they had to concern themselves with was how to milk it without attracting too much attention. The first course of a huge dinner yet to come had just been served.

Nothing succeeds like success. Future politicians didn't see any good reason why they should reinvent the wheel. Elephant was on the menu again when the Social Security Act was passed in the 1930s.

The Congressional Record clearly establishes that in the debate on the mechanics of administering the new program through the use of assigned numbers, solemn assurances were provided by supporters that use of such numbers would be only limited to the program. Under no circumstances, they said, would they be used as government identification numbers for citizens. This issue was of specific concern among the American people. Many of the nation's population were first-generation immigrants. They still had vivid memories of the totalitarianism they had left in Europe. They still retained a deep-seated and long-standing distrust of government and with good justification. Even a remote implication that such numbers would be used as national identification numbers to identify citizens by a potentially oppressive federal government would have killed the program before it ever saw the light of day.

Anyone old enough to remember the passage of the first income tax law will recall how Congress promised that the rate would never exceed two percent.

Today, Social Security numbers are now assigned routinely as personal military identification numbers, driver's license numbers, tax return numbers, passport numbers and numbers assigned to stock transactions, just to name a few applications of a number that wasn't supposed to be used for those purposes at all. Now, under the provisions of the Tax Reform Act of 1986, every American child over the age of five who is declared as an exemption must have a Social Security number. Such a development is almost inconceivable when the original intent of the program to protect the elderly is considered, or when the original debate is examined. If we reach a point when tattoos are the dessert, we will know that we will have eaten the entire elephant.

Finally, our current Congress knows how to cook, prepare and serve elephant just as well as did their predecessors. Under the provisions of the same act, tax reform was sold to the American people.

Recognizing that they could not increase taxes to keep up with their penchant for spending the money of those who elected them to office, they sold tax reform to the American people by lowering the basic income tax rates. In the process, they abolished a substantial accumulation of deductions. This conveniently gave the impression to the common working man that the new act would soak the rich because they would no longer have a complex tax law's "loopholes" to manipulate to their advantage.

Yet, any competent CPA or tax attorney would be the first to say that this is the first serving of the elephant. With the deductions gone, anyone who believes that future congressional action will not gradually raise income taxes is politically naive.

With Congress' established record of feeding the American public in small increments that which their fellow Americans would not normally swallow, the American voter must be more alert than ever to continued assaults on our freedom and security through the tactic of graduated subterfuge.

I do not smoke. Unlike some of my fellow Americans, I do not object to those who do. What I do object to though is having my intelligence insulted by those who presume to suggest that they know what is best for me better than I do, and who are going to see to it that I benefit from their best judgment.

Congressman Mike Synar (D-Oklahoma) is a classic example of such intellectual arrogance. He is currently attempting through legislation to restrict the right of the tobacco industry to advertise, and thereby restrict my right to make my own decision.

He makes a persuasive argument, because he is articulate, to those who don't realize they are being fed elephant meat a spoonful at a time. He quotes health statistics and implies that the tobacco industry is the personification of the devil incarnate. He insists that only through restricting the right of the tobacco industry to advertise their product can the nation reduce the use of what he terms "a dangerous product when it is used in the manner in which it is intended."

I frankly resent his clear implication that I am not intelligent enough to make my own decisions. But more importantly, I resent being force-fed political elephant meat.

The First Amendment to the Constitution is crystal clear to even a partially literate elementary school dropout. Its operative phrase, "Congress shall make no law. . . abridging the freedom of speech. . . ." leaves no room for vacillation or interpretation. There are no qualifying phrases designed to provide job security for lawyers. There are no hidden terms. There are no ten-penny words that are incomprehensible to the less sophisticated. The words are brilliant in their simplicity, precise, and applied specifically to Congress itself.

Synar and his supporters argue that the same courts have ruled that corporations shouldn't have the same rights as do individuals. But why shouldn't they have the same rights? Legislated protection against harmful products on the open market is one thing, but to legislate against the dissemination of ideas regardless of their source is something else entirely.

The fact is that there is a much larger issue involved than merely a difference of opinion between a few politicians who are milking the headlines for all they can get, and an industry under siege. The real issues are that this is not only another example of unwelcome paternalism on the part of those who "know what is good for the rest of us," but it also possesses the clear potential of being the hors d'oeuvres for another main course of elephant meat.

The real issues are that this is not only another example of unwelcome paternalism . . . it also possesses the clear potential of being the hors d'oeuvres for another main course of elephant meat.

Synar's position on this issue is almost a joke in his home state. The only product meant to be smoked that is raised in his Oklahoma second congressional district is already illegal. Strangely, he doesn't seem to be spending the same amount of energy requesting federal grants for under-funded local, county and state law enforcement agencies to clean up his own district's marijuana plantations. The fact that his district produces more marijuana than the rest of the state combined is a fact that he conveniently avoids mentioning in his attacks on tobacco advertising.

Instead, he claims that tobacco is injurious and only through restricting tobacco advertising will the people be protected. Literally millions of Americans have been killed and maimed in automobile accidents as a direct result of mechanical failures or misuse of automobiles. In fact, more have died on our highways than have died in all of our wars. But does he propose limiting the automobile industry's advertising? What about the drug, aviation, electricity or even the toy manufacturers? Are they next?

We've already gone through Prohibition once. It was an abject failure. Alcohol has virtually no food value. Its sole purpose is as a depressant drug. It deadens the brain cells temporarily and reduces the reactions of the user. As a direct result of alcohol, we bury at least 50,000 Americans every year because someone thought he or she could drink and drive. But does he propose any limit on their advertising? Not yet, at least.

The philosopher George Santayana once observed, "Those who don't know their own history are doomed to repeat the mistakes of previous generations."

Only a fool attempts to predict the future. But the sorry congressional record of feeding Americans an elephant a dinner plate at a time should speak for itself.

Rick Dawson
Salem, Oregon

Occupation: Attorney
Interests: Movies, reading, theater
Entered the Competition because: "I have a strong
belief in the Constitution and the First Amendment
in particular; could I write a short essay in support
of those beliefs and be persuasive?"

THE TOBACCO ADVERTISING BAN—A POLITICAL CONSENSUS OR A SMOKESCREEN FOR INTOLERANCE?

Some of my best friends are liberals. I'm sure some of yours are, too. If not, they are easy to recognize. Liberals are those people who are always trying to protect you from your own vices. Given sufficient political power liberals would outlaw large fuel-inefficient luxury cars, ban cholesterol, and would force everyone to vote. In method they do appear much like conservatives: always desiring to ban or outlaw activities. As such, it's not always easy to tell a liberal from a conservative, especially when each stands on the high road and is trying to do good. Conservatives, though, are not trying to protect the wicked from their own vices but to protect the innocent. As such, conservatives are always trying to protect people from *other people's* vices, or more appropriately, to protect the innocent from the seduction of the vices rampant in society at large. Among these vices are evolution, sex education, secular humanism and communism, all of which would be banned by conservatives if given ultimate power.

It may come as somewhat of a surprise when both conservatives and liberals agree on a particular ban. The proposed ban on cigarette advertising evidences such a conviction by both the right and the left and deserves particular scrutiny. Liberals support the ban as a means for inflicting severe economic distress on an industry they dislike. Liberals would really like to ban smoking itself, but have been unable to muster the political clout to do so. Conservatives, on the other hand, view the ban as a means to protect innocent and vulnerable minds from an otherwise unscrupulous, liberal, sexually titillating mind-control organization called the media. With such political consensus how can the proposed cigarette advertising ban be wrong?

Enter the First Amendment, that constitutional guarantee of free

339

speech. Is the First Amendment a legal bar to the proposed ban? Moreover, *should* it so operate when it would effectively thwart the will of the people?

In the arena of political speech the First Amendment's role is clear. Judges tell us the First Amendment is one of the cornerstones of our democracy side by side with the Madisonian checks and balances, separation of powers and republicanism (I use the word republicanism in its purer political science definition meaning "government by elected officials" and not as it is more commonly used today to describe the Republican party's philosophies.) The First Amendment is designed to create a "marketplace of ideas" where all thoughts can freely be expressed so that an enlightened populace can choose the best ideas, and their spokesmen, to run the government. But the judges have not been able to tell us the role of the First Amendment as it applies to advertising and speech not associated with the political arena. Historically, this "commercial speech" has been given lesser protection and is seen as less desirable than even ordinary political speech.

But commercial speech does have as important a role to play in our free market economic system as political speech has to the operation of government. To the same extent free political speech guarantees that the best ideas and spokespeople are adopted by government, so does free commercial speech guarantee the continuing vitality of our chosen economic system: capitalism. Capitalism, stripped of any negative political connotations, is simply a system based on supply and demand that allocates scarce or finite resources. Capitalism is neither good nor bad, but like most systems has its pluses and minuses. Economists would probably readily agree that at the very least capitalism is the most efficient transfer system. Goods and materials could hardly move any faster, from where they are to where they are needed, than in a free market economy. Unfortunately, the system can be criticized as being unfair because it may result in a disproportionate concentration of wealth in a few individuals. Yet despite this and other faults, capitalism endures in America today. Each generation has adopted and reaffirmed the system, either by passive consent or (in the case of my generation) by out and out embracement of money and wealth and profit. This consent needs to be taken seriously, at least as seriously as our consent to be governed by our republican political system. Because like our political consent, our consent to capitalism means we accept the trade-offs. Our political consent for a government with checks and balances, separation of powers and free speech is a cumbersome, slow and nearly immobile government. It takes years to pass the average bill through Congress. But the benefit resulting from these institutional mechanisms

340

is a stable government unlikely to become either tyrannical or to dissolve into anarchy. In short, the price Americans pay for stable government is slow government. A similar trade-off exists with our adoption of capitalism. The price we pay for an efficient allocation system is unfair accumulation of wealth. And the attempt to ban tobacco advertising brings to light another price of the market economy — the fact that some resources can be squandered, wasted or even used in harmful ways. There's the rub. A free market economy will allow the production of any product so long as there exists a demand for it.

Those who want the tobacco advertising ban understand the principle. The ban on advertising is designed to artificially reduce the demand for tobacco simply because the amount of advertising is proportionally related to the amount of demand for the advertised product. Stop the advertising, stop the demand is the theory. The savings in reduced medical costs and societal obligations might be large, but the costs will be greater. Because any savings, in either the political or economic arenas, at the expense of free speech is not a savings but a liability.

Where does a ban on advertising stop? Is tobacco the only vice worthy of such a measure, or does the advertising of abortion also run afoul of political sensibilities? How about advertising disguised as fundraising for fundamentalist organizations? What legitimate reason is there to protect these forms of advertising once it's okay to ban tobacco advertising?

The First Amendment has a long history of protecting the minority from the majority. The very essence of the amendment's protection lies on a fundamental premise that the citizenry of this country are capable and enlightened enough to distill the worthy speech from the unworthy. In a "marketplace of ideas" the best ideas will eventually achieve a consensus despite having been a minority and radical position originally. Bad speech and bad ideas, on the other hand, will be hotly debated and their "badness" will become evident to all. The First Amendment reflects the understanding that the cure for bad speech is not censorship but more speech. The cure for bad advertising is the same—more advertising. And in probably every way tobacco advertising epitomizes the success of the First Amendment's model. Allegedly harmful advertising for a known harmful product, cigarettes, has been vigorously countered by equally challenging "advertising" from heart and lung associations, the AMA, the Surgeon General and ordinary public service announcements. Why, the Surgeon General even gets to "advertise" on each and every pack of cigarettes sold today about the very hazards of the product inside.

341

And the counteradvertising has been a success. There can't possibly be a smoker in this country who doesn't know smoking is dangerous. Smokers are not ignorant of the dangers; nor are potential smokers like teenagers who go through yearly health classes in school watching morbid films on smoking and lung cancer and death.

But the demand for tobacco continues nonetheless. Those who smoke don't continue to smoke because of the allure of cigarette advertisements, but because they want to. Smokers nowadays are hardcore. It is doubtful whether a legal ban on even the possession of tobacco would seriously discourage smoking habits.

The solution is the same now as it was when our founding fathers debated the First Amendment. Trust to each person to listen, be exposed to and choose from all possibilities and trust they will choose wisely. An odious political message, like an allegedly odious product, will eventually be exposed by the collective wisdom of the populace for what it is. Advertising in and of itself does not blind the average person to the merits, or lack of them, of the advertised product. In the end, truth will out.

We should refuse to support or condone any action that so degrades the American people and undermines the First Amendment.

In a free market economy demand is one half of the supply/demand equation. Advertising plays probably the single most important role in shaping demand. But forbid the advertising, warp the demand curve, then the free market economy may not be able to best allocate resources.

The lesson is a hard one. Faith in the wisdom of the people to ultimately choose correctly necessitates an incredible tolerance. And nothing tests that tolerance more than speech. For the true test of free speech is not tolerance for ideas we agree with, but tolerance for ideas we hate. But it is that very tolerance which reaffirms the faith in the people themselves. Those that would ban the advertisement of tobacco products, or any advertisement or speech apparently assume you and I are incapable of making the right decision on our own, whether it be in the way we vote politically or the product we buy at the market. We should refuse to support or condone any action that so degrades the American people and undermines the First Amendment.

Elizabeth S. Henderson
Philadelphia, Pennsylvania

*Occupation: Electrical Engineering Design
Consultant
Interests: Reading, writing short fiction and science
fiction
Entered the Competition because of: "Fear,
frustration and indignation that the U.S. Congress
should consider a ban that would modify the
guarantee of the First Amendment. The contest
presented a forum for my protest."*

> [A ban's] dynamic is fueled by a fear of something from which the public "must" be protected, and its effectiveness is assured by some means of persecution.

A CLEAR AND PRESENT DANGER

Because freedom of expression is the rule, and not the exception, in our society, we tend to forget harsh lessons the past has taught, that freedom and suppression are two mutually exclusive, noncoexistent ideologies. Of the two, a choice of one was demanded of us. We chose freedom of expression as our way of life.

With our choice inheres a responsibility for constant vigilance, constant readiness to defend freedom from the pernicious, persistent encroachment of suppression, which invades the territories of the First Amendment to smother the freedoms protected therein. Because, if any given freedom should be lost to the forces of suppression, the First Amendment as a whole would be doomed. For that reason, we propose that the censorship of freedom of expression is a substantive evil which poses a clear and present danger to the First Amendment as a whole.

The legislation currently under consideration by Congress, which would impose a ban on tobacco advertising, gives legitimacy to that proposition. In full awareness of the consequences such a restraint would impose upon freedom of expression, Congress turns a deaf ear to the ringing command of the First Amendment that "Congress shall make no law . . . abridging freedom of speech or of the press. . . ." Consequently, any legislation that would ban any legitimate advertisement must fly in the face of that sweeping command because such legislation would contain the abridgment of speech and press which the First Amendment forbids.

A ban is an instrument of censorship, and censorship is a drive to suppress. Its dynamic is fueled by a fear of something from which the public "must" be protected, and its effectiveness is assured by some means of persecution. The drive to protect the public from whatever the fear may be causes the censors to adopt a police-authority role which overrides individual rights and freedoms as the censors determine what is good and what is bad for the public. A conspectus of censorship interests includes every freedom under the protection of the First Amendment.

Historically, censorship came into being when man began to think and formulate ideas. Unfortunately, nearly every idea can be an incitement for suppression through some means of persecution. But, ironically, the consequences of censorship contributed dynamic to the impulse of liberty and tolerance. Much of our history attests to the struggle of freedom against the forces of suppression. Fortunately, in each instance, freedom prevailed. But the forces of suppression are never quite defeated and the struggle goes on and on.

Religious ideas were the first targets of censorship and persecution was meted out for blasphemy and heresy. Religious censorship got off to a bloody start under the Roman Empire and flourished more than one thousand years as it raged across Europe seeking and slaughtering heretics. The heretics were the proponents of whichever religious beliefs were unpopular at the time. And they were all unpopular at one time or another. Even the Archbishop of Canterbury and the Bishop of Worcester were burned at the stake. Oliver Cromwell banned Christmas in 1652 because of its pagan origins. Then in 1689 when intolerance became intolerable, the religious carnage abated with The Intolerance Act, granted by William and Mary.

Political ideas became the next targets of censorship, and liberty in our fledgling republic was dangerously threatened. In 1798, just seven years after the ratification of the Constitution, Congress adopted the Alien and Sedition laws that practically nullified the provisions of the First Amendment. But by the time Thomas Jefferson became president, Congress wiped the offending statutes off the books and restored freedom to the citizens who had been thrown in jail and fined.

Our history records other perilous times when censorship threatened to take control of our way of life.

Our history further records other perilous times when censorship threatened to take control of our way of life. The Civil War brought civil liberties and freedom of expression under restraint. In 1917, during World War I, Congress adopted the Espionage Act, which carried prohibitions far beyond any act of espionage. Then, in 1940, Congress adopted the Smith Act along with a satellite of other restrictive statutes which served as peacetime sedition laws, changing the quality of freedom for every American citizen.

Nor shall we ever forget those dark days of the early 1950s, when the freedoms of the First Amendment were eclipsed by the power of one man, Senator Joseph P. McCarthy, who, with his committee, launched a witch-hunt to seek and persecute subversives.

Since nearly everyone was suspect, thousands of citizens lost their jobs, were stigmatized and persecuted, while military officers and civilian officials were hunted, hounded and publicly stripped of their dignity. It was a nightmare that numbed the nation and rendered the First Amendment powerless. Finally, in 1954, the United States Senate formally condemned McCarthy for "conduct contrary to the Senate tradition," and brought that peculiar terrorism to a halt. That such an incredibly chilling scenario could be performed on the stage of democracy served to dramatize the vulnerability of the First Amendment under a seige of suppression. But not until later in the decade, when the Supreme Court reviewed the Smith Act and found the sedition sections unconstitutional, were the liberties of the First Amendment restored, and freedom of expression again became the rule.

Literary ideas have always attracted active censorship. Across the centuries, from Homer to Hemingway, there have been many literary martyrs whose works were banned, burned or expurgated when some authority found the work offensive. The writings of Confucius, the Talmud, the English translation of the Bible and the English translation of the New Testament, all have been consigned to the flame.

In more recent times, the interest of literary censorship centered on obscenity. But the definition of obscenity posed a serious problem for the censors.

And by reason of difficulty the definition of obscenity became the pivotal point around which the struggle for literary freedom of expression revolved.

The first reported decision on literary censorship in the United States occurred in Boston in 1821. It involved John Cleland's *Memoirs of a Woman of Pleasure*, a book commonly known by the name of the heroine, Fanny Hill. When the book first appeared, two booksellers were thrown in jail, the book was banned by the postal authorities and the Customs Bureau. The book vanished. Meanwhile, censorship maintained a lively interest in obscenity despite the difficulty of defining it.

In the years between 1842 and 1956 Congress enacted twenty antiobscenity laws, the constitutionality of which were never challenged until 1957 when the Supreme Court issued an opinion that contained the definition of obscenity and a test.

The definition is, ". . . all ideas . . . having the slightest redeeming social importance have the full protection of the guarantee. . . ."

And, ". . . the test is whether to the average person, applying

347

contemporary community standards, the dominant theme of the material, taken as a whole, appeals to the prurient interest."

With the establishment of criteria for defining and testing obscenity, the power of decision shifted from the censors to the writers, where it belonged. But the greatest literary triumph was to come later.

More than a century had passed when, in 1963, *Fanny Hill* appeared again. This time, the book was published and advertised in New York. Promptly, the Massachusetts court condemned it, but the New York court gave the book its blessings. In the midst of this legal controversy, *Fanny Hill* came before the Supreme Court in the spring of 1966. The Court put the book to the test and found that "taken as a whole," the book did indeed contain some "redeeming social importance." With this finding, the Massachusetts court decision against *Fanny Hill* was struck down and since then, the First Amendment has stood squarely in the way of obscenity laws. They cannot reach a book containing even a modicum of social importance, meaning, literary merit. Thus, literary censorship became a dead issue. But the distance between literature and motion pictures is a very short step and the censors took it in stride.

Thomas Edison first introduced what was to become motion pictures in 1894, and by 1907 Chicago adopted an ordinance giving the chief of police authority to preview all films and issue or withhold license, according to his judgment of immorality or obscenity. This practice was prior restraint, and it was challenged two years later, but upheld by the Illinois court. By 1915, the issue of prior censorship had become such a grave concern for all levels of government, that it made its way to the Supreme Court. At that time, the Court held that motion pictures were not protected by the free speech guarantee because they were merely spectacles. When the movies began talking in 1927, the status of the medium remained the same. But in 1951 *The Miracle* changed the course of events for motion pictures. *The Miracle* had received a license and opened in New York, only to have the license revoked on charges of "blasphemy" and "sacrilege." The New York Court of Appeals upheld the "sacrilegious" findings.

Now, after thirty-seven years of silence on motion picture censorship, the Supreme Court spoke. It agreed to hear the case considering only whether motion pictures were a medium of speech, and whether the censorship standard of "sacrilege" in the New York law was permissible. When the Court spoke, it said ". . . it cannot be doubted that motion pictures are a significant medium of communication of ideas. . . ."

This placed motion pictures within the free speech and free press guarantees of the First Amendment. The previous decision was struck down.

With reference to prior restraint on free speech the Court held that such a limitation could only be recognized in exceptional cases, and the burden of demonstrating such a restraint would rest with the state. The state could not demonstrate. So the Court proceeded with its opinion concerning "sacrilege," declaring,

> . . . the State has no legitimate interest in protecting any or all religions from views distasteful to them which is sufficient to justify prior restraint upon expression of those views . . . whether they appear in publications, speeches or motion pictures. . . .

The entire genre of communication gained status.

When *Lady Chatterley's Lover* reached the Supreme Court, the Court held that the licensing standard construed to ban the film was in effect a bar to the discussion of ideas.

That decision stripped the censors of all authority to ban, bar or cut films because they contained unconventional ideas or sexually immoral themes. This left motion pictures relatively free of censorship. But it also left the censors free to find another target on which to concentrate their interest.

Congress found the targets! In 1967 Congress passed a law which permitted homeowners to insist that there be no second mailings from anyone who sent anything the homeowner considered "erotically arousing or sexually provocative." However, when this law was challenged the conventional mailers did not take heed. They felt safe in their operations, that is, until the postmaster began receiving notices objecting to respectable mailings. Then the conventional mailers knew that they, too, had been caught in the net of censorship.

In 1970, the case *Prohibition of Pandering Advertisements in the Mails* reached the Supreme Court. Chief Justice Warren Burger in a unanimous decision ennunciated a new doctrine. The ". . . right to be left alone should be placed on the same scale with the right of others to communicate. . . ."

Agreed! But the Chief Justice further declared,

> . . . the power of the householder is unlimited, . . . he or she may prohibit the mailing of a dry goods catalog because he objects to the content or indeed the text of the language touting the merchandise. . . .

This broad spectrum of the Court's opinion was ominous of future attacks on advertising. It was the handwriting of warning on the wall.

Now there should be no surprise that Congress has tobacco advertising under scrutiny for a possible ban. It was merely a matter of time and logistics before some other aspect of advertising would be brought under the attack of censorship. The most vulnerable elements of advertising had really been identified by Chief Justice Burger when he intoned "the content or indeed the text." From this, the censors took their cue to seize upon these elements as the object of their interest.

Nonetheless, it seems incredible that Congress should consider a ban on any legitimate advertising, because it would place Congress in the untenable position of opposing standing laws that place the communication of ideas within the mandate of speech and press.

Consider an advertisement comprises words, or words combined with pictures, or words combined with pictures accompanied by sound. Whatever the composition, taken as a whole, the advertisement constitutes a medium of communication that expresses an idea. The expression of ideas is speech. Speech is protected by the First Amendment. The First Amendment denies Congress the privilege of abridging speech. Only grave and imminent danger can justify the suppression of speech.

Justice Oliver Wendell Holmes made that point clear in 1919 in an eloquently phrased opinion delivered for the Supreme Court in which he established the "clear and present danger" test. Justice Holmes declared,

> . . . the question in every case is whether the words used . . . are of such nature as to create a clear and present danger that they will bring about the substantive evils that Congress has a right to prevent. . . .

The answer to the question, if applied to a tobacco advertisement, would be a resounding "No." There is no "clear and present danger" in a tobacco advertisement which Congress has a "right to prevent." And any other law abridging free speech for any reason must be challenged as unconstitutional.

A ban on tobacco advertising would inherently cause more harm to society than all the "good" it would intend to create. It would restrict the right of the individual to exercise his free choice according to his interests. It would interfere with the press by imposing censorship restraints on the "content and text" of the advertisements in its publications. It would introduce political controls that could cause the collapse of the pluralistic balance of our free market system. And, it could cause our economy to sustain incalculable damage as a direct result of an acute depression induced in the tobacco and advertising industries. Even though the ban may be conceived with the good intention of protecting the health of the public from harmful effects of tobacco consumption, such legislation would also provide the censors with unrestricted license to ban anything they fear to be harmful to public health. Because the dynamic of censorship is such that, if a ban on tobacco advertisement should be permitted to go unchallenged, it would be just a matter of time before the "content and text" of other advertisements would be banned because the censors feared the touted products to be harmful to public health. And there would lie the threat to all advertisements.

A ban on tobacco advertising would inherently cause more harm to society than all the "good" it would intend to create.

Driven by a righteous determination to protect public health, and armed with legislation that would, no doubt, carry some means of persecution, the censors could reach right into our private lives and strip away our freedom of decision and choice. Under the onslaught of rampant censorship, freedom of expression would become mute, and the First Amendment would be powerless to honor its guarantee.

An exemplification of extreme suppression is encapsulated in the phrase André Vishinski wrote in the Laws of the Soviet State: "In our state, naturally, there can be no place for freedom of speech, press and so on. . . ."

These few words formulate a succinct description of the very effective suppression mechanism which maintains status quo in the Soviet State. That suppression mechanism, if impacted against our free society, along with a sufficiently harsh system of persecution, would be very effective in changing our way of life into something resembling the Soviet State. That is what the struggle is all about!

A ban on tobacco advertising would be a step in that direction because it would advance the encroachment of suppression further upon the territories of the First Amendment. Nor would it stop there. Freedom of expression is under attack. The threat should be enough to galvanize us into the kind of action that will stop the encroachment before it is too late. For if we lose our freedom of expression, the First Amendment will surely be overcome by the forces of censorship, and the clear and present danger of suppression will ultimately prevail.

Guy J. Wells
Providence, Rhode Island

Occupation: Attorney
Interests: Reading, tennis, travel
Entered the Competition because: "I am deeply
concerned about erosion of First Amendment rights
and I love competition."

Well-meaning supporters . . . forget that "every journey begins with a single step" and fail to look very far down the road they would walk.

*Congress shall make no law respecting the
establishment of religion, or prohibiting the free
exercise thereof; or of abridging the freedom of speech
or of the press; or the right of the people peaceably
to assemble, and to petition the government for redress
of grievances.*
—*First Amendment to the Constitution
of the United States*

No responsible scholar will argue that there is any document which so shapes the way we live in America as the first ten amendments to the Constitution, aptly named the Bill of Rights.

They protect us in our homes and on the street; they secure us in our churches; and most importantly, they guarantee our right to hear, see and voice diverse opinions on every subject imaginable. And it is this free exchange of ideas that has transformed this country from a group of colonies clinging precariously to life on the Atlantic edge of the continent to an industrial giant literally spanning the world and reaching out as far as the moon.

And on the date these amendments became law, autocratic governments all over the world shuddered. It marked the first time in the history of man that a ruling power willingly gave up to its people rights that had always been believed to be the prerogatives of the sovereign. Never before had a government so limited itself except by threat of force. The Magna Carta, long hailed as the first step toward real democracy, was, after all, literally signed at the point of a sword.

But the drafters knew what they were doing. Monarchical despotism was not to them an abstract proposition or something that happened to someone else thousands of miles away. It was real because they had lived with it. They knew its length and breadth and depth.

They had seen it in action whether under a tsar in Russia, a Louis in France or a Stuart or a Hanover in England. There had been good rulers, of course, and bad rulers, but rulers nonetheless.

They had just fought a revolution which bloodied the colonies from Breed's Hill in Boston to Yorktown on the James.

And within the memory of their immediate ancestors they had seen a popular revolution against the excesses of the first two Stuart kings lead to a dictatorship so oppressive that they were later happy to trade the Cromwellians for two more Stuarts.

And those of them who were students of the classics saw ominous parallels in the revolutions of ancient Greece and Rome which invariably turned out one despot only to raise another in his place.

So they resolved to give the people of this fragile and bloodied little nation an insurance policy designed to forever preclude the usurpation of *their* revolution by the government it brought forth—the Bill of Rights.

It is not an historic accident that the first of the ten amendments dealt with freedoms of religion and the press.

Since before the Middle Ages, state-dictated religions had been the cause of more bloodshed than territorial ambition, lust for treasure and the like. England had been ripped apart by the Catholic-Protestant wars. The French slaughtered Huguenots and the flower of Europe had perished wholesale in the fruitless Crusades.

Most of the drafters' colonial forbears had come to the Americas as a result of religious persecution by governments, and the authors deemed it vital that that shadow never fall across the face of their new land.

Of equal importance to the authors was the permanent preservation of the notion that ideas be freely and openly circulated, unfettered by the whims of a government that disagreed with them.

They well remembered the Redcoats sacking bookstores in Boston, Philadelphia and New York, smashing printing presses and imprisoning pamphleteers; ripping broadsides off walls and harassing those who read them.

They had seen newspapers burned down and their publishers jailed. And all in the name of the king—thousands of miles and weeks of sailing away. And a king who was not really English but German, who suffered frequent bouts of insanity and who really would have been happier as a farmer than a monarch.

Now the king was gone but the spectre of another form of despotism haunted the drafters.

Today those who would abridge, modify or water down some of the first ten amendment rights argue that the original Constitution ratified in 1788 contained no Bill of Rights and the Convention had indeed rejected the inclusion of one by a ten-to-zero vote by states. Ergo, they say, they can't be too important.

Such a notion is historical nonsense. The framers believed that since the new Constitution gave no powers, particularly to Congress, to abridge those rights described in the Declaration of Independence as "fundamental," an enumeration of them was superfluous.

In *Federalist Papers* No. 84, Alexander Hamilton argued that original bills of rights such as the Magna Carta were stipulations between kings and their subjects and since there was no more king and the American people had surrendered nothing but retained everything, there was no need of particularizing anything.

The states (nine of which were required to ratify the Constitution) were not as sanguine, however, and the omission of such a bill almost sank adoption of the new Constitution.

Eight of the new states had bills of rights in their constitutions and they along with the other five—always suspicious of central government—could not accept the argument that unless restrained by specific prohibition the federal government would modestly refrain from doing anything not specifically delineated in the governing document. Needless to say, history has proven the merit of such reservations.

Indeed the intrusion of the executive, judicial and congressional branches into virtually every area of personal life not forbidden by the Constitution and its amendments has been swift, inclusive and pervasive.

Despite the protestations of the members of the Constitutional Convention, public outrage at the failure to include a Bill of Rights was immediate and imperative.

The debate was furious.

One can imagine the consternation of the framers. Though a product of compromise, they believed—correctly as it turned out—that they had produced a document which, as Thomas Jefferson pointed out, "is unquestionably the wisest ever yet presented to men."

But the general populace was outraged not because of what was in it but because of what was not—a bill of rights.

Clearly there were other issues—slavery as an example—which were the subject of debate, but the insulation of the individual from excesses of the federal government was clearly the pivotal question.

The affirmative vote of nine states was required to ratify. Ultimately all thirteen ratified. But four states attempted to condition their ratification on a guarantee of speech and press freedom. These, of course, were Virginia, New York, North Carolina and, naturally, Rhode Island.

As a result of this popular outcry at the first session of Congress in 1789, a bill of rights was proposed, passed and ultimately ratified, becoming part of the Constitution on December 15, 1791.

There is currently in Congress some small sentiment for banning the advertisement of tobacco products. Well-meaning supporters, armed with some rather suspect medical opinions, urge that such proscription is really a "healthy thing," "affects very few people" and represents only a "small" incursion on First Amendment guarantees. They forget that

357

"every journey begins with a single step" and fail to look very far down the road they would walk.

Once the first chip has been chiseled out in the name of "health" the second is easier, and so on.

Since 55,000 Americans die every year in automobile accidents, does it not follow that automobile advertising should be banned?

And might not the party in control of Congress decide that since the economic policies of the opposition, if implemented, would lead to fiscal disaster, the vocalization of those policies was inimical to the country's "economic health" and should thus be silenced?

And so it goes.

Apologists will argue that this is just a ban on business advertising and has nothing to do with the exchange of ideas—political, moral or intellectual. Two important points escape them. First, the amendment does not define what speech is protected—all speech is, and, second, who decides what an idea is, anyway? One must remember that the media politicians use to promote their candidacies—press, radio and television—are precisely the same as the ones used by business to promote their products. To deny the maker of a legally sold product the use of those media is as legally, morally and intellectually indefensible as denying such use to a Republican, Democrat or Bull Mooser.

Those who would, however well-meaning, support such an imposition on the right of the individual to hear and to know would do well to remember the bloody price that was paid for that right. They would do well to wonder why the farmers of Lexington and Concord, the young boys at Valley Forge, the soldiers of Princeton and Trenton, volunteers all, left their homes and families to fight a king that had been their monarch all of their lives and their ancestors' lives to secure those rights.

They should ponder, if just for a moment, that no dictatorship, no autocracy, has ever dominated its people before dominating the expression of ideas.

And it might be instructive if they were able to ask themselves what answer would they get from the men who died at Saratoga and Brandywine, Bull Run and Chattanooga, the Marne and Château-Theirry, Okinawa and Normandy if they asked "Would you mind if we just diluted a little bit the freedoms you bled for, left widows and sons and daughters for? Would you mind if we let the members of Congress decide what we can hear or say or see? After all, Washington and Jefferson, Adams and Madison died a long time ago—so did you—and this is just a little bending of the First Amendment. It probably won't happen again."

But history teaches us that it will happen again and again.

And sooner or later the great shield of freedom will be so eroded as to become a gauzy tissue protecting no one but those who would misuse it.

Sooner or later the great shield of freedom will be so eroded as to become a gauzy tissue protecting no one but those who would misuse it.

Seventy-five years after the Revolution an astute observer of mankind wrote of the printer:

> Without him tyrants and humbugs in all countries would have their own way. He is a friend of intelligence and thought. A friend of liberty, of freedom, of law, indeed, the friend of every man who is a friend of order.
>
> Of all inventions, of all discoveries in science and art, of all the great results in the wonderful progress of mechanical energy and skill, the printer is the only product of civilization necessary to the existence of free men.
>
> —Charles Dickens, c. 1850

Those words become no less true with the passage of time.

The fact that serious people are suggesting such an incursion today is not so much an indictment of them as malefactors as a demonstration of how far we have grown away from the very real world of the drafters and how little we understand of the imperatives that moved them. Having lived under the protection of the First Amendment for almost two hundred years, we cannot imagine life without it. They didn't need to imagine life without it—they had lived it.

Proponents should take heed from the admonition of the sage: "He who does not learn from history is doomed to repeat it."

Mary Kay Beall

Hilton Head Island, South Carolina

Occupation: Writer/Editor
Interests: Biking, reading, walking on the beach
Entered the Competition because: "I was
interested in the issue; it was a provocative one
and worth addressing."

> If there is a question in our minds, any question at all, as to the validity, the lawfulness or the morality of the government's handling of its responsibilities toward us, we must in good conscience speak out.

WHEN THE NEEDS OF THE MANY OUTWEIGH THE NEEDS OF THE FEW

This proud nation of ours was born out of the yearning of a small body of individuals to enjoy certain basic freedoms to which they felt entitled. When these freedoms were denied them, they took issue with their government, withdrew, endured hardship and suffered deprivation in order to form a new and better country . . . America.

The colonists struggled. They struggled with the elements, with the Indians, with one another. Many suffered and died while these shaky newborn settlements were fighting to survive. Over a period of time, they devised what to them seemed an ultimately satisfactory form of self-government. We call it democracy. They elected leaders to whom they delegated the decision making process on their behalf. And then the leaders continued the struggle, fervently trying to verbalize their most basic hopes and dreams for this new country, trying to protect forever and ever the fragile seed of liberty which they had so tenderly sown and so lovingly nurtured.

The process of defining our structures of law and our means of governing continues today. It is a process which will never be completed. Times change, mores changes, people change a bit, and the laws must speak to those changes as effectively as possible. But the basic rights laid out for us by our forefathers are a constant. They are a blueprint for the building of a nation "conceived in liberty and dedicated to the propostion that all men are created equal." Through all of the intervening years since those first basic freedoms were defined on paper and later defended on the battlefield, we have tried to honor the single fundamental premise on which we built this country: that every basic right guaranteed to us in the Constitution applies to every person.

If we hold *this* truth to be self-evident, if we recognize that this is the foundation of our system of government, then we must also recognize that it bears defending. "Liberty is always unfinished business!"* If we take our liberties for granted, we run the perilous risk of losing them. We must never forget that "We, the people" are one body. If any citizen's freedoms are endangered, then all of our individual and collective liberties are vulnerable.

In a democratic system, the government has several basic responsibilities . . . to formulate the law, to interpret the law, to administer the law and to respond to the collective voice of the people. But it is easy to overlook our own responsibilities . . . the responsibilities to be informed, to make our voices heard and to be vigilant in protecting and maintaining our own freedoms. Our government has strength and power only insofar as we allow ourselves to be governed. If there is a question in our minds, any question at all, as to the validity, the lawfulness or the morality of the government's handling of its responsibilities toward us, we must in good conscience speak out.

Liberty is like the air we breathe. We don't think about it much as long as there is plenty to go around and the quality is unimpaired.

Liberty is like the air we breathe. We don't think about it much as long as there is plenty to go around and the quality is unimpaired. But the sweet breath of Liberty can easily be tainted before we know it. Censorship is but one of many insidious contaminants that can invade our moral environment with little warning and leave an ugly residue in its wake. Like a sly serpent, it rears its head in the garden of our Liberty and tempts us to taste the forbidden fruit of power. It is the embodiment of self-righteousness. To borrow the logic of Commander Spock (*Star Trek II: The Wrath of Khan*), it is an act which defies "the needs of the many" . . . to serve "the needs of the few."

While each one of us may have the strongest of feelings about what is proper, what is healthy and what is morally acceptable, we do not have the right to impose those values on others. That is what freedom is all about. If we as individuals, or if any government, take up the standard against a citizen, a business, a church or a sect, then other individuals and groups are in peril.

Any advertising ban administered by the government in a free

* American Civil Liberties Union, *Annual Report, 1955–1956.*

market economy is a blatant act of censorship and challenges the foundations of a democractic society. The product to be sold is not at issue here; if any product can be censored in any way, then all products are at risk. The issue is simply that of protecting the basic liberties granted to all of us by the Constitution. If we as individuals take issue with a particular book, a film, a play or a product, we have the right to speak our minds about it. We have the right to refuse to read the book, view the film, attend the play or buy the product. We do not, however, and never should have, the right to make those choices for others, no matter how good we feel it would be for them. Neither we nor our government should set ourselves up as arbiters of any standard to which others are compelled to conform.

Quite simply, "the needs of the many" to make decisions for themselves must "outweigh the needs of the few" who feel certain that they know what is best for all.

It is crucial to our form of government that as citizens we retain the right to see and to hear and to judge issues for ourselves. When the government dictates what we cannot read, what we dare not say, what we must not buy, where we shall not worship or what we may not advertise, we have forfeited our most precious possession. The individual liberties that we enjoy today are not really individual at all; they are part and parcel of the great concept, Liberty, upon which this extraordinary country was founded. Thus, if any single liberty is threatened or destroyed, the others are undeniably compromised.

Given the opportunity, any one of us might be sorely tempted to censor something for someone else . . . in their best interest, of course. Individuals and governments may well impose censorship with the very best of intentions. They may believe that by removing certain books or films or products from the public eye they are acting in the best interest of the public and protecting them from inherent dangers and evils. Good intentions or not, the end result is the same. Someone's liberty is eroded and endangered. And though some may claim censorship as a cure for the evils that surround us—and there are plenty of them to be sure—it poses a threat with implications more far-reaching than the imagination can dare to comprehend.

Censorship is to be avoided at all costs, whatever our own personal prejudices may be. The price we will pay for censorship in any sector of our lives is far greater than any of us can afford. Quite simply, "the needs

365

of the many" to make decisions for themselves must "outweigh the needs of the few" who feel certain that they know what is best for all. If the road to hell is truly paved with good intentions, then censorship may well be the first stop along the way.

John E. Getz
Brookings, South Dakota

Occupation: College Professor
Interests: Reading, music, hiking, camping,
photography, do-it-yourself projects
Entered the Competition because: "I believe the
fundamental freedoms guaranteed by the Bill of
Rights must be zealously protected."

> Those who oppose the New Prohibition ought not be categorized as apologists for the tobacco industry but as people who are concerned about fundamental American freedoms. . . .

FREEDOM OF COMMERCIAL SPEECH

Like a puff of smoke, a proposal to ban the advertising of tobacco products in the print media has been, at least to the purveyors of those products, intruding, annoying, lingering.

Like a puff of smoke, it may be soon gone.

Those who oppose the New Prohibition ought not be categorized as apologists for the tobacco industry but as people who are concerned about fundamental American freedoms; not, specifically, about the freedom to smoke but about the freedom to speak.

The proposal is, of course, merely the latest in a long series of attempts by one group to silence another. The United States was founded on the principles of free speech in spite of a one-hundred-and-fifty-year history of repression of colonial speech, and ever since, some of its citizens have sworn allegiance to the concept of basic rights even as they have sought to deny those rights to others.

The first American newspaperman to feel the heavy hand of official repression was hapless Boston printer Benjamin Harris. He brought out a tiny sheet in 1690 with the idea of making it a monthly newspaper—the first one in the colonies. But he had neglected to clear his plan with the authorities, and they promptly shut him down. His *Publick Occurrences Both Forreign and Domestick* lasted only one issue. It was more than a dozen years before the second American newspaper appeared.

Harris was the victim of a system of prior restraint. It required printers to obtain government authorization before producing any material. The British monarchy enlisted the Church of England to help it keep a lid on the spread of the written word, and for generations it succeeded in doing so. Eventually, though too late for Harris, the system collapsed of its own weight.

The Harris case, James Franklin's conflict with colonial authorities in 1722 and John Peter Zenger's trial for seditious libel in 1735 were points of articulation in the evolution of the free speech/free press concept in America. The very first addendum to the new Constitution was this guarantee: "Congress shall make no law . . . abridging the freedom of speech, or of the press. . . ."

Yet the ink was barely dry on the document before the Alien and Sedition Acts were passed by a Congress suddenly anxious to stifle political speech. The acts ran contrary not only to the First Amendment but to the thinking of the American people as well, and soon died. Subsequent attempts by authorities to silence annoying voices also have run contrary to the Constitution and to the people, and also have died.

Congress now proposes to silence tobacco processors and distributors, contending that they are hawking lethal wares. The congressional action is directed toward their speech rather than toward their product. So directed, it is a clear violation of the First Amendment.

A discussion of the constitutional implications of the proposed tobacco advertising ban requires the omission of considerations that are beside the point.

One such tangential issue is the medical: the relationship between smoking and health problems. Whether tobacco consumption causes cancer, heart disease, emphysema, high blood pressure, strokes, tumors and any and all other maladies researchers have linked it to simply is not a constitutional matter. The number of people annually killed by diseases said to have been the result of smoking is not a constitutional matter. Graphic, compelling stories about teen-agers who suffer the agonies of mouth and jaw cancer from the use of smokeless tobacco are not a constitutional matter. Medical concerns must be addressed, but in the proper forum. In short, advertising does not cause cancer—but suppressing free speech could bring about a societal "illness" of grave import.

Another tangential issue is the economic one. Certainly the millions of dollars spent every year on tobacco advertising in the print media has a huge impact—on the media, on the advertisers, on the agencies that serve them. Tobacco advertising provides or contributes to the livelihoods of tens of thousands of people. A ban on tobacco advertising would bring about a shift in spending of tidal wave proportions, with untold ramifications. But none of this is a constitutional matter.

Yet another tangential issue is advertiser motivation. Critics contend tobacco manufacturers are enticing young people into establishing harmful tobacco usage habits. They denounce advertisements that portray cigarette smokers as youthful, vibrant, healthy, athletic, exuberant, sexy, sophisticated and affluent. But the advertisers deny that they are directing their message toward adolescents or toward nonsmokers. They say they seek only to encourage people who already smoke to 1) switch

370

to their brand or 2) remain loyal to their brand. Either way, it doesn't matter. The identity of the advertising target has no bearing on the free speech debate. Motivation is not a constitutional matter.

Severing such issues from the discussion serves to strip away emotionalism. Even though emotion, in the form of an overpowering desire for liberty, played a role in the development of the free press/free speech concept, the defense of that concept must be conducted on the basis of rational thinking.

The framers of the Constitution envisioned an open government accessible not exclusively to a ruling aristocracy but to every class of society. It is likely those early champions of individual liberties had no real idea of how far their philosophical reach ultimately would extend. Judicial interpretation of the First Amendment over the course of two centuries has made Americans the freest to express their thoughts of all the people in the world.

Traditionally, the dangers to free speech and free press have fallen into two broad categories: prepublication restrictions, or prior restraint, and postpublication penalties that are so severe as to amount to censorship. Such dangers are manifested when people presume to speak against the government (sedition), against individuals (libel) or against morality (obscenity). The Supreme Court has addressed all of these issues in landmark rulings involving freedom of expression.

But the upholding of high principles has focused largely on noncommercial speech. What about advertising?

Generally and increasingly, the justices of the Supreme Court have endorsed the concept of an open marketplace of ideas, encouraged the robust debate of public issues and empowered the media to talk about controversial issues with at least some degree of fearlessness.

But the upholding of high principles has focused largely on noncommercial speech. What about advertising?

Commercial speech once was held—and continues to be held, to a diminishing degree—to be less worthy of constititional protection than other forms of speech. It was on that rationale that fifteen years ago a ban on advertising tobacco products on the airwaves was enacted and upheld. Significantly, however, the Supreme Court did not make its own statement when it affirmed a lower court's decision regarding the ban. By implication, the higher court agreed that the ban did not amount to an infringement on free speech, but merely to a control on marketing methods.

371

The justification for that decision might have had its genesis in a 1942 case involving the distribution of handbills in New York City, then prohibited by city ordinance. The Supreme Court ruled that the free speech guarantee of the First Amendment covered the dissemination of information and opinion, but not advertising. And thus the content of advertising messages could be controlled by government.

But the commercial speech principle seemingly established forty-five years ago has steadily eroded. Ever since handbill distributor F. J. Chrestensen lost his case, the Court has been modifying its position.

For instance, in 1971—the same year cigarette advertising was pulled off radio and television—a weekly newspaper in Virginia published an advertisement for abortion services. The newspaper's managing editor subsequently was convicted of violating a state statute prohibiting such advertising. The Supreme Court reversed the conviction on the grounds that the message of the offending advertisement was of public interest. Although commercial, it involved the dissemination of information and opinion, the Court said. "The relationship of speech to the marketplace of products or of services does not make it valueless in the marketplace of ideas," wrote Justice Harry Blackmun.

A few years later, a pair of lawsuits involving the advertising of prices of prescription drugs reached the Supreme Court. The justices ruled that advertising itself is the dissemination of information. Advertisements tell people who is selling what at what price. Wrote Blackmun:

> So long as we preserve a predominantly free enterprise economy, the allocation of our resources in large measure will be made through numerous private economic decisions. It is a matter of public interest that those decisions, in the aggregate, be intelligent and well informed. To this end, the free flow of commercial information is indispensable. And if it is indispensable to the proper allocation of resources in a free enterprise, it is also indispensable to the formation of intelligent opinions as to how that system ought to be regulated or altered. Therefore, even if the First Amendment were thought to be primarily an instrument to enlighten public decision-making in a democracy, we could not say that the free flow of information does not serve that goal.

In light of such rulings, concludes Professor Thomas Tedford of the University of North Carolina, the Constitution "protects advertising that communicates to the general public 'truthful information about entirely lawful activity.'"

Legal challenges to the freedom of commercial speech have continued into the 1980s. Those cases that have reached the Supreme

Court have expanded constitutional protections for advertising. The Court, says Tedford, "overruled the Chrestensen doctrine and rewrote the law concerning commercial expression." Government, in other words, is not permitted to tamper with truthful advertising of legal products, but is allowed only to control false and deceptive advertising and advertising of illegal products.

The emerging law of the land regarding commercial speech is almost exactly parallel to that regarding noncommercial speech: Judicial interpretation of the free speech/free press guarantee of the First Amendment is ever broadening.

If Congress should ban the advertising of tobacco products in the print media, it would deny the manufacturers and distributors of those products their rights of free speech. And if the present trend of constitutional interpretation continues, the ban—eventually, and with significant expense to the American taxpayer—would be found to be in conflict with the First Amendment and would be overturned.

The crux of the matter is that tobacco products are legal products. As long as they continue to be legal, their purveyors have the right to advertise them truthfully and straightforwardly. If tobacco marketing were to be prohibited as alcohol sales were (unsuccessfully) from 1920 to 1933, the debate would take a different turn.

Those who oppose the use of tobacco should attack the product that they deplore, not a liberty that they in other circumstances hold dear.

The connection between an attack on "loathsome tobacco" and American freedom is neither long nor remote nor convoluted—but frighteningly direct.

Freedom of speech and freedom of the press in the United States are not now, nor ever have been, absolute. But for two hundred years, speech has become steadily less restricted rather than increasingly more restricted. The pattern, more inevitable than fortuitous, is essential for the preservation of liberty. Should people be allowed to speak less freely rather than more freely they would be thrust into the chains of intellectual bondage.

Still, defending the tobacco interests can be difficult. First Amendment scholars occasionally find themselves in a similarly difficult position of defending pornographers. For both groups, it is imperative that a spirited defense be mounted, because the issue is neither tobacco nor pornography, but liberty.

373

The marketplace of ideas includes ideas that are reprehensible as well as ideas that are uplifting. To preserve the latter, a blanket of protection must be extended to the former. To eliminate the former would be to endanger the latter.

Inroads against commercial speech imperil noncommercial speech. Inroads against noncommercial speech imperil democracy. Inroads against democracy imperil American society, the freest society in the world.

The connection between an attack on "loathsome tobacco" and American freedom is neither long nor remote nor convoluted—but frighteningly direct.

Linda M. Hatcher
Mount Pleasant, Tennessee

Occuptation: Editor/Journalist
Interests: Reading, writing, spending time with my
Little Sister in Big Brothers/Big Sisters, attending
college part-time, serving as Treasurer of Area
Chamber of Commerce and First Vice President of
Business and Professional Women
Entered the Competition because: "I strongly believe
in the subject—the protection of the First
Amendment. In my work, I serve as a disseminator
of public information and as a check on government.
Every time I watch the presses run, I realize that the
First Amendment is the basis of ALL our freedoms."

The American Civil Liberties Union and the American Advertising Federation joined tobacco companies in proclaiming the proposed measure unconstitutional.

CENSORSHIP ANYWHERE IS A THREAT TO THE FIRST AMENDMENT EVERYWHERE

Martin Luther King said, "Injustice anywhere is a threat to justice everywhere."

Although the late civil rights leader was referring to injustice against blacks, his statement applies to threats today against the First Amendment.

Governmental regulations are increasingly encroaching upon First Amendment rights, which were described by the writers of the Bill of Rights to mean no law should be made "abridging the freedom of speech or of the press."

One of the most dangerous challenges currently facing the First Amendment is proposed legislation which would censor the tobacco industry in advertising.

In December 1985, the American Medical Association proposed a total ban on cigarette advertising.

The American Civil Liberties Union and the American Advertising Federation joined tobacco companies in proclaiming the proposed measure unconstitutional, citing Supreme Court decisions allowing "truthful advertising for legal products protected under the free-speech provision of the First Amendment."

Senator Bill Bradley introduced into Congress a proposed tax measure against tobacco companies, which would limit cigarette advertising illustration to the product package and copy to the brand name and price.

Banning commercial free speech anywhere will lead to threats against free speech everywhere. Inherent in proposals such as Bradley's and the AMA's is the attitude of one group appointing themselves as

377

lifestyle dictators to other groups. Even more apalling is the harm censorship of commercial free speech can cause the First Amendment.

If proposers of such measures succeed in getting anti-tobacco advertising legislation passed by citing health threats, why should companies with products high in salt be allowed to advertise under the provisions of the First Amendment's protection of free speech? After all, too much salt can lead to many health problems such as high blood pressure.

Passage of censorship measures in the tobacco industry will lead to censorship of the commercial free speech in other free markets. Almost every product can have a negative case constructed against it, and there are always individuals or groups who want to impose their condemnation of products or ideas upon others.

For example, take fast food hamburger chain advertising. It is widely known that a typical fast food hamburger meal is highly caloric, which can lead to obesity, which can lead to heart problems. Such a fast food meal is also high in cholesterol (also bad on the heart) and lacking in proper nutrition (nutritional deficiencies cause overall health malfunctions).

That's different than tobacco advertising, critics argue. But it is not different: fast food advertising creates a desire for food that, when abused, is unhealthy. However, adults have the right to make their own food choices, just as they have a right to decide whether to smoke or not.

Very obviously, a censorship or ban on cigarette advertising would not long remain restricted to cigarettes. Our justice system is largely based upon legal precedents from decisions in legal cases from the past. If cigarette advertising is limited or prohibited, other groups opposing the advertising of other products will have a legal precedent upon which to limit the commercial free speech of other companies.

Dr. King was correct in saying one injustice often leads to another. Without the protection of the First Amendment, however, King could not have left us his inspiring legacy of wisdom and reform, and he could not have promoted the justice of his people.

There were certainly those who would have silenced King; those who found his usage of his freedom of speech contrary to their beliefs. But under the great protection of the words of the First Amendment, King was safe—it took a bullet to silence him, not censorship sanctioned by a dictatorial government.

Just as not everyone agreed with King, not everyone agrees with cigarette smoking. But it is just as dangerous to silence or censor cigarette advertising as it would have been to silence or censor King. It is in protecting the right of others to voice opinions contrary to ours that we become a great nation, not in protecting only expression with which we agree.

Many great thinkers of our past have been aware of the critical importance of protecting the First Amendment.

Benjamin Franklin said the freedom of speech guaranteed by the First Amendment should be unrestrained, as long as a person or group "does not hurt or control the right of another." Cigarette advertising has been proven to reach an established adult market—an adult market with the right to smoke. These ads do not "control the right of another" to not smoke. But banning or censoring tobacco ads would certainly control the right of commercial free speech of tobacco companies.

Cigarette advertising has been proven to reach an established adult market—an adult market with the right to smoke.

In 1964, Supreme Court Justice William O. Douglas said that speech must be an indistinguishable part of illegal activity before it can be subject to penalty. Is cigarette smoking illegal? No. Then based upon what a justice of the nation's highest court has said, the commercial free speech of companies promoting tobacco products should not be penalized by censored advertising.

A society which allows legislators or other groups to dictate the commercial representation of legal adult choices, like smoking, will soon find itself unable to allow or disallow other areas of free speech or, eventually, any other right.

We are a country built upon the premise of free choice and free speech; without these rights, no other freedoms could be created, fought for, maintained.

Diversity of lifestyle has been the driving force for a system of justice which allows for individuality. When we begin to let one group decide what is proper for another group, freedom becomes a relative word, an elusive concept, and the freedom of one too easily becomes the imprisonment of another. The ability of one group to get tobacco ads censored will not only discriminate against the free commercial speech of tobacco companies, but we also leave wide open the door to infringement upon others' liberties.

The breakdown of the sweeping power of the First Amendment could too easily occur: For example, if cigarette advertising is censored or banned, the legal precedent has been set for narrow commercial freedom of speech.

Let's say that after the cigarette advertising was enacted, a vege-

tarian group learns of the decision. They decide that the legal definitions of censorship of cigarette ads will support their goal of censoring
hamburger fast food restaurant advertising. This vegetarian group is
adamantly certain of the harmful effects of hamburger chain meals, and
they feel morally obligated to save everyone else from the harmful effects
of the fast food.

The group lobbies successfully for censorship of the restaurant
advertising. Such establishments can only show a picture of the burger
box and show the name of the restaurant. (The vegetarian group successfully argued that previous ads created in customers a desire for the
unhealthy meals that might not otherwise have occurred.)

Another health-oriented group knows that soft drinks are too high
in sugar, have too many calories, and can lead to serious kidney disor-
ders. They know of the advertising censorship of cigarettes and hamburger fast food chains, so they know they have past legal decisions in
their favor. They succeed in getting enacted censorship on soft drink
advertising.

**Fight against censorship of commercial free speech;
remember, you are also fighting for your own freedom of
speech.**

Soon, groups everywhere would be trying to control the free
choices of other adults. It would not end with advertising. A First
Amendment weakened by censorship of commercial free speech would
leave room for censorship in other areas of free speech. For example,
news editorials revealing shady political deals would certainly be
deemed by the exposed parties as undesirable and harmful. A frayed
First Amendment would allow removal of stories which revealed political wrongdoing.

If we allow chinks in the armor of the First Amendment like the
proposed censorship of tobacco advertising, we are leaving room for the
chisel of other First Amendment abusers. More and more censorship
chisels could fill the gaps left by the chinks, and the First Amendment
would soon collapse upon a weak foundation.

We cannot allow threats to the First Amendment protection of
freedom of speech and press, and this includes commercial free speech.
The First Amendment protects every right we as Americans cherish.

As a journalist for a newspaper, I am keenly aware of the importance of the First Amendment. Without the protection of free speech, a

writer is continuously under the shadow of fear of reprisal. A writer under fear leaves most writing unwritten.

Writing would be left unwritten about political corruption, for example. Without the fear of newspaper exposure and public censure, government servants become public masters. They become free to abuse their public trust without fear of public exposure through the press.

If you fail to see the danger inherent in public officials with no public accountability, ask a Russian citizen. Only, don't be surprised if they are afraid to answer. They are not familiar with freedom of speech—Russia is not renowned for a First Amendment, America is. But for how long? Attacks on our freedom of speech, such as the proposed tobacco advertising censorship, make this a question of critical magnitude.

Fight against censorship of commercial free speech; remember, you are also fighting for your own freedom of speech. Censorship of free speech anywhere is a threat to First Amendment rights everywhere.

Sandy Dollarhide
Orange, Texas

Occupation: Store Owner
Interests: Writing, learning new things just for the sake of learning, fishing, target shooting
Entered the Competition because: "The First Amendment is not just one amendment among many, it is part of our Bill of Rights. Without those rights, the Constitution would not have been ratified."

AN ESSAY ON THE FIRST AMENDMENT: FREE SPEECH FOR SOME

The Constitution of the United States is the oldest surviving document of its kind. The reason our Constitution has outlived the rest is due to the inclusion of the first ten amendments which guarantee the protection of certain rights. In fact, many states refused to ratify the Constitution unless a bill of rights was included. Thus, the Bill of Rights was drafted by the authors of the Constitution, and first among those rights was that of free speech.

Freedom of speech is probably the right we most often take for granted and this is due mainly to Americans' everyday exercise of that right. We're collectively quick to disagree with a talk-show guest, or rebut an article in a newspaper, but it would never occur to most of us to remove the right of that person to speak his or her mind.

Lately, however, more and more Americans have found comfort in abridging the rights of others in a form that can only be described as *convenient bigotry*. Many often justify this bigotry by quoting Oliver Wendell Holmes' famous statement that the First Amendment did not include the right to falsely shout "Fire" in a crowded theater. Most of us would nod our heads and agree that Mr. Holmes had made a valid point, but did he? It would seem on closer examination, that Mr. Holmes suffered from the same constitutional misconception that the rest of us do: that the freedom *to* is the same thing as the freedom *from*, and that is a very false concept indeed. In other words, let us hypothetically grant the First Amendment freedom *to* falsely shout "Fire" in a crowded theater to some maladjusted knothead. Does that mean we have also granted him freedom *from* the consequences of that action? Of course not!

Our vocal miscreant may find himself on the receiving end of lawsuits and criminal charges. A panicky crowd could lead to injuries and property damage, and if a fatal heart attack should result, the practical joker might have to laugh off a manslaughter charge. Thus, the freedom of speech is preserved, and so is justice. But Oliver Wendell

385

Holmes was actually only one of many who would impose restrictions on guaranteed rights "for our own good." These types of abridging tactics should be known as the Underwear Laws.

I use the term Underwear Laws, because its roots sink deep into our childhoods, or at least mine. If my aunt sent me five dollars for my birthday, my mother would buy me some underwear with it, "for my own good," of course. Underwear Laws are designed to keep us serenely childlike. These laws keep us from having to rely on our own common sense. The mandatory use of seat belts and the fifty-five-mile-per-hour speed limit are good examples. Common sense tells us that excessive speed and lack of seat belts kill thousands each year, but thanks to our paternal government, we don't have to be bothered with common sense any more. If we're naughty we get fined or have our highway funds taken away, sort of like being sent to our rooms and having television privileges revoked. There is, however, at least one instance where the elastic snapped, and our nation found its underwear down around its ankles. This was not only embarrassing, but it proved to be quite hazardous as well.

Prohibition, the granddaddy of Underwear Laws, ushered in a generation of scofflaws, blood and speakeasys. People who would never have considered drinking found themselves listening to jazz and drinking watered-down whiskey in a little basement nightclub to which they gained entrance by whispering "Joe sent me" to an eyeslot in the door. This often romanticized era left a trail of corpses on both sides of the war, and when the law was finally repealed and the dust cleared, the only legacy left behind was organized crime. An elite group of criminals who discovered that there's big money to be made from poorly conceived, suffocating laws. Some Underwear Laws are so poorly conceived, in fact, they actually become an unintentional boon to the business or product they are attempting to control. The Gun Control Act of 1968 is an excellent example.

The GCA 68, in part, stated that firearms could not be shipped or received through the mail unless the sender and recipient both had an FFL (Federal Firearms License), further, an FFL could only be obtained for the purpose of *dealing* in firearms. This meant that big catalog stores such as Sears could no longer send guns through the mail, so if someone wanted a gun for hunting season, he might as well visit a neighborhood gun shop rather than traveling all the way to town to shop at Sears. Small gun shops quickly became big businesses, and gun dealing became quite lucrative. In less than twenty years, from 1968 to 1986, we went from a nation of fewer than five thousand gun dealers to a nation of nearly one quarter of a million gun dealers, and all of this due to proski

lawmakers who felt equipped to tamper with the Second Amendment. Now the First Amendment is on the carving platter of Congress. It seems our government feels we have regressed to infancy, and will choke on any pretty bauble dangled in front of us because we have not developed an adult sense of reasoning. It follows, of course, that if our government believes our reasoning is locked in a crib, then it is our government's parental duty to make choices for us. It comes as no surprise then that Congress is considering legislation that, if passed, would ban all forms of cigarette advertising.

The true horror of this bill is the amount of people who will nod their heads and support it, *for our own good*, without ever once considering its constitutionality. It does not seem to matter to these parental lawmakers that cigarettes are a legal consumer item and should therefore be granted the same First Amendment rights that protect toothpaste, deodorant or bug spray. No doubt health will become an issue in the debate even though it should not have any bearing on the issue.

If the proposed bill concerned a ban on the manufacture and sale of cigarettes, then health would be the major, if not the only issue; however, the benefits or detriments to consumer health should not be an issue in this floor fight. Congress should concern itself solely with the constitutional issue: Should cigarette manufacturers be denied their First Amendment rights? If Congress answers yes, the inevitable question will be "What next?"

"WARNING! This motion picture contains scenes of graphic cigarette smoking."

"WARNING! This motion picture contains scenes of graphic cigarette smoking. Parental guidance is suggested." The above warning may sound ludicrous, but isn't Hollywood the next logical target? Nowhere has the cigarette been more visible than in American film. It has dangled from the fingers and lips of Hollywood's giants, and may in itself constitute a form of advertising. A warning label on, say, *The Maltese Falcon* may sound humorous, even if it were to eventually become a reality. What is not so funny though, is the idea that whole scenes which depict cigarette smoking could be cut from a film. If this seems too outrageous to even be a viable turn of events, consider the fact that actor Gene Kelly insisted on doing a dance number with the Nicholas brothers in one of his films. He insisted because it had come to his attention that black acts, like the Nicholas brothers, often ended up on the cutting room floor in some Southern theaters. He reasoned that if

387

they wanted to cut the Nicholas brothers out of the film, they would have to cut him out as well. Though that was an era of selective censorship prompted by bigotry, it was followed very quickly by the McCarthy era, which had a profound effect on television and films of the day. Most Americans under the age of thirty do not realize that it was during this time that the phrase *under God* was added to the Pledge of Allegiance, and that Superman not only had to fight for "truth and justice," but he also had to fight for "the American way"! Then came the sixties, and several films had whole scenes cut from them: scenes depicting blacks in derogatory or stereotypical roles. Ironically, the NAACP was cutting out almost the identical scenes that Southern theater owners had excised years earlier. With the seventies came the purge of the popular "hic-coms," or rural comedies, in favor of more *relevant* programing. It may be hard to believe today that any of the networks would ax a top-ten show, but it happened. This decade, thus far, has been mild by comparison.

It's true there have been requests for warning labels on rock albums, and demands for bans on pornography, but the only true change to come about was the addition of the number thirteen to certain PG rated films. There are only a few years left to this decade, so if the next scissor-happy bunch is going to be the anticigarette people, they'll have to hurry if they want a stamp of censorship on the eighties. But first, of course, they'll have to be successful in their bid to censor the Constitution.

It can only be hoped, and fervently, that this bill fails, and that citizens, like myself, who do not smoke cigarettes will be among the most vocal in upholding the First Amendment, because if we do not speak up, the congressional fight will turn into a Super Bowl with smoking and nonsmoking sections, spectators and contestants. Passage of the bill will be deemed a victory against smoking instead of a defeat of the First Amendment, and that is the real tragedy.

The bicentennial of the Constitution will be celebrated in 1987. The passage of this bill would be a poor birthday gift. How ironic to live in an era where an automobile manufacturer can brag in an advertisement that his car can go from "zero to sixty" in a certain amount of time, but it is illegal to test his claim. Of course we could get close by testing it from zero to fifty-five. It is also amusing to see an over-the-counter cough remedy being touted as nonnarcotic. They might as well claim that their product contains no unicorns, since it is illegal for any over-the-counter medicine to contain narcotics, but still these commercials with their half-truths, no-truths, and unprovable "facts" still persist.

Why in light of all of this is the cigarette singled out? Is it a question of health? Not likely. If it were a matter of health, then why weren't products containing saccharin barred from television? Since aspirin can cause a potentially fatal illness known as Reye's Syndrome, why do aspirin products continue to advertise without a warning? Excessive use of acetaminophen can cause kidney damage, but that fact somehow escapes Madison Avenue.

Perhaps we give medicine a pass because we feel the good it provides outweighs the bad, but if we go with that reasoning, then why do we summarily approve of coffee, carbonated soft drinks, beer or even eggs? Each of these items has some laboratory black mark against it, and they hardly carry any overpowering good to them. These legal consumer goods, which are protected by the First Amendment, give us choles-terol, jittery nerves and drunken drivers. The reason they exist, for good or ill, is because we like them, and the reason they advertise is because we have a free enterprise system; which means there is more than one brand of coffee, soft drink, etc., and the various manufacturers want you to choose their product over their competitors. If Schlitz were the only beer, or Brim the only coffee, there would be no reason for these companies to advertise; they would have the market all to themselves. Even Hershey, after years of spurning television, realized they would have to advertise to stay competitive.

Russia must feel complimented by a government which grows stronger as its citizens become more submissive. After all, isn't imitation the sincerest form of flattery?

Commercials, or ads in the print media, are carefully targeted to a specific consumer group. It is not by accident that children's programs are littered with toy and cereal commercials, or that beer and shaving creams are pushed during ball games. Cigarettes, like alcohol, or auto-mobiles are adult products, and their advertising is targeted accordingly. I have never seen a Winston ad in an issue of *Jack and Jill*, or Bacardi Rum in *Humpty Dumpty*. If the reformers of the First Amendment want to use children as the focal point of their reasoning, then all other companies that produce products for the adult consumer market should watch the Congress very closely, because they may be next.

This is not a hollow warning. More and more we have become a nation content with our government's growing shadow of authority over us. We drive fifty-five, not because we want to, but because we have to. We wear seat belts, not by choice, but by dictum. How ironic then is Russia's complaint that America, through movies and commercials, is making fun of the Soviet Union. Russia should ignore the media representation of their country, and look instead to the citizens of the United States. Russia should be comforted by citizenry that actually demand their freedom of choice be usurped by their government. Russia must feel complimented by a government which grows stronger as its citizens become more submissive. After all, isn't imitation the sincerest form of flattery?

John S. H. Smith
Salt Lake City, Utah

Occupation: Historian
Interests: Reading, travel
Entered the Competition: "To support the
constitutional principle at stake."

> The real danger was not the elimination of free choice, but rather the substitution of a "freedom to make the correct choice."

AMERICAN LIBERTY AND THE "PERFECTIONISTS"

The greatest dangers to Liberty lurk in insidious encroachment by men of zeal; well-meaning but without understanding.
—Justice Louis D. Brandeis

There is a malady abroad in America today. A political disease that the founding fathers were not unfamiliar with, and who thus sought to contain its effects by carefully limiting the opportunities for zealots to impose their vision of a "perfect" America on the people. The complexity and majestic deliberateness of our constitutional processes have one simple aim . . . to ensure that the rights of the individual are in harmony with the needs of society, yet free from the trivializing demands of faddish cliques who would seek to abridge the meaning of American freedom by subverting constitutional legality to "save us from ourselves."

The urge to "perfect" individuals has been present almost from the beginning of American history. The Puritans of Massachusetts Bay Colony derived their name not only from their wish to "purify" the religious practices of the Church of England, from which they would eventually separate themselves, but also from their fundamental belief that their mission in life as individuals and as a church was to carry out God's will to create a perfect society in the wilderness. This "city on a hill" would be a beacon to all mankind; therefore no effort was too great in disciplining all aspects of life to achieve this "perfection."

The Puritans set impossibly high standards for themselves and would fail in their larger purpose, but the general objectives and the distinctive style of legalistic moralism of the Puritan commonwealth would become a dynamic element in the political and social agendas of the new nation of America—with consequences both good and bad.

393

The good can be found in the close relationship between individualism and responsibility created by Puritan values, resulting in a civic conscience that would slowly ripen into the positive concept of political and economic freedoms enshrined in the Constitution. The bad can be summed up very neatly by H. L. Mencken's appraisal of the assertiveness of Puritanism, suggesting that its pervasive interference in the lives of others was provoked by "the haunting fear that someone, somewhere, may be happy."

In this comment, which suggests the meanness of spirit the Puritans displayed toward all whose behavior did not measure up minutely to established propriety, Mencken echoes the much earlier wisdom of Michel de Montaigne, "To forbid us anything is to make us have a mind for it." For, in truth, Puritan censoriousness provoked reactions that doomed their spiritual objectives by suffering those aims to be diminished by pettiness and intolerance. The Pilgrim community at Plymouth, later to be absorbed by like-minded Puritan Massachusetts, vividly demonstrated the absolutist nature of bigotry when they destroyed Thomas Morton's settlement at Merrie Mount. The crime of the citizens of Merrie Mount? Light-mindedness! Drunkenness! Dancing around a maypole! Such merrymaking was a clear abomination in the eyes of those who claimed to know God's will. The maypole was chopped down.

This lack of regard for human frailty, this enmity to man's instinct for simple pleasures, was sternly defended by the Puritan divines as necessary if society was to be purged of those weaknesses that would undermine the community of God which they sought to build. But the fanatical level of this commitment was the agent of destruction of their attempted ideal society. Their democracy was flawed and incomplete because only full members of the Puritan church could participate in the political life of the colony; those without the required level of religious commitment were denied participation in government. Inevitably this sapped the vitality of the great experiment of the faithful by creating dissension and further alienating the secular-minded.

Less than fifty years after the founding of Massachusetts Bay Colony, the issue was addressed by those of the second- and third-generation Puritans who could not, or would not, cope with standards set by their elders. These mellow Puritans forced the creation of a Half-Way Covenant in 1662 that was clear evidence of the failure of the absolutist nature of the earlier covenant. Those evolving Americans-to-be of the Massachusetts Bay Colony, beneficiaries of the democratic example of town-meeting government and of the subversively liberalizing influences of the literacy demanded by the Puritan church, had grown increasingly irked by the oppressive conformity and public display of piety demanded of them. Having established the value of the liberty of conscience, the Puritans had proceeded to deny the full operation of that privilege within their society—and thus they destroyed themselves. Puritans had said "Thou shalt not" too often and too insistently, and this misguided attempt at perfectionism doomed them and their society.

The founding fathers were keenly aware of the violence that the dogmatic beliefs of special interest groups could unleash upon the republic they were striving to create. Respect for compromise as the moderating mechanism to ensure a fair balance among competing interests was their guiding principle. Whether it was the institution of the electoral college to forestall the emergence of a demagogue, or the limiting of power through the operation of checks and balances among the branches of government, or establishing a free press as the watchdog of our liberties, their concern was to preserve for society—and, ultimately, the individual—the freedom of choice in all things. They clearly understood that the real danger was not the elimination of free choice, but rather the substitution of a "freedom to make the correct choice" as determined by those zealously dedicated to making us do what is good for us *whether we like it or not!*

This usurpation of individual freedom can be cloaked in the most inviting, the most seductively phrased, arguments. Dictatorships throughout the world have all made use of the hollow concept of "freedom to make the correct choice." It is more efficient and certainly easier for a nation to be guided by an elite claiming superior knowledge. But those so manipulated are deprived of opportunity for true moral growth that is offered when citizens are governed by their own conscience, and where public policy is determined by a process of compromise among different points of view.

Said T. B. Macaulay in 1830,

> Nothing is so galling to a people not broken in from birth, as a paternal, or in other words a meddling government, a government which tells them what to read, and say, and eat, and drink, and wear.

Well, we are that kind of people! The Constitution was written so as to nullify any efforts in the direction of unwelcome paternalism. Suspicion of the malign effects of too much government control over personal lives suffuses every line. An uncannily prophetic Thomas Jefferson would later write, "Were we directed from [the city of] Washington when to sow, and when to reap, we should soon want bread." He recognized, as did the authors of the Constitution, the limitations of "efficiency" in ordering human affairs. He believed that the bulwark against the stealthy theft of our liberties was a free press. "Our liberty depends on the freedom of the press, and that cannot be limited without being lost."

In many ways the threat to free expression, both in the press and in forms of personal behavior, was less the actions of government than it was the thoughtless tyranny of conventional majority opinion. Speech and choice have been circumscribed by what was thought to be acceptable, through selective appeals to popular ideas and so-called scientific wisdom that would support claims to act in the public interest. Bigots, bluenoses and racists could cover up their autocratic designs with this cloak of respectability and did so, as the study of illiberal nativist movements in American history has shown.

The Prohibition movement was one such conspiracy to deny the right of free expression to Americans. The historical origins of political prohibitionism in the nineteenth century are well-known; a combination of understandable reaction to the social evils of excessive drinking, and of the influence of Protestant sects which had adopted a theological position equating abstention from alcohol with Christian virtue. The rise of the women's movement to some extent paralleled that of Prohibition, for women as wives and mothers were the chief victims of drunkenness. But in retrospect, Prohibition can be viewed as a diversion of the awakening political energies of women. For the conventions of the time made the campaign against alcohol a more socially approved cause than the fight for actual political rights for women.

With the advent of the Progressive Era, prohibitionism benefited from the unspoken assumptions of those involved with promoting the progressive causes of the period. Bluntly, this meant that the least responsible members of society—meaning robber barons as well as the disadvantaged working class—had to be disciplined by a progressive middle class. Arguably, this middle class represented a core of values thought to be under attack by the un-American trends of the late nineteenth century, namely the new industrial wealth and the new immigration. The middle-class response was to utilize its strength to reform society along those lines necessary to reproduce their idea of the American dream. Progressivism was the classic conundrum—illiberal liberalism; self-serving paternalism, if you will. These progressives argued that Prohibition would improve society, and utilizing patriotic arguments against the war time use of grain for the manufacture of alcohol, were able to achieve the victory they sought over the "degrading" habits of others.

Need it be said again that the Eighteenth Amendment was disastrous? It led to gangsterism and the rise of organized crime. It made a mockery of the law by criminalizing behavior that was not wrong in the eyes of many. It corrupted the organs of government. It did nothing to eliminate alcoholism or any other social evil. It was an outrageous infringement of the right of self-expression. It was a smug exercise of social control, a Big Brother manifestation of government. The right to "the pursuit of happiness" had been made secondary to the goal of a perfect America.

Do not surrender the initiative, or the moral high ground, to the proponents of legislated goodness.

Evidence of the popularity of Prohibition as a perfectionist legal device can be found in the extension of the idea to smoking. Tobacco was as vulnerable a target as alcohol, sharing many of the same vague associations with sin and "imperfect" behavior. Evangelist Billy Sunday stirred his followers to action, thundering, "Prohibition is won; now for tobacco." Between 1896 and 1921 no fewer than fourteen states prohibited the sale of cigarettes entirely, with the last of these laws remaining in force as late as 1927. The No-Tobacco League of America and the Clean Life Army of the Anti-Cigarette International League were already in the fray against the evil weed, although the obvious difficulties in enforcing anticigarette laws made their successes temporary, as legislatures usually repealed such laws within one or two years of their enactment.

An example of the disregard of constitutional legalities and the operation of perfectionist progressive legislation was the experience of the state of Utah. The rhetoric of the anticigarette forces was typical of the moral certainty assumed by the self-righteous. "The cigarette smoker is not a degenerate because he smokes cigarettes. Quite often he is a cigarette smoker because he is a degenerate." The intention was to label smoking an offense to public morals, thus justifying the intervention of law. The arguments strain credulity, but were advanced fearlessly because of the moral certainty of their proponents. "The tobacco habit leads to vice, and is frequently the forerunner of crime. This is because tobacco is a drug, and dulls the moral sense." The protection of youth was frequently invoked to legitimize prohibition. "I have seen bright boys turned into dunces and straightforward, honest boys made into cowards by cigarette smoking." Virtue, citizenship, youth—all that was sacred had been shown to be in danger. At the stroke of a pen an unproductive habit had been eliminated, and the moral tone of Utah raised. Or had it? The Utah *Citizen* editorialized, "A cigarette does not mean life, but to some it may mean liberty, and the pursuit of happiness."

The cigarette law foundered in Utah, as it had elsewhere. Why? Because it was a piece of uncalled-for social engineering, an invasion of privacy, an absurdity. Prominent citizens were humiliated by public arrest and the police turned into figures of fun. Religious animosities, combined with political polarization, threatened to recur in a state where tensions between church and state had been resolved less than a decade before.

Fortunately, the dangers were recognized, and the law was changed within two years. It had passed in the first place because a vocal and organized minority had overwhelmed the state legislature with a seemingly unchallengeable moral imperative. This is what must be done for the good of the people! That not all of the people supported such a high-handed limitation of personal freedom was ignored. And that is the message to a still-threatened America. Do not surrender the initiative, or the moral high ground, to the proponents of legislated goodness.

Americans must armor themselves against the weapons of faddish virtue and doubtful science, for the fight is on to mold us all into an ideal . . . what?

The desire to control the lives of others is a disease—a political malady. Americans must armor themselves against the weapons of faddish virtue and doubtful science, for the fight is on to mold us all into an ideal . . . what? To limit freedom of expression in the promotion of tobacco use would further validate the political respectability of prohibition. The defense of liberty must be constant, and the smallest threat countered with firmness and resolution. The freedoms enshrined in the Constitution must not be diminished. Remember the words of an unknown patriotic observer of the Constitution's formative process:

> The Preservation of Liberty is a Point equally nice with the Preservation of a Ladies Chastity; the first Assaults are to be repell'd with the utmost Fortitude. A Maidenhead, a Fort, or a Constitution, that begins to capitulate, will soon surrender. If the Outworks are once given up, the Citadel cannot be long maintained.

Leo O'Connor
South Burlington, Vermont

Occupation: Writer
Interests: Reading, gardening
*Entered the Competition: "To stress the importance
of the First Amendment to the Constitution as the
chief instrument in protecting the rights of the
nation's citizens."*

The web that is woven by moral guardians would strangle
freedom of expression.

THE FIRST AMENDMENT: TOUCHSTONE OF AMERICAN LIBERTY

But for the stubborn resolve of George Mason, one of Virginia's delegates to the Constitutional Convention, the Bill of Rights, as Americans know it, probably would not exist.

During the sometimes heated debate that preceded the adoption of
the Constitution, Mason, one of the authors of Virginia's Declaration of
Rights, was among a minority of delegates who opposed the document
as it was written. Arrayed against such luminaries as Alexander Hamilton, John Jay and James Madison, Mason argued that a bill of rights
should be included in the Constitution. But Hamilton contended that
the Constitution itself was a bill of rights and said that state constitutions would augment it by guaranteeing broader protection for their
citizens. He did not believe, for instance, that there should be a provision in the Constitution on freedom of the press, expressing his doubts
about the ability of the delegates to define the phrase and saying any
attempt to interpret it "would leave the utmost latitude for evasion."
"From this, I infer, that its security, whatever fine declarations may be
inserted in any constitution respecting it, must altogether depend on
public opinion, and on the general spirit of the people and the government," he wrote in *The Federalist*.

Mason was adamant. He was an advocate of strong local government and a weak central authority. Because large and indefinite powers
were granted to the new federal government by the Constitution, he
argued that it must include specific guarantees of individual rights as did
the Virginia constitution, which he drafted in 1776. Without a bill of
rights, he believed, it would be possible for a strong central government
to exercise virtually unlimited authority over its citizens. It was not so
much that he questioned the intentions of those delegates who supported
the Constitution as it was written as it was a fear of the motives of others
who might run the government in the future. Either a bill of rights would
be included or he would refuse to sign the Constitution, he said.

When the delegates assembled to give formal assent to the Constitution on that September day in 1787, George Mason had clearly been outvoted. There was no bill of rights. His powerful convictions would not permit him to sign the document. At the same time, he warned the other delegates that he would continue his campaign to include guarantees of individual rights in the Constitution. And he embarked on his crusade even before the states ratified it.

His persistence paid off in 1789 when the Bill of Rights was put before Congress for its approval and when it was adopted two years later. It constitutes a milestone on the route toward individual liberty, a model for other nations that choose a democratic form of government. That the United Nations used the Bill of Rights as a framework for its Universal Declaration on Human Rights is proof that those principles are just as relevant in the twentieth century as they were in the eighteenth. By guaranteeing American citizens against unwarranted intrusions by government into their lives, the Bill of Rights is an unequivocal statement in defense of the right of privacy. Moreover, it assures the people that government essentially belongs to them and not to those who exercise temporary power. Mischief makers are precluded from misusing their authority by arbitrarily voiding the basic rights of the citizens. Demagogues and tyrants cannot carry out their schemes as long as the Bill of Rights exists.

While the nation will celebrate the bicentennial of the Constitution this year, there is an even greater reason for celebration in 1991 when the Bill of Rights will be two hundred years old. However important the other provisions of the Constitution may be, the first ten amendments are more relevant in the daily lives of Americans.

The First Amendment is the touchstone of the Constitution, protecting as it does the people's rights to religious freedom, free expression and peaceful assembly. There can be no official state religion; citizens are free to belong to any denomination, or none at all. They can express their opinions without fear of being arrested for doing so, even when they are critical of government policies. The press is given broad latitude in fulfilling its obligations of keeping the people informed. When citizens disagree with the government, they can take to the streets to demonstrate their disapproval. Standing as it does at the head of the Bill of Rights, the First Amendment is the key to the other rights enumerated in the first ten amendments. Without it, the Constitution would be little more than a pale shadow of itself. It, in essence, is a demand that government respect human dignity and individual rights.

Nothing underlines its significance more than the numerous efforts to dilute it or abolish it in the two centuries since its adoption. Those who wish to erode the concept of personal liberty know that they must begin by canceling the First Amendment. Before they can set in motion schemes to undermine the government, they must first stifle the right to freedom of expression, for free speech and freedom of the press are formidable roadblocks on the path that leads to repression. "The only security of all is a free press," said Thomas Jefferson. "The force of public opinion cannot be resisted, when permitted freely to be expressed." Jefferson's views were shared by James Madison who said, "To the press alone, checkered as it is with abuses, the world is indebted for all the triumphs which have been obtained by reason and humanity over error and oppression."

That there have been many assaults on the First Amendment since its inception is a fact of history. Using the pretext of good intentions, politicians with shoddy motives have tried to persuade the public to surrender the right to free expression, contending that, for one reason or another, the fate of the nation was at stake. Indeed at times it appeared that citizens were willing to accept some restraints on the theory that giving up a little liberty was harmless. Fortunately, more perceptive individuals sounded the alarm and the deceptive schemes were thwarted. Yet excuses for restricting free speech are heard even today: national security, higher standards of morality, protecting people from the consequences of their own mistakes, concern for public health.

Would-be censors, wrapped in cloaks of righteousness, yearn to impose their standards on others by determining what citizens can hear, read or see. Most are moral busybodies who often see evil where there is none. Their objectives are to create a homogeneous society where everyone talks alike, thinks alike and acts alike. All other behavior in their version of Utopia would be deviant. Yet their ideal world would be a sterile place, closely resembling those closed societies which are so repugnant to free people. Nevertheless, the censors, morally mistaken though they may be, fervently pursue their goals. They conduct campaigns to strip the nation's libraries of books, many of them literary classics, that they contend are offensive. Claiming that magazines plant the seeds of sin in vulnerable minds, they demand the removal of certain types of periodicals from the racks of newsstands and other stores. They would control television programming to insure that the public would be protected from seeing what the censors believe it should not see. The web that is woven by moral guardians would strangle freedom of expression. If given free rein, they would consign the First Amendment to the trash bin of history.

Where they would stop, no one knows. Once they succeeded in controlling freedom of expression, would they then invade the realm of ideas? Would they demand that books, magazines and newspapers that contain material that conflicts with their particular ideology be removed from libraries and bookstores? Would they attempt to rewrite the Constitution so that people who voiced unpopular opinions would be jailed? Behind the façade of righteousness lurks the specter of repression. It is a frightening prospect.

Only by being vigilant can free men and women avoid such an eventuality. Unfortunately, however, too many citizens are indifferent to the assaults on liberty. And the conduct of the government is equally discouraging. At times it seems to be allied with the zealots. When an attorney general appoints a commission on pornography with the avowed intention of reaffirming his convictions that the government must exercise censorship, civil libertarians must shudder at the consequences for freedom of expression. To proscribe the publication of even one magazine is for the government to take a giant step toward controlling the free flow of information. "I am really mortified to be told that in the United States of America, a fact like this can become a subject of inquiry, and of criminal inquiry too. . . that a question about a sale of a book can be carried before the civil magistrates," said Thomas Jefferson in 1814. "Are we to have a censor whose imprimatur shall say what books may be sold, and what we may buy? . . . It is an insult to our citizens to question whether they are rational beings or not."

And when Congress proposes to restrict certain types of advertising, it too is going beyond the scope of its authority and flirting with the idea of abrogating the First Amendment. It, in short, is acting as a self-anointed censor. Meddling in the legitimate activities of the private sector is unjustified and unjustifiable. Banning tobacco advertising, for instance, would set a perilous precedent. Worst of all, such a measure would deprive a group of citizens of their right to do what other citizens can do without restrictions. Even though the proposed legislation may appear to be aimed only at the tobacco industry, it will only be a matter of time before other businesses will be denied their constitutional rights. The argument over whether smoking is harmful to the public health is irrelevant when it is put in the context of the larger issue: the arbitrary cancellation of the right of free speech by the Congress. To suggest that citizens are incapable of making intelligent choices is to say that they are inferior to those who govern the country. Whatever the effect of tobacco advertising on their behavior, consumers, in the end, must be allowed to make up their own minds about smoking in the same way as they decide what detergents or dog food to buy. Choice is what a democracy is all about. Powerful as advertising may be, rational people

404

must be conceded the right to resist it and choose their own courses of action.

Prohibiting tobacco advertising could signal the beginning of campaigns against other forms of advertising. Alcohol could well be the next target. Considered one of the most serious problems of modern society, alcoholism destroys families and careers. Drunken driving has snuffed out the lives of millions of innocent people. Having decided to protect citizens from the dangers of smoking, congressmen might well vote to impose bans on liquor advertising. Denial of freedom of expression to one segment of the economy is bound to have a snowball effect. Other businesses and industries surely will be next.

The First Amendment cannot be interpreted selectively for any purpose; it means clearly what it says, no more, no less.

The First Amendment cannot be interpreted selectively for any purpose; it means clearly what it says, no more, no less.

To reinvent it to conform to the standards of one group or another is to set the stage for its destruction. Legal speech—and the courts have ruled that advertising falls in that area—cannot be proscribed even if proscription is perceived as a means of protecting people from the consequences of their own mistakes. Neither Congress nor the courts can shape the First Amendment to fit the peculiar biases of the moment. If that were so, it would not have survived the vicissitudes of history. In a nation that lives by the rule of the law, twisting the law to serve what may be perceived as good intentions cannot, and should not, be tolerated. To allow that to happen would be to consent to the dismantling of democracy.

Proponents of a ban on tobacco advertising might argue that there is precedent for such legislation, since the Supreme Court in 1972 upheld a similar measure to prohibit such advertising on television. They might say that theirs is nothing more than a logical step to extend the ban to other media. Questions must be raised, however, about the Court's decision in that case because it appeared to conflict with the rights of individuals and businesses to free speech. The decision was puzzling on a constitutional basis. By denying the tobacco industry free access to television, the Court clearly contradicted its own precedents for the protection of free speech in all its forms. In decision after decision in the past, the Court staunchly defended First Amendment principles to the exclusion of other considerations. That the Court abandoned its role as the arbiter of the law to cast itself as the guardian of public health lent the impression that the justices felt they could reinvent the First Amendment to conform to popular opinion. Little wonder then that Congress now feels it has a license to invade areas that lie beyond the bounds of its authority.

Neither Congress nor the courts can shape the First Amendment to fit the peculiar biases of the moment.

To dilute the First Amendment by restricting freedom of expression in any way is to betray the principles that drove George Mason during his campaign to include a bill of rights in the Constitution. It is to negate the convictions of Jefferson and Madison who believed that liberty was not something to be taken lightly by the government and the people, that the inalienable rights of the citizenry cannot be canceled to satisfy the whims of various interest groups.

Only by stoutly defending the right of freedom of expression can Americans keep faith with the founders of the nation and insure that their precious legacy will be preserved.

Stephen P. Halbrook, Ph.D., J.D.
Fairfax, Virginia

Occupation: Attorney
Interest: Marathon running, sports shooting,
hunting, swimming
Entered the Competition because: "Government
censorship of printed matter violates the freedom of
the press. The Bill of Rights will be preserved only if
citizens speak up."

There is probably no freedom our founding fathers sought to
make perpetual that some legislator is not at this moment,
albeit perhaps with good intentions, scheming to destroy.

CAN THE FIRST AMENDMENT SURVIVE A BAN ON TOBACCO ADVERTISING?

As Americans prepare to celebrate the bicentennial of the Constitution and Bill of Rights, various politicians are busily at work in Congress trying to restrict virtually every right the people have enjoyed for these two hundred years. There is probably no freedom our founding fathers sought to make perpetual that some legislator is not at this moment, albeit perhaps with good intentions, scheming to destroy. Yet by focusing public attention on the liberties guaranteed under our written charters, the bicentennial may be a turning point which will revitalize freedom in America.

This analysis addresses the proposal that Congress ban the advertising of tobacco products. This is only one of hundreds of pending proposals to outlaw previously legal conduct. The writer of this article is a nonsmoker. Yet all Americans have an interest in preserving the First Amendment freedoms of speech and the press, and a ban on advertising lawful products would be a particularly egregious abridgement of those rights.

The proposed ban on tobacco advertising will, if enacted, lead to similar bans being applied to all kinds of products. Advertising of fantasy "action figures" must be prohibited because they may encourage violence among children. Americans should not be encouraged to buy ladders because they cause such a large proportion of household injuries. Sugar-laced cereals, meats with high fat content and other foods which contribute to obesity and heart disease must not be advertised. There will be no end to the products that our censors will protect us from.

Moreover, if Congress can determine what products we may learn about through advertising, why may it not also decide what political ideas the people are exposed to through advertising? Economist Ludwig Von Mises said it best in *Human Action* (1949): "If one assigns to the government the task of making truth prevail in the advertising of

409

perfumes and toothpaste, one cannot contest it the right to look after truth in the more important matters of religion, philosophy, and social ideology."

Even if the proposed advertising ban does not abridge the rights to freedom of speech and the press (which it does), it is unclear what authority Congress would have to enact the ban under its limited, enumerated powers defined in the Constitution. The following analyzes two critical areas to determine whether such an advertising ban passes constitutional muster. First, would the ban be permissible under current Supreme Court precedents on the First Amendment? Second, what was the intent of the framers of the First Amendment when they said that "Congress shall make *no law*. . . abridging the freedom of speech, or of the press"?

The leading Supreme Court decision on the First Amendment protection of commercial advertising is *Virginia State Board of Pharmacy v. Virginia Citizens Consumer Council, Inc.*, 425 U.S. 748 (1976). Freedom of speech protects both the speaker, including an advertiser, and the listener, who is entitled to receive advertising. Speech which does "no more than propose a commercial transaction" is still speech, and it is entitled to First Amendment protection even though the advertiser has an ecomonic interest. As the Court stated:

> Moreover, there is another consideration that suggests that no line between publicly "interesting" or "important" commercial advertising and the opposite kind could ever be drawn. Advertising, however tasteless and excessive it sometimes may seem, is nonetheless dissemination of information as to who is producing and selling what product, for what reason, and at what price. So long as we preserve a predominantly free enterprise ecomomy, the allocation of our resources in large measure will be made through numerous private economic decisions. It is a matter of public interest that those decisions, in the aggregate, be intelligent and well informed. To this end, the free flow of commercial information is indispensable.

Some social planners believe that they, as a ruling elite, should make the "right" choices for the common people, who should be denied information about products (such as tobacco) the social planners do not like. The Court stated: "There is, of course, an alternative to this highly paternalistic approach. That alternative is to assume that this information is not in itself harmful, that people will perceive their own best interests if only they are well enough informed, and that the best means to that end is to open the channels of communication rather than to close them."

410

Similarly, in *Central Hudson Gas and Electric Corp.* v. *Public Service Comm.*, 447 U.S. 557 (1980), the Supreme Court noted that in recent years it "has not approved a blanket ban on commercial speech unless the expression itself was flawed in some ways, either because it was deceptive or related to unlawful activity." Advertisements of tobacco products are not misleading per se, nor is tobacco unlawful in any state.

Since speech and press are fundamental rights, well-established Supreme Court jurisprudence would hold that they may be balanced or restricted only for a compelling governmental interest. *Central Hudson* addresses this concern by requiring that the restriction must in fact substantially advance the state interest and must be narrowly drawn.

A ban on tobacco advertising could not meet these strict standards. First, the extent to which advertising (in contrast with peer influence or individual choice) "causes" nonsmokers to become smokers is low; rather, advertising affects brand selection by preexisting smokers. Secondly, if the state wishes to discourage smoking, it may pursue less drastic alternatives than a First Amendment violation—such as a public education campaign.

In a five-to-four opinion, the Supreme Court recently upheld a partial ban on casino advertising in *Posadas de Puerto Rico Assoc.* v. *Tourism Co. of Puerto Rico*, 92 L.Ed.2d 266 (1986). The Court upheld a prohibition on such advertising aimed at residents of Puerto Rico, on the theory that the gambling itself could be banned, and thus the advertising of gambling could be banned as well.

In *dictum*, the Court stated: "Legislative regulation of products or activities deemed harmful, such as cigarettes, alcoholic beverages, and prostitution, has varied from outright prohibition on the one hand . . . to legalization of the product or activity with restrictions on stimulation of its demand on the other hand. . . . " This analogy mixes apples with oranges, because cigarettes have never been banned, unlike alcohol and prostitution.

Under the *Posadas* rule, if a *state* could ban tobacco, then the *state* could ban advertising of tobacco products. Yet it is uncertain that a state may prohibit consumption of tobacco, given the right to privacy, the liberty interest in freedom of choice, and the retention by the people in the federal Ninth Amendment and various state bills of rights of all rights not explicitly enumerated. Indeed, tobacco was in common use when the Bill of Rights was adopted.

Posadas in no way suggests that if a *state* could and did ban tobacco, then the *federal government* could ban tobacco advertising. Nor does the Congress have any enumerated power to prohibit tobacco or any other product for that matter, although it may regulate interstate commerce and tax various products. The federal government had no constitutional power to prohibit the manufacture, sale or transportation of intoxicating liquors until the Eighteeth Amendment was ratified. Nor could it prohibit tobacco production and consumption without a constitutional amendment authorizing it to do so.

The United States is a federal system, in that the Congress may pass legislation authorized by the limited, enumerated powers in Article I, Section 8 of the Constitution. None of those powers would justify a ban on tobacco or advertising of tobacco. The states have broad powers to legislate for the common good and may pass general criminal codes. Even then, the states are barred under the First Amendment and equivalent state guarantees from abridging freedom of speech and the press.

A review of the intent of the framers of the Constitution and Bill of Rights confirms that the framers meant exactly what they said when they wrote that Congress shall make "no law" abridging the freedom of speech or of the press. Two hundred years ago, anyone who suggested that Congress had a constitutional power to do things like ban tobacco advertising would have been considered a lunatic. This author has reviewed hundreds of newspapers published in the 1787–91 period, when the Constitution and Bill of Rights was debated and ratified. Bulk tobacco and smoking pipes were frequently advertised commodities.

Two hundred years ago, anyone who suggested that Congress had a constitutional power to do things like ban tobacco advertising would have been considered a lunatic.

The chief objection to the Constitution as originally proposed was that it had no bill of rights. Alexander Hamilton argued in *The Federalist* No. 84 that an enumeration of rights is "less applicable to a Constitution like that under consideration, which is merely intended to regulate the general political interests of the nation, than to a Constitution which has the regulation of every species of personal and private concerns." In short, the Constitution was intended to secure national defense and to prevent the states from enacting restrictions on trade against each other, not to interfere with such activities as informing consumers about and providing them with products in the marketplace.

Hamilton's further remarks seem to have been tailor-made to preclude any misinterpretation that the Constitution, even without a bill of rights, empowered Congress to regulate, much less prohibit, the freedom of the press:

I go further and affirm that *bills of rights*, in the sense and to the extent in which they are contended for, are not only unnecessary in the proposed Constitution but would even be dangerous. They would contain various exceptions to powers which are not granted; and, on this very account, would afford a colorable pretext to claim more than were granted. For why declare that things shall not be done which there is no power to do? Why, for instance, should it be said that the liberty of the press shall not be restrained, when no power is given by which restrictions may be imposed? I will not contend that such a provision would confer a regulating power; but it is evident that it would furnish, to men disposed to usurp, a plausible pretense for claiming that power. They might urge with a semblance of reason that the Constitution ought not to be charged with the absurdity of providing against the abuse of the authority which was not given, and that the provision against restraining the liberty of the press afforded a clear implication that a power to prescribe proper regulations concerning it was intended to be vested in the national government. This may serve as a specimen of the numerous handles which would be given to the doctrine of constructive powers, by the indulgence of an injudicious zeal for bills of rights.

Predictably, today someone wants Congress to ban advertisements of products that have been legally in demand, advertised, and consumed in this country since the colony of Virginia was settled in the seventeenth century. The argument by the proponent of this measure, Congressman Mike Synar, in the December 1986 issue of the *American Bar Association Journal* that tobacco advertising is not "protected under the First Amendment" is enough to evoke a rousing "I told you so!" from Alexander Hamilton's grave.

The argument by Congressman Mike Synar that tobacco advertising is not "protected under the First Amendment" is enough to evoke a rousing "I told you so!" from Alexander Hamilton's grave.

When James Madison, the father of the Constitution, proposed the Bill of Rights to Congress in 1789, what became the First Amendment read in part: "The people shall not be deprived or abridged of their right to speak, to write, or to publish their sentiments; and the freedom of the press, as one of the great bulwarks of liberty, shall be inviolable." This language shows the absolute character of the right protected, and exactly what is inviolable: speaking, writing and publishing.

Congressman James Jackson objected to a Bill of Rights because,

413

however expressed, politicians would later try to restrict the rights enumerated by misconstruction and argue that the rights not listed do not exist. Moreover, Congress had no power over speech or the press: "The gentleman endeavors to secure the liberty of the press; pray how is this in danger? There is no power given to Congress to regulate this subject as they can commerce, or peace, or war." Jackson and his colleagues would be horrified to know the powers some today presume Congress to have.

Madison's draft was reworded by the House committee on amendments to state: "The freedom of speech and of the press. . . shall not be infringed." Madison had no problem with this change, remarking that "the right of freedom of speech is secured; the liberty of the press is expressly declared to be *beyond the reach of this Government.* . . . " Clearly, it was intended that Congress would have no authority to regulate or prohibit free speech or a free press.

As finally adopted, the language of the First Amendment could not have been clearer: "Congress shall make *no law* . . . abridging the freedom of speech, or of the press. . . . " "No law," despite the seeming inability of some contemporary lawmakers to read, means exactly what it says: *no law.*

The first major analysis of the Bill of Rights was published in 1803 by St. George Tucker, a friend of Madison and of Thomas Jefferson. Discussing the freedom of speech and press, Tucker began with "one of the great fundamental principles of the American government, that the people are the sovereign, and those who administer the government their agents, and servants, not their kings and masters. . . . " The First Amendment guarantees to the people the rights to "speaking, writing, printing, or by any other mode of publishing, which they may think proper. . . . [T]he smallest infringement of the rights guaranteed by this article, must threaten the total subversion of the government."

The founding fathers saw very clearly the dangers of abridging freedom of speech and press by restricting ideas or messages with which one disagrees or dislikes. Tucker quoted U.S. Supreme Court Chief Justice John Marshall as stating that this liberty has sometimes been "carried to excess; that it has sometimes degenerated into licentiousness, is seen and lamented; but the remedy has not been discovered. Perhaps it is an evil inseparable from the good to which it is allied: perhaps it is a shoot which cannot be stripped from the stalk, without wounding vitally the plant from which it is torn. However desirable those measures might be which correct without enslaving the press, they have never yet been devised in America."

414

Nothing has changed since the above was written regarding government's inability to censor the press without enslaving it. Nor is there any way government can prohibit discussion, speech or advertising concerning perfectly legal products and activities without threatening free expression in all forms, not to mention the economic freedom of consumers. If freedom of speech and of the press, a limited federal government with enumerated powers, and a free enterprise economy are to survive another century, it may well be only through a rediscovery of the principles of liberty so well expounded by our founding fathers.

William H. Ryan
Mount Vernon, Washington

Occupation: Executive Director
Interests: Landscape gardening, sailing, reading
Entered the Competition because: "I am strongly
interested and concerned about the topic of
government intervention in the marketplace—
whether it is the marketplace of goods,
services or ideas."

> Call [the First Amendment] a carefully crafted edifice if you will, an arch of the indispensabilities of freedom. Pull out one and it's tumbledown time.

IS FREEDOM JUST A BREAKFASTFOOD?

> *Congress shall make no law respecting an establishment of religion, or prohibiting the free exercise thereof; or abridging the Freedom of Speech, or of the press; or the right of the people peaceably to assemble, and to petition the government for a redress of grievances.*
> *—The First Amendment*

Freedom.

Now there's a word to wrestle with. There's a word that has called forth a billion words to explain it, and explain it away. It shows as many phases and faces as the moon: freedom of speech, freedom of assembly, freedom of the press, freedom of religious practice. And like the moon, over the ages, freedom evokes fear and superstition from those who seek to be feared, joy from those who crave light in man's dark night.

Do you remember e.e. cummings' opening line, "as freedom is a breakfastfood. . . "? It's a line to make one wonder if that poet of irony and wonder, joy and anger had just scanned the First Amendment when he penned it. The questions which cummings' line provokes are myriad.

Is freedom just a breakfastfood? Is the First Amendment just a long-ago-ingested, long-digested potpourri of ingredients with no nutritional value for the body politic after two centuries? Did the writers of the Bill of Rights cynically word-solder together the various "freedoms" demanded by their separate constituencies, then tack this freedom ornament on the Constitution, just to purchase that document's passage by those who feared federalism? Did cummings see freedom as an insubstantial, sugarcoated cereal, to be hawked by demagogues to hungry colonials? Or did he speak ironically? Did the poet hold freedom to be vital, permanant, indivisible?

cummings has his own answer, to which we will return.

In the meantime, it remains worth our while to wrestle with this word, this concept, this freedom which cummings challenges us to engage.

The questions beckon: Is freedom, particularly as articulated in the First Amendment, a mishmash of artificially related ingredients? Together, do they add up to only an insubstantial abstraction? If you remove one of the ingredients, one of the so-called freedoms, does the meal remain? Is there a necessary wholeness to freedom? And was the First Amendment, or even the entire Bill of Rights, just a frosted afterthought, enticing the separate states to substitute union for confederation?

The latter question is well answered through review of any solid American history text. While the Constitution might have been launched, it would neither have remained upright nor would have sailed without a Bill of Rights. Giants of integrity such as John Hancock and Sam Adams, along with the critical ratifying state of Massachusetts and those that followed after, said, in effect, "No Bill of Rights, no Constitution." And at the top of the rights agenda was what we know as the First Amendment, that curious conglomeration of freedoms.

Or were they curious? A random amalgam to attract allegiance and the attention of the generation popularly enamored of "The Rights of Man"? Or is there a pattern there, an integration of parts which both makes a whole and without all of which there is no whole? And does the whole make up something which our grandfathers would have said, "sticks to your ribs"?

If we reread the words, the order, the direction of the First Amendment, we need few commentaries or texts. Purpose is plain here. Meaning is clear. More than a pattern exists in this seminal paragraph, more even than an order. A sort of building is going on here, an erection of a hierarchy of values. Call it a carefully crafted edifice if you will, an arch of the indispensabilities of freedom. Pull out one and it's tumbledown time.

The overall framework of the First Amendment—its context and direction—is evident: It is directed to government, not to individuals, private societies, businesses or corporations. It is a caveat to government, a warning not to begin to chip away at the whole of freedom by removing pieces of freedom. The men of the eighteenth century knew that governments, not private associations or individuals, have the final power to shrink, to extirpate the citizens' freedom. Government, finally, makes the law, enforces the law. Government possesses the final monopoly on the police power. Thus the words begin, "*Congress* shall make no law. . . " The words do not begin, "XYZ, or XYZ corporation shall make no law. . . ."

420

The pieces of freedom, the quintessential ingredients, are next enumerated so that the impingement or theft of any single one can be clearly seen as a hole in the whole. The missing piece will be conspicuous by its disappearance.

First the foundation: freedom of religious choice. This is the basis of man's whole system of belief and action. What a person believes and thinks and hopes about the Ultimate Things will ultimately determine the goals, the quality, the self-achievement of his or her life. Monopolize the "way" to God (and only government possesses the power to enact and enforce monopoly) and many will not find their way to God because they are not free to search for their own individual paths. Block all paths but one and different men, being different, will not discern their Purpose, their Final Truth.

And of what value is the freedom of religious belief without the next building block, the freedom to *exercise* that belief? Thus the amendment's first critical link between the personal and the social, the individual and the shared, the world of thought and the world of action. I think and arrive at belief. Belief about the nature and purpose of man in the universe. But I am not free unless I can exercise that belief openly, publicly. Yet freedom does not stop here; *your* freedom depends upon being able both to exercise your belief *and* observe, compare and perhaps share my belief. The proof of the freedom of thought emerges in its expression. The proof of its expression becomes manifest in its communicability. Freedom *is* an abstraction unless it can be exercised. Freedom is an equally empty right unless its expression is mutual, shared, comparative—sometimes even competitive. Who will learn and who will teach, who will grow and who will reform their lives without the ability to acquire, exchange, renew and review their thoughts?

The logic of those who drafted the Bill of Rights two hundred years ago does not allow escape: Freedom of thought must be exercised. It will be shared, communicated, or it will wither. The next freedom, "Freedom of Speech," follows inexorably. Note that it is capitalized in the original. Properly so. The bond between idea and expression, between thought and speech is imperative for the life of freedom; they are divisible only by coercion. Abort Freedom of Speech and its twin, its mother freedoms die.

On to freedom of the press, to all those forms of public communication which we call today the "media." Like branches, these modes of social, widespread communication grow organically, ungrafted, from the trunk of Freedom of Speech. In many tongues—published literature, product advertising, videotapes, television and the traditional newsprint, they speak not only of the freedom of speech, but of the

421

freedom of hearing, learning, thinking. Tie off one tongue and you have pierced one eardrum.

It becomes ever clearer the more one examines this thing called freedom that it is even more than a patterned order. It *is* organic, symbiotic. Its roots are deep but its manifestations, the proofs of its health, are prosaic and ordinary as twigs and leaves. Strip off the leaves from only one small twig of a new branch: one small death. Only a twig. Keep stripping, carefully, one by one. In the season of flourishing growth. Watch. Ever see caterpillars kill a tree over the course of a summer?

Tie off one tongue and you have pierced one eardrum.

Perhaps not. Perhaps, in two hundred years we have wandered far from a forested world where observance and observation of the particularities, the smaller evidences, meant the difference between survival and oblivion. Perhaps we think, in these our times, that a great, stark, naked trunk, still supported by ancient, decaying roots, is a living tree.

We think, for instance, that we would mount the barricades against "thought control." "Orwellian," we call it. We express indignity at "censorship," outrage at "muzzling" of the press or other media. We scorn the generations which banned and burned D. H. Lawrence, James Joyce, Henry Miller. In our righteous, deep-rooted commitment to the exercise of religious freedom, we have even purged religious exercise from our public schools. Why, we simply *adhere* to the tree of freedom; we *cling* to the great, stark trunk.

With some minor—very minor—exceptions. Some trimming of unruly leaves and branches. To make the tree of freedom a little more to our personal liking, shape it a little more to our group's interest or taste.

And the pruning tool we use is the best, sharpest, most efficient. Always has been. It's our government. "Congress," as it's called in the First Amendment.

Let's take the instance of product advertising. A very small and, you might say, *inferior* form of media freedom or freedom of speech. For it's the language of the marketplace, the speech of the vendor, the producer of goods and services. It's not the speech of world leaders or world-class thinkers. It's often tasteless, raucous, offensive to you or me or both of us. But it happens to be the only way the producer or vendor can communicate with someone who might need or want what the producer offers. Just as significantly, it happens to be the only way, with any degree of efficiency, in which the person in Oregon, or in Newark or in Buffalo, can learn about something he needs and wants from a producer in White Plains. I need to speak and you need to hear in order to learn what we need and don't need.

But you and I don't like the free speech of the marketplace. It's too loud, or too corny. Or even too effective. So let's regulate it, prohibit it. Let's ban the billboards, limit access to television. And, because you and I haven't the power to enforce our opinions or tastes, let's use government. Let's have "Congress make. . . [a] law prohibiting. . . . " Take what analogy suits you: It's only a small ingredient, a small part—out of the meal, the recipe, the tree. Only a small stone has disappeared from the edifice.

As there is a logical building of freedom in the First Amendment, there is a progression in its dismantlement to remind one of the closing of a vise. Within the encroachment of the right to advertise is the particularly pointed case of the tobacco industry.

The progression marches as follows: competitive advertising, followed by coercive advertising, followed by no advertising.

The progression marches as follows: competitive advertising, followed by coercive advertising, followed by no advertising.

First, the government spoke out against the use of tobacco, especially cigarettes. Although we had no say in the cost or exercise of our government's right to advertise, and although the media dared not grumble at the government's "public service messages," it was a freedom of speech of sorts, where the free communication of competing ideas could enhance our ability to choose.

Some chose to quit smoking. Some chose to keep smoking. Some chose to start or not start smoking. It's the way of freedom.

But for those who wish to control, some is not enough. So the government, using law as force, coerced the tobacco companies into running *antiproduct* ads on their *own* products. The companies, of course, were forced to bear the cost of speaking out publicly (advertising) against themselves.

Well, perhaps you could say that it was more efficient; the potential buyer could be informed both for and against a product on the product's own label. And in the way of the marketplace, where the free man chooses freely between many and competing speeches, some chose to quit smoking, some chose not to begin. But some chose to exercise their hearing, their seeing and their choice another way. And some is still not enough.

So Congress is now considering "prohibiting," as the First Amendment terms it, the advertising of tobacco altogether. Having failed to win by the rules, those who seek a single "way"—their way, bend the rules. Failing that, they break the rules. Finally, failing to win all, they tumble down the rules. They erect Rule.

What shall we say? What would Sam Adams or John Hancock say as they held in one hand the First Amendment, in the other a "law prohibiting" free speech in the marketplace?

"It's only tobacco"? Or is it, this freedom, only breakfastfood? Nothing to get *exercised* about.

What does the poet say about this? How does cummings speak, whose personal and professional life was dedicated absolutely to the freedom to express his unique, radical style, his unpopular beliefs, his dread and distaste of war, force and especially, government coercion? Two stanzas should suffice:

> as freedom is a breakfastfood
> or truth can live with right and wrong
> or molehills are from mountains made
> —long enough and just so long
> will being pay the rent of seem
> and genius please the talentgang
> and water most encourage flame
>
> as hatracks into peachtrees grow
> or hopes dance best on bald men's hair
> and every finger is a toe
> and any courage is a fear
> —long enough and just so long
> will the impure think all things pure
> and hornets wail by children stung

Shall Congress make a law prohibiting the free speech of the marketplace? Does the water of such a prohibition most encourage the flame of freedom? Or does it drown it? As in a bowl of soggy breakfastfood.

Susan T. Dean, Ed. D.
Cross Lanes, West Virginia

Occupation: Special Assistant (Technical Affairs) to the Governor
Interests: Swimming, classical piano, bluegrass banjo, writing, needlework
Entered the Competition because: "I enjoy the challenge of structured writing. Writing on a predefined topic is an enjoyable intellectual challenge."

Rather, these representative Americans seek to erode and
destroy a major American enterprise through a methodical
plan for government-imposed obscurity.

ON PROCESS AND CHOOSING IN AMERICA

Choice. The freedom to decide. This simple notion served as sole
impetus for an historic revolution and is the ideological foundation of
the largest free society in the history of civilization.

Choice. Millions have died for it. Untold others from every region
of the globe have endured persecution, poverty and family separation to
seek it within the boundaries of America.

What is it about freedom of choice that so intensely bonds a people
of stark cultural, ethnic and philosophical diversity? What are the
commonalities that unite America's people in this singular theme
despite differences and disagreements throughout the spectrum of day-
to-day living? And what must the government of and by the people of
this land of choices do to insure the preservation of that which made
and nurtures America?

The authors of the United States Constitution recognized that
only through the unrestricted flow of ideas and information could a
people be expected to make informed choices. They knew that informed
decision making—an exposure to and understanding of all available
alternatives—was requisite to survival in and of an organized free
society.

The First Amendment is much more than a perpetual guarantee
that Americans will have the freedom to choose. It provides assurance
that those who would endorse an idea, a practice or a product will be
free to disseminate information openly to all who would receive it
through speech, assembly and an uncensored press. It warrants that
the process of choosing may be accomplished in an information-rich
environment.

In this society of free choice, the art of persuasion is the most
significant tool for those who would sell ideas, products or services.
Evangelists, politicians and businessmen alike rely on effective persuasion to swell the rosters of believers, to promote candidates and statutes,
and to market the wares of American enterprise.

427

The outcomes of persuasion are the heart and soul of the moral, social and economic systems which are America. Selective response to persuasion is the exercise of the very freedom which spawned America's creation. Unstifled persuasion substantively reinforces an otherwise superfluous cohesion of a people united only by the birthright to differences.

Censorship erodes the free flow of information, and thereby subverts the citizens' right to choose. Government imposed limitations on persuasion make a mockery of America's inherent freedoms. If religions, political entities or businesses are arbitrarily prohibited their right to provide information—to persuade—every citizen is effectively denied the guarantees of the First Amendment to the United States Constitution. By controlling the flow of persuasive information, a government can serve only to narrow, and finally eliminate, the freedom of choice upon which America was founded.

Free and uncensored persuasion is the process which lends credence to choice. And the freedom of choice—of informed choosing—is the process for which the cornerstone of America is hewn.

In a 1956 article entitled "What's American About America?", * historian John Kouwenhoven discussed his perplexity that a people so diverse would share an impelling unity in being "American." He sought to define and describe that elusive characteristic which made us all uniquely Americans.

Kouwenhoven began by analyzing several things apparently common to the American way of life, such as chewing gum, jazz, the Constitution, skyscrapers and soap operas for their elements of appeal. He concluded that, while much of that which is American is made up of "apparently irreconcilable opposites," all of America subscribes to *process* rather than *conclusion*.

He postulated that chewing gum is American because it can be chewed for a moment or forever. This favorite confection affords its user the process of chewing as opposed to the finality of satiation.

Jazz was portrayed as a loosely-organized musical style attending more to momentum than melody. The jazz performance, though laced with distinct patterns of rhythm and tone, is without harmonic resolution.

The Constitution was said to be an "infinitely extendible framework for the process of reconciling liberty and unity over vast areas and conflicting interests." This treatise represents not the detail of law, but stands as foundation for the process of governance.

* Kouwenhoven, John A. "What's American About America?", *Harper's Magazine*, July 1956, pp. 25–33.

Skyscrapers were labeled as process architecture because they lack a conclusive cornice. A skyscraper could go on forever. And soap operas were said to offer but a compendium of interwoven scenes which assure the writers ample material for future episodes.

During the thirty years since the publication of "What's American About America?", other telling indicators of America as process and Americans as subscribing to "infinite extendibility" have evidenced themselves. Examples of these are lotteries, computers and the ubiquitous home mortgage plans.

Lottery jackpots have grown to the tens of millions of dollars. Hoards of Americans from the myriad of cultural, ethnic and socio-economic strata of America anxiously await the weekly drawing now held in roughly half the states in the union. Most never win, but continue to be lured to the process of the draw—to the ongoing element of chance.

Computers are being produced in America to manipulate ever-growing amounts of information in machines once consuming a warehouse, then shrinking to the size of a desktop, then to a portable device and getting smaller. Attention to the prospective applications of super-computers is distracted by an intense infatuation for the development of technology. The process of increasing machines' capacity for information while minimizing the space required to store it resembles a chemical reaction gone berserk by conservative standards.

The home mortgage was once amortized quite simply and concluded very directly. This very American transaction has become fair game for process-attuned businesses to complicate with balloons and variable interest rates to the point where the actual amount to be repaid, or the time frame for repayment, is indiscernible even to the most sophisticated buyer. Americans seek to buy a home and to borrow money to buy the home with little concern other than the process and momentum of repayment. The question is not when and at what rate the loan will be repaid, but one of ongoing due dates and amounts of payments owed.

Do all Americans play the lotteries? No, but those who do recognize the odds. They understand the game and freely choose to spend a dollar for even a minuscule chance of winning the jackpot.

Do all American businesses keep pace with the rapidly changing computer technology? Most do not, yet none are unaffected by the application of high technology to the American marketplace. Businesses freely choose to employ or ignore technology after being liberally saturated with advertisements and unrestricted information concerning its costs and benefits.

Is there one best mortgage plan or company for the potential home buyer? Certainly not, though lenders may freely tout the advantages of their programs and services to all who will listen. Some potential home buyers will choose not to buy at all, but do so after being afforded the opportunity to evaluate the persuasive materials of all who seek to lend to them.

One could scarcely argue the pervasiveness of lotteries, computers and home mortgages throughout American society. These things are distinctly and obviously American. Yet there are religious fundamentalists who decry the evils of gambling in any form, even through carefully controlled and government-managed lotteries. Some Americans mistrust computers and believe their impact is largely one of the depersonalization of society. There are even some Americans who think all commodities, even houses, should be paid for with cash.

Controversy surrounds much of that which is American. In 1956, many Americans would not choose to live or work in a skyscraper. And while scores protested the invasion of the skyline by towers termed shapeless and gangling, the fact that skyscrapers existed as a significant element in American society could hardly have been argued. That which is American in 1987 should be expected to foster no less discussion and dissonance than that which came to be American thirty or two hundred years ago.

The use of tobacco is undeniably a part of the American scenario. Tobacco may be likened to chewing gum in that it affords Americans an activity of process in chewing or smoking. As with skyscrapers and jazz in 1956, the use of tobacco in America has given rise to controversy and discontent among some Americans.

Quite predictably, a number of Americans respond to the persuasion of tobacco advertising, while other Americans freely choose to ignore it. And, quite naturally, some who disapprove of the use of tobacco make loud complaints about its availability to others.

In response to the noise, a few government officials would ban the materials of persuasion of businesses seeking to sell tobacco in the marketplace. They understand the role of persuasion in the exercise of free choice, and they realize the potentially devastating effect of suppressed persuasion on the fate of ideas, products and services.

These elected leaders have deliberately avoided a head-on confrontation with their constituencies of thousands of tobacco farmers, laborers, executives and retailers. They have chosen not to direct their biases to the voting Americans who choose to buy and use tobacco. A direct attempt to halt the free enterprise of growing, processing and selling tobacco is not even considered.

Rather, these representative Americans seek to erode and destroy a major American enterprise through a methodical plan for government-imposed obscurity.

Perhaps these officials don't smoke or approve of smoking themselves. Perhaps they harbor political or financial alliances with other business entities in competition for the finite set of American dollars to be spent on the luxuries of process indulgences. Or perhaps they simply feel that a government can make better choices for its people than the people would make for themselves.

Congress is being bombarded with a new breed of persuasive materials. These do not seek to convince the American not to buy tobacco, but attempt to impugn the American businessman's constitutional right to advertise freely. This persuasion deals not with the choices of Americans, but with the very essence of America.

In America, advocates of anything are guaranteed the freedom to both persuade and be persuaded. Therein lies the process of freedom of choice. The special interest groups who would lobby Congress to draft laws of total absurdity have a First Amendment-guaranteed right to do so. Each member of our society, whether congressman, farmer or businessman, is entitled to the same inalienable freedoms.

Individual members of the legislative branch of government in America are indeed afforded the right to personal differences just as any among us. But in the formal and official capacities of United States congressmen and United States senators, these citizens serve not as individuals, but as those honored by their selection to represent the whole of society—to represent America. As congressmen and senators, regardless of personal preferences, their foremost charge is to uphold and preserve the freedom of choice which is America.

The United States Constitution created the framework for America's governance and, in so doing, provided for the establishment of representative governing assemblies. The First Amendment implores the selected representatives to guard America's freedoms mindfully. "Congress shall make no law. . . ." In this society of diversity and inconclusiveness, there is no ambiguity whatsoever in the guarantee of process ordained by our founders and mandated of their successors.

Those who drafted the First Amendment had firsthand experience with a government which made for its people the choices of religion, culture and lifestyle. Some had been physically in the midst of the bloodbaths of the Revolutionary War. And when it was over, they left for their progeny the opportunity to build America—the privilege of being American. They protected against subversion by guaranteeing the process of freedom of choice. And they fortified the promise by issuing to all an irrevocable license to persuade.

The legacy of America's founders has weathered civil crises, wars, social change and economic fluctuations for over two hundred years. Now there are those who would deface it by hampering the flow of information—the right to persuade—concerning tobacco products today and who knows what tomorrow.

Those who drafted the First Amendment. . . protected against subversion by guaranteeing the process of freedom of choice. And they fortified the promise by issuing to all an irrevocable license to persuade.

If the freedom to choose fails to be protected by those selected to govern, the American process is left vulnerable to virtually any organized group of Americans with shared likes or dislikes—to groups of special interest and selective ambition. Once the *process* is subjugated the first time, a ban on tobacco advertising would soon be followed by censorship of a host of products and ideas unpopular or undesirable to some few Americans who might vigorously seek to impose their own choices.

The open forum which lends credence to difference, once violated, would fail to support the reasoning upon which a free society depends. And the disorientation created by government's de facto assault upon a major American enterprise would begin an erosion of ideological foundations for those Americans whose economic survival is threatened by censorship of rightful persuasion.

The differences which make us American would methodically, though subtly, be eliminated. Eventually, government would feign to shape and polish its people identically, as pebbles are ground by the force of monotonous yet unrelenting waters.

Tobacco companies and all businesses within our system of free enterprise are guaranteed the right to advertise. Americans are guaranteed the right to choose. And Congress is forbidden to interfere. *These are the processes which are America.*

What would become of America if the right to choose were tempered, constricted and finally obliterated? What would become of freedom and difference? And what would an America be were process to give way to conclusion?

Helen D. Hering
Wausau, Wisconsin

Occupation: Antique Dealer
Interests: Reading, writing, poetry, editorial work
*Entered the Competition because: "I believe strongly
in equal rights for all, and I would welcome the
beautiful, sensible ads again, especially on TV."*

THE MUZZLE PUZZLE

During a visit to Poland several years ago I had the opportunity to see firsthand what government-controlled media was like. Their television fare consisted of two channels—take your pick—both force-fed by the Communist government. Into those two channels was funneled, along with propaganda, only what the government wanted the people to see and hear. Most of the people never even bothered to turn their sets on until late night, when they might catch an American film.

Their newspapers and magazines contained the same watered-down propagandistic material. One could sometimes see people standing or sitting in some corner glancing at them, chuckling to themselves at the blatant brainwashing attempts.

Even though the Poles are fiercely patriotic and intelligent enough to tell the difference between honest news and propaganda, they were betrayed at Yalta, along with their neighbors in Hungary, Czechoslovakia, Lithuania, Latvia, Estonia and East Germany, and are now denied the freedom to choose their own television programs, their own reading material and other forms of communication.

Seeing their lack of well-rounded, diversified advertising and programming, their hunger for honest, straightforward news from the outside, and their chafing under the "truth blackout," I thought to myself: "GOOD GOD, LET THAT NEVER HAPPEN IN AMERICA!"

It should never happen here, because we had Thomas Jefferson and his compatriots instead of Vladimir Lenin. Where Leninism makes every man a slave, Americanism makes every man a free participant to live as he chooses.

Our Bill of Rights was carefully, anguishingly crafted by those brave pioneers to guarantee Americans, among other things, the freedom of speech and of the press. Not for a certain length of time. . . not only under certain conditions. . . not subject to the biased opinions of self-appointed "do gooders," but forever! And to everyone!

So what's the problem? Are they telling us that Americans are no longer capable or intelligent enough to decide what we want to see and read so the Congress must decide what is good for us and what is not?

I am not a politician, so I don't have to bend to pressure of those self-appointed messengers of doom or the bulge-wallets who demand

435

special favors. Nor am I a puppet in the game of "AMA Monopoly."

I am not a corporate executive, so I don't have to fret over profits and losses, competition, unfair practices or undue restrictions.

I am not a Wall Street manipulator, so I don't have to live by the bible according to Dow Jones. I don't have to make sure that everyone listens when I speak. The mad, mad world of ups and downs is not my cup of tea.

I am not a doctor, so I don't have to be a pawn in the battle of one industry against another (drugs, alcohol, tobacco, pollutants, insecticides, abortions and the list goes on and on). I do not have to pretend to care whether a person chooses one lifestyle or another.

I am not a Philadelphia lawyer, so I can't find ways and means to twist the laws, find advantageous loopholes, or use my expertise to help clients circumvent the Bill of Rights.

I am not an advertising executive, so I can't devise ads that will sell products, sway opinions or perform some other function. I can't influence a whole nation to accept my beliefs or prejudices.

BUT, I am a consumer, and I can finally express my opinions on the subject of censorship, thanks to you, Philip Morris! I can speak from the perspective of the home front, from my vantage point in front of the tube or with a newspaper or magazine for company. On this I am an authority, and I shall give it both barrels.

"Congress shall make no law abridging the freedom of speech, or of the press. . . . " Can anything be more clear, more binding, more protective? Who in our society dares feel qualified to put himself above the law?

That law should declare unconstitutional the law prohibiting cigarette advertising on television. It should prohibit Congress from making any further laws concerning cigarette advertising in any of the media.

Have our congressmen become so weak and pliable that they can be coerced into serving the whims of a few at the expense of the entire nation? Have they become so overconcerned with small unimportant issues, so overzealous in trying to solve everything with more laws and restrictions that they ignore the most vital issues of our time, like national defense, which should be everyone's top concern?

Example 1: Prayer in schools. How many days, weeks, months Congress spent arguing the pros and cons of this nonissue! That they would let one pitiful individual throw a monkey wrench into the entire operation of our government indicates a loss of direction somewhere along the way. How could they waste so much high-salaried time on something that never should be an issue! Our Constitution clearly, emphatically states that church and state must remain separate. Were they so afraid of losing their own popularity that they were too weak to throw it off their agenda? The cases of any prayer-in-school issue arising anywhere in the country are so few and far between as to be almost nonexistent. Yet they blew it up all out of proportion and made a big issue out of it and accomplished nothing.

Example 2: Mandatory seat belts in cars. They have passed laws requiring the manufacturers to put them in all cars. Fine. *Let it go at that!* Smart drivers use them. But if somebody chooses to fly through the windshield in an accident, let that be his or her prerogative! The belts are there—leave the choice of using or not using them up to the people. Again. . . use your time dealing with more important issues. Period.

And now the AMA and other activists are calling for a total ban on all cigarette advertising. (The AMA is a powerful monopoly with a stranglehold on medical care in this country, and should have its own power stripped for the good of society. Then we wouldn't be so far behind European countries in medical advances, and we'd have had a cancer cure long ago.) Their respect for free speech ends where their prejudices begin. "Because some smokers get lung cancer and die. . . " is their argument.

Cars kill people—many, many people—yet the car manufacturers are allowed to advertise them.

Many desperate people kill themselves with overdoses of over-the-counter drugs, yet they continue to be advertised.

Alcoholic drinks kill or destroy the lives of many people, yet they can be advertised openly.

So why cripple only the tobacco industry with restrictions and bans? Fair is fair. If the products are legal, advertising them should be legal. We cannot claim otherwise. The tobacco manufacturers already comply with government law by placing warnings on every package, every ad. That fulfills any obligation the government need consider necessary for the protection of its citizens.

Before taking further action to muzzle the cigarette manufacturers, I suggest they put it to a referendum at the next election and let *the people* decide if the First Amendment to our Constitution is no longer valid. If given a voice, I believe they would vote to lift the ban on television advertising also.

Research shows that ads don't just sell products. . . they build images. They inform, they compare brands. . . and build images. Consumers react favorably to some ads and unfavorably to others, and we are free to ignore them if we don't like them.

This consumer really misses those beautiful Western sunset scenes that told us we were in "Marlboro Country." I miss the lovely northwoods wildlife scenes that brought us "From the land of sky blue waters comes the beer refreshing. . . Hamms." And I hear echoing down the years the stentorian cry, "Call. . . for. . . Phi—lip. . . Mor—riss," and it brings a lump to my throat.

This does not mean that I ran right out and bought those products. It means that I really appreciated those beautiful ads, and will always have a warm spot in my heart for the companies that provided those many pleasant moments.

In these days of disgustingly loud, raucous, freaky ads on television, we would really welcome those beautiful ads again! Now we can only be grateful for the few pleasures we find in such ads as Ernest and Julio Gallo, Luvs, and Coldwell Bankers.

Yes, ads do build images and impressions, and they last a long, long time. And always the choice remains with the consumer—to buy or not to buy those products. And that's as it should be.

I, therefore, would urge Congress to restore all television advertising rights to the cigarette manufacturers, and let the American people choose whether they want to smoke or not.

In the name of freedom they allow Nazis to organize and march through our streets. They allow Communists to speak in our schools, to assemble and flourish, and they let other treasonous elements go unchecked. . . all in the name of freedom!

How can they, then, in clear conscience, deny the rights of free speech and press to one industry, especially one that is so vital to our economy? They would muzzle the tobacco industry because of the pressure of prejudice. Whom will they muzzle next?

If we are not watchful, this tightening of censorship will sneak up on us insidiously and, one by one, take away our freedoms of expression, and undermine our Bill of Rights.

And if we allow our Democracy to be strangled by Bureaucracy, we will no longer have a government "of the people, by the people, for the people"!

That yoke of oppression weighs heavily on those people in Poland and the other captive countries. I have seen their fear, their hunger, their sadness, their futility. . . and that's why I cry out from a fearful heart—

"GOOD GOD, LET THAT NEVER HAPPEN IN AMERICA!"

Thomas E. Higham
Rawlins, Wyoming

Occupation: Locomotive Engineer
Interests: Fishing, bow hunting, backpacking,
camping, tennis, city-league basketball, reading in
Latin the classical Latin literature
Entered the Competition: "Because of an abiding
interest in the First Amendment."

The tobacco industry is actually forced to advertise *against* itself!

FREEDOM OF SPEECH: WILL WE LOSE IT?

Mark Twain once said, "It is by the goodness of God that in our country we have those three unspeakably precious things: freedom of speech, freedom of conscience, and the prudence never to practice either of them." The statement is both humorous and thought provoking. No matter how much we Americans use, or do not use, our freedom of speech, we all cherish the right, though we may sometimes take it for granted. What many of us sometimes fail to realize is that our freedom of speech is not now, and never was, an absolute right, but rather it is dependent on various circumstances and considerations, and is constantly being defined and redefined by our courts. We all know that we do not have a right to yell "Fire" in a crowded movie theater (unless of course there is a fire), or slander someone, or give a speech intended to foment the violent overthrow of our government. These limitations on the right of free speech all have obvious merit, but in these days and times, in the hubbub and confusion of the complicated society in which we live, a fear arises that unwarranted limitations may be inadvertently placed on our basic rights. When our vision becomes blurred or distracted by the multiplicity of modern life, a kind of social entropy can result, in which not only our integral values, but our basic constitutional rights that we have long taken for granted, are at stake.

In such a heterogenous and dynamic society as ours, with the wide diversity of beliefs and interests we have, a judge or justice often finds himself walking the razor's edge between conflicting factions when it comes to constitutional issues such as the right to the freedom of speech. It's a tough business deciding such things as what literature should be outlawed, and who can say what, where and when, while at the same time holding to the underlying principle that, as much as possible, a free exchange of ideas should be allowed. Concerning pornography, one judge uttered the now-famous statement, "I don't know how to define pornography, but I know it when I see it,"—hardly a practical basis on which to decide what is pornography and what is not. It is inevitable that when we begin to legislate morality, or ethics or lifestyles, we run headlong into a nebulous gray cloud of uncertainty.

If we cannot always be like a perfect deity when we decide what

441

should be forbidden to men and what allowed, we should at least attempt to be consistent—treat similar cases in a similar fashion. The truth is, however, that we are not consistent, and consequently not always fair. A good example is the way in which the advertising of tobacco is treated. It is singularly noticeable that of all the products which have been designated as potentially harmful to our health or happiness, tobacco has had, by far, the most vigorous constraints placed on it by the government. The tobacco industry is actually forced to advertise *against* itself! Each package must bear a warning of a certain minimum size which is designed to discourage the consumer from using the product, as must each magazine advertisement. I know of no other product which has been federally mandated to advertise against itself. If a warning on a pack of cigarettes, why not a warning on a bottle of whiskey, or a can of beer or a gun? If a cigarette can be harmful, so can liquor or a tranquilizer, for that matter. If a warning label should be put on one of them it should be put on them all; if one potentially hazardous product is to be restricted in its advertising, so should they all be, in just proportion. It makes no difference if one uses tobacco himself, or one drinks or one hunts; advertising is a form of free speech, and all types of commerce deserve protection under the First Amendment, or none do. It's a question of equity; if we must make arbitrary judgments we should at least apply our moralistic injunctions with reasonable consistency.

But why, when any potential hazards of a product are already commonly known by the general public, should the members of an industry and the consumers be harassed at all? In such cases, continued intervention of government is an unnecessary expense to taxpayers and to commerce, and is an undesirable abridgement of freedom of speech.

But why, when any potential hazards of a product are already commonly known . . . should the members of an industry and the consumers be harassed at all?

Some people would completely prohibit the advertising of tobacco products. This step would have far-reaching legal, social and economic ramifications. First, it would establish a dangerous legal precedent, for it would deny to business the constitutional right to freedom of speech. Not only are individuals endowed with the right of free speech, but likewise are churches, clubs and all other legal associations of people—including businesses. It is impossible to give men singly such a basic right and not give it to men collectively. To say that the tobacco industry cannot advertise is to say that American business is not entitled to the right of freedom of speech, and one can only shake one's head in wonder at the disregard for the First Amendment that such a position implies. If the federal government can silence the tobacco industry, it can do the same to any business, no matter how large or how small, whether it consists of thousands of employees or just one person.

There would also be a social consequence to the banning of advertising by the tobacco industry. It would be a blow to free enterprise and the personal opportunity which it represents to Americans. We don't all make it big in the world of entrepreneurship—many of us don't even try—but we can all look around us and see those who have risen to great heights from humble beginnings. It is important to know that the opportunity is still there. To deny the right of free speech to business would quell the spirit of independence and freedom that free enterprise has traditionally meant to Americans.

As a pragmatic consideration, a ban on advertising by the tobacco industry would cause serious economic repercussions. The first and most inevitable effect would of course be that millions of dollars of advertising revenue would be lost. Following this, we might likely see farmers, manufacturers, wholesalers and retailers hurt financially, and this would in time result in increased unemployment, less income tax and tobacco tax revenues, and increased government expense for unemployment and social welfare programs.

Americans don't need or want the kind of government protectionism which insulates them from the advertising of lawful products.

Supreme Court Justice Hugo L. Black once called the First Amendment "the heart of the Bill of Rights." He said of it:

> The framers knew, better perhaps than we do today, the risks they were taking. They knew that free speech might be the friend of change and revolution. But they also knew that it is always the deadliest enemy of tyranny. With this knowledge they still believed that the ultimate happiness and security of a nation lies in its ability to explore, to change, to grow, and ceaselessly to adapt itself to new knowledge born of inquiry free from any kind of governmental control over the mind and spirit of man.

It is the American ideal to control one's own destiny, without government intervention. Basic to this ideal is the right to freedom of speech, as guaranteed by the First Amendment. The right should not be lightly denied to any individual or lawful organization, and certainly not on an arbitrary basis, as a ban on advertising of the tobacco industry would be. Americans don't need or want the kind of governmental protectionism which insulates them from the advertising of lawful products, especially when it involves the abridgement of a basic constitutional right. In the end, we will all retain the right of freedom of speech, including businesses, or we may all lose it.

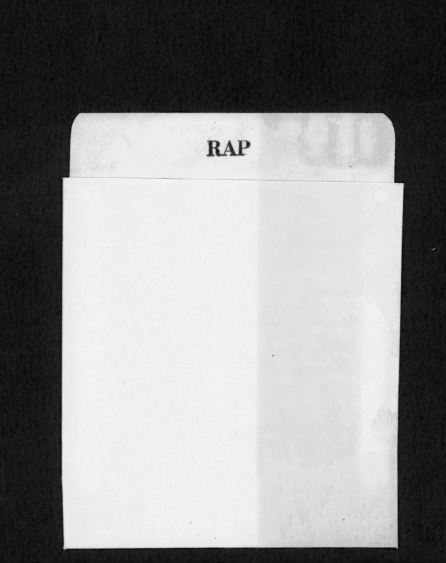

RAP